Contents

PERSPECTIVES ON ACADEMIC GAMING & SIMULATION 3

Perspectives on Academic Gaming & Simulation 3

TRAINING & PROFESSIONAL EDUCATION

The Proceedings of the 1977 Conference of SAGSET,
the Society for Academic Gaming and Simulation
in Education and Training

Edited by Ray McAleese

Kogan Page

sagset

SOCIETY FOR ACADEMIC
GAMING AND SIMULATION
IN EDUCATION AND TRAINING

Acknowledgements

The Editor wishes to thank contributors for co-operation in editing their papers, members of Grampian SAGSET for help in preparing the manuscript, Mrs Sheila Riach for typing the manuscript, and my wife Sybil for compiling the Index. Any deficiencies in the work are the responsibility of the Editor.

First published 1978 by
Kogan Page Limited
120 Pentonville Road
London N1 9JN

Distributed in the United States of America by
Nichols Publishing Company
Post Office Box 96
New York, NY 10024

Copyright © SAGSET and contributors 1978

SAGSET is the Society for Academic Gaming and Simulation
in Education and Training. Its permanent address is:
The Secretary, SAGSET
Centre for Extension Studies
Loughborough University of Technology
Leicestershire LE11 3TU, England

Printed in Great Britain by
Biddles of Guildford

ISBN 0 85038 104 5

Introduction

The 1977 SAGSET Conference

The Eighth Annual Conference of SAGSET was held in the Kepplestone premises of Robert Gordon's Institute of Technology, Aberdeen, on 1-3 September 1977. It was attended by 108 delegates, including visitors from the Netherlands, Israel, the USA and New Zealand. At first sight, Aberdeen might not appear to be an obvious choice of venue for an international conference on gaming and simulation, but there are a number of very good reasons why it was chosen.

(a) Aberdeen is becoming increasingly recognised as one of the leading centres in Britain for the development and exploitation of academic games and simulations. A number of local educational establishments, particularly Robert Gordon's Institute of Technology (RGIT), have been extremely active in this field over the past few years, and have produced several games that have achieved recognition at both national and international level. Furthermore, the local Education Authority (Grampian) has pioneered the integration of such exercises into the school curriculum.

(b) A local branch of SAGSET (Grampian SAGSET) had been in existence in Aberdeen since 1975, so that the organisational machinery needed to plan and run the conference was already firmly established.

(c) RGIT and Aberdeen College of Education had expressed a willingness to act as joint hosts to the conference by making available their adjacent Kepplestone premises, with the Institute hosting the actual conference and the College providing all the residential accommodation needed.

(d) Despite the northerly location of Aberdeen in the UK, it is comparatively easy to reach because of its excellent rail and air communications. In recent years, many major conferences have been held in Aberdeen, including several connected with the offshore oil industry.

(e) Aberdeen is a beautiful city of great historical interest. It is also a major tourist centre and the acknowledged oil capital of Europe. Because of these attractions, several delegates made the conference part of a holiday in Aberdeen, and a number were accompanied by their families.

The choice of theme and target population: SAGSET was formed to promote both the educational and the training applications of gaming and simulation, but it is fair to say that previous SAGSET conferences have tended to concentrate on the former sector. In an attempt to redress this imbalance, a policy decision was made by SAGSET Council in September 1976 that the 1977 conference

7

should have, as its main theme, *'the application of gaming and simulation in training'*. It was subsequently decided that the first two days of the conference would be largely devoted to this theme, with the final day being set aside for educational applications, particularly those relevant to the teaching situation in schools.

The first two days of the conference were designed to attract, both as contributors and as delegates, people who (i) develop games and simulations for use in training, (ii) use games and simulations in their existing training programmes and (iii) work in areas in which gaming and simulation could make a useful contribution to training. The success of this policy can be judged by the wide range of organisations which were represented at the conference. These included the Army School of Instructional Technology, Linguistics Systems Engineering, the RAF School of Education, the Scottish Police College and the UK Atomic Energy Authority as well as a number of Scottish banks.

The final day of the conference was so structured as to appeal both to practising teachers and educational administrators and to educationalists active in the field of gaming and simulation. The conference was timed so that this final day fell on a Saturday, thus allowing the former to attend without disrupting their normal work. There was a special reduced conference fee for local teachers. As a result of this policy, 18 local teachers attended the final day, and the conference was also attended by the local Director of Education and several senior members of his administrative staff. In addition, over 30 further and higher education lecturers attended the full conference.

Publicity: Six months before the conference was due to take place, an advance publicity leaflet was prepared and 1,400 copies circulated to individuals and bodies likely to be interested. Bodies such as the Council for Educational Technology and the Scottish Council for Educational Technology were supplied with copies for display and distribution. At the same time, the conference was advertised in a number of appropriate journals, such as *Programmed Learning & Educational Technology* and *SAGSET Journal*. Three months later, a specially prepared leaflet publicising the educational day of the conference was distributed to all schools and further education establishments in the Grampian region via the local Education Authority; this incorporated a registration form for the final day. Two weeks before the start of the conference, a press release was issued through the Liaison Officer at RGIT. As a result, the conference received coverage in both the local and national press and on television and radio. The success of the publicity programme can be judged by the fact that attendance at SAGSET 77 was significantly greater than at any previous SAGSET conference and well above the most optimistic forecast made by the organisers.

Planning: From the onset, overall responsibility for planning and running the conference was vested in Grampian SAGSET Committee, on which a wide range of local educational and industrial establishments were represented. The Chairman of Grampian SAGSET become Conference Secretary, with the Vice-Chairman taking on the role of Programme Secretary. Throughout the planning of the conference, major policy decisions were referred back to the organising committee. The Conference Secretary, who had overall responsibility for all aspects of the conference, was particularly concerned with the logistical and organisational details and with liaison between the organising committee,

SAGSET and the two host bodies.

The Programme Secretary was responsible for all aspects of the conference programme, especially the programme of papers; this involved corresponding with potential contributors and arranging for delivery of abstracts and papers to deadline. The Programme Secretary was assisted in his work by a small Programme Committee, two members of which took on responsibility for the programme of demonstration and participation sessions and for the provision of computer facilities. Another member of the organising committee took on responsibility for all aspects of the organisation of the exhibition which it had been decided to incorporate in the conference. This work involved contacting potential exhibitors (both commercial and educational), arranging facilities, and, in many cases, setting up the actual exhibits.

One important feature of SAGSET 77 was the conference desk, which was permanently manned throughout the three days of the conference. This acted as a focus of interest for delegates, and was extensively used as an information desk, notice board and distribution centre for papers and other material. The full texts of all papers available at the time of the conference were lodged at the conference desk and could be borrowed by delegates at any time.

Structure of the conference: The practice at all previous SAGSET conferences had been to have a fairly rigid linear programme with (as a consequence) a relatively small total number of papers, demonstration sessions and participation sessions. In the case of SAGSET 77, however, it was decided to organise the conference on a much larger scale and to have a full programme of papers in conjunction with a wide selection of other activities. This was done by having a small number of plenary sessions (including a keynote address by a specially invited speaker at the start of each day) and by organising the remainder of the conference in four parallel streams, namely: (i) a programme of formal papers, (ii) a programme of scheduled demonstration and participation sessions, (iii) a programme of *ad hoc* demonstration and participation sessions, discussion sessions, films, etc, and (iv) the exhibition, which was open throughout the conference.

To assist delegates in the planning of their activities, a loose-leaf booklet containing the full conference programme together with abstracts of all papers and scheduled demonstration and participation sessions was issued on registration; this booklet also contained ample space for note-taking.

The above arrangement had a number of intrinsic advantages and disadvantages, and the general consensus of opinion was that the former greatly outweighed the latter. In particular, the wide range of available activities allowed each delegate to select that programme best suited to his/her specific situation or interests. In addition, the flexible nature of the programme enabled *ad hoc* sessions to be incorporated at very short notice. The inevitable disadvantage was that delegates had to be selective, and could, therefore, sometimes miss sessions in which they were interested; the conference programme was, however, designed in such a way as to reduce such conflicts of interest to a minimum.

The programme of papers: As mentioned above, each day of SAGSET 77 started with a keynote address designed to set the scene for the subsequent programme of papers and other activities. This was followed by a series of one-hour sessions, each containing either one or two papers; all these sessions were organised on fairly formal lines, having a designated chairperson who introduced the speaker(s) and controlled the subsequent discussion. In planning the programme of papers, an attempt was made (a) to group together papers with similar themes and (b) in so far as this was possible, to allocate a full hour to those papers likely to lead to prolonged discussions and to 'double up' those which were largely descriptive in nature. The above arrangement allowed an extremely full and varied programme of papers to be arranged, but had the inevitable disadvantage that there was all too often insufficient time for in-depth discussion to develop. In many cases (particularly the double paper sessions) the chairperson had to curtail discussion in order to keep to the timetable; such discussions were, however, frequently resumed on an informal basis later.

Demonstration and participation sessions: Unlike the programme of papers, all the demonstration and participation sessions were informal, with no chairperson and no formal discussion session; the method of organisation was entirely at the discretion of the presenter. In addition to the scheduled programme, a wide range of special activities were organised, including the playing of a number of games brought to the conference by delegates and the showing of films illustrating various aspects of the use of gaming and simulation. Throughout the conference, two computer terminals (connected by telephone to the College of Education's multi-access computer on the other side of Aberdeen) were available to delegates through a simple booking system. Using these terminals, delegates could try out a variety of computerised games and simulations, a list of which was included in the wallet of documents provided on registration.

One of the features of SAGSET 77 was that facilities could be made available to any delegate who wished to organise an *ad hoc* session of any sort — whether it was a playing session, demonstration session, discussion, or the showing of a film — and several delegates took full advantage of this arrangement. For example, one delegate made use of the conference to obtain data for an MEd thesis by circulating a questionnaire on the educational uses of games and simulations; this was completed by over 40 people.

The Agecroft Trophy: One innovative feature of SAGSET 77 was that it incorporated, as an ongoing demonstration session, a full-scale inter-school competition which extended over all three days of the conference. In this competition, teams of sixth-form science pupils from three local comprehensive schools played THE POWER STATION GAME (a role-playing simulation exercise concerned with the choice of type and siting of a new power station) for the Agecroft Trophy, presented by the Agecroft Training Centre of the Central Electricity Generating Board. The competition was sponsored by the Institution of Electrical Engineers, who had published the game jointly with RGIT. During the first two days of the conference, the three teams (each comprising six pupils) had the task of preparing the strongest possible case for building the type of station to which each had been allocated (coal, oil or nuclear). This involved the pupils in detailed technical and economic calculations and also in determining the most suitable site for their station. At all times, conference delegates were encouraged to drop in on the competition in order to watch the pupils in action and discuss the game with both the participants and the organising teachers; many took advantage of this opportunity. The climax of the competition took place before lunch on the final day, when the three teams presented and defended their cases in a plenary session of the conference to which parents, teachers and fellow pupils were also invited. The presentations were assessed by a panel of seven judges (all drawn from among the conference delegates) chaired by Grampian Region's Director of Education, who subsequently presented the Agecroft Trophy to the winning team.

In addition to the benefits provided to the participating pupils, the Agecroft Trophy Competition gave conference delegates the opportunity to observe a large-scale simulation game in action and thus appreciate the great potential educational value of such exercises. In addition, the competition provided a focus of interest for the local press, and thus helped to bring the conference to the attention of the educational community and public at large.

Exhibition: During the early stages of the planning of SAGSET 77, a considerable amount of discussion took place as to whether or not there should be an exhibition associated with the conference, and, if so, whether it should include exhibits from commercial bodies as well as from educational establishments and individual members of SAGSET. It was eventually decided to mount an exhibition as an integral part of the conference programme and to invite exhibits from all the sectors mentioned above. In order to achieve the above aim, the main part of the exhibition was housed in the refectory in which meals and refreshments were served, with other exhibits being located in the reception area. This arrangement produced an atmosphere of informality which almost certainly resulted in more than usual interest being shown in the various exhibits, of which ten were from educational establishments and six from commercial bodies. The general opinion of both delegates and exhibitors was that the exhibition was a great success, and that the format employed could well serve as a model for future conferences.

Social activities: SAGSET 77 incorporated two social events, namely, a civic reception on the evening of Day 1 and a conference dinner on the evening of Day 2. The civic reception was provided by Aberdeen Town Council and was held in Aberdeen Town House. The conference dinner was held in the main Conference Centre at Kepplestone. As is the case with all conferences of this type, the various social activities arranged by delegates apart from the main programme proved to be a valuable part of their total experience.

Henry I Ellington, Conference Secretary
and Eric Addinall, Grampian SAGSET

The Society for Academic Gaming and Simulation in Education and Training (SAGSET)

Although the power of play in education has long been acknowledged, and indeed may be traced back via Bruner, Piaget, Dewey and Rousseau to Plato, it is only in recent years that serious thought has been given to the practical problems and possibilities inherent in its application. As teachers, lecturers and industrial trainers sought to explore less didactic forms of learning they found that little systematic work had been done to collect and exchange information and ideas.

One of the characteristics of simulation and gaming, however, is that it is *experiential*. There is a limit, therefore, to the information about it that can be conveyed by the written word. It is necessary for practitioners to meet, discuss and try out games. It was largely to fulfil this need that SAGSET was formed.

The Society was started in 1969 by a small band of enthusiasts, led by Pat Tansey of the Berkshire College of Education. It held its first conference in

August 1970 and rapidly established itself as a focal point for activities and publishing in the field.

From the start, the interests of its members have spanned the whole universe of education and training from primary school to university and from trade unions to senior management. Again, right from its beginnings, the Society's approach to the subject of gaming and simulation has been from two distinct viewpoints. In both publications and conferences, therefore, there are contributions which emphasise the theoretical basis of gaming and simulation, which explore common conceptual frameworks, and which debate the problems of evaluation and assessment; at the same time there are always contributions which look at the practical aspects of gaming, the hardware, the difficulties of timetabling, scoring, debriefing, and the dynamics of the group in action. Equal emphasis is placed on the need for practical help in running gaming exercises and on the need to build from a sound academic framework.

The Society publishes a quarterly journal (*SAGSET Journal*) which carries articles on use and design, reviews of games and simulations, references and news about courses and conferences.

Other publications include subject area resource lists, conference proceedings under the series title *Perspectives on Academic Gaming & Simulation* and an anthology of articles under the title *Aspects of Simulation & Gaming*. It also acts as the European distributor for the well-known books by Stadsklev on simulation gaming in social education. Through its contacts with other national and international organisations and by means of its annual conference, local meetings and widespread membership, the Society tries to encourage and develop the responsible use of gaming and simulation as a teaching technique. It also endeavours to offer support and encouragement to those who use these methods and provide them with a forum to discuss their ideas and problems.

SAGSET COUNCIL (1977–1978):

Morry van Ments	*Loughborough University of Technology* (Chairman)
David Walker	*Loughborough University of Technology* (Secretary)
Henry Ellington	*Robert Gordon's Institute of Technology* (Treasurer)
Eric Addinall	*Robert Gordon's Institute of Technology*
Malcolm Cornwall	*Brighton Polytechnic*
Tina Eden	*Royal College of Art*
Ian Gibbs	*Home Office Unit for Educational Methods*
John Ginifer	*Longmore Teachers Centre*
David Jaques	*University Teaching Methods Unit, London University*
Jacquetta Megarry	*Jordanhill College of Education*
John Smith	*RAF School of Education*
Michael Smythe	*Institution of Electrical Engineers*
Trevor Bennetts HMI\	*Department of Education and Science Assessor*

Information about the Society and details of membership may be obtained from: The Secretary, SAGSET, Centre for Extension Studies, University of Technology, Loughborough, Leicestershire LE11 3TU.

Morry van Ments,
Chairman, SAGSET

Chapter 1

Overview:
some questions for readers

Ray McAleese, *University of Aberdeen*

The first chapter in this collection of papers identifies three themes that merit closer examination. First, the rational justification of games/simulations is examined. It is suggested that different authors use differing criteria for the selection of *experiential learning* as a teaching medium. Some of the extant justifications are examined. As a second theme, the competitive — co-operative dichotomy is examined. It is suggested that too often the competitive element of games/simulations is glossed over or even emphasised as a strength when more thought should be given to the effects that such learning have on the student and on social structure. Third, the question of transfer is considered with respect to evaluation. It is suggested that neither the range nor the complexity of learning transfer is considered and that in absolute terms little is known of empirically based models of learning transfer or the identification of transferred skills.

It is not the purpose of this chapter to undertake a definitive review of the area of games and simulations. Apart from being a daunting task that even the bravest tackle with some temerity (Goodman, 1973; Shirts, 1976), it is not this author's intention to go further than the papers in this work as a primary source of stimulation, although other evidence is used to add weight to claims made. Further, Chapter 5 (Retrospect and Prospect, Megarry) is an invaluable synthesis of some of the wider issues that concern the reviewer. No set of papers selected as they are and presented at a national conference can do more than serve as a slice of the totality of games and simulations.[1] Indeed, the very selection of the conference theme itself limits the range of the papers. With this caveat or academic 'exclusion clause', the author has been able to identify three themes that run across the professional/management/education divide. These three are *justification, goal-structure* and *learning transfer*. In other words, taking the 25 papers in this book, three questions crop up time and time again as the reader proceeds through the contributions:

What justification had the author(s) for using experiential learning?
What explicit and/or implicit goal-structure was adopted by the game or simulation described?
What attempt was there to establish a learning transfer from the simulated to the real situation?

Therefore, a series of questions will be posed that the reader should attempt to answer or at least be conscious of when reading the papers.

Justification

There are times when it seems that training innovators are so unsure of their actions that they must rush to justify why they do what they do and why they adopt the tactics they do. It is nevertheless right that users of games and/or simulations need to examine why they chose that particular teaching/training strategy. In the general field of educational technology there is a growing awareness that media classification or selection has been tackled with less than precision over the last quarter of a century. Only in recent years have serious attempts been made, using the postulates of Aptitude Treatment Interaction (Salomon and Clark, 1977; Heidt, 1978) to examine the nature of the task, the learner and the *medium*.[2] Although most of the authors in this volume draw the readers' attention to the *raison d'être* for games and/or simulations, they do not agree on their criteria for selection. This is not surprising given the variety of reasons that authors can select: involvement (Teather, 1973), producing learning 'gestalt' (Duke, 1974), involving a heuristic active learning process (Taylor, 1976), among many others. Underlying the various justifications is a dimension that can be called the 'experiential learning dimension'. As long ago as 1910 John Adams (Adams, 1910) in *Exposition and Illustration in Teaching* identified the abstract-concrete continuum which leads to the direct purposeful experience in Dale's 'Cone of Experience' (Dale, 1954).[3] More recently, when Cruickshank and Mager (1976) suggested guide-lines towards model building, they considered Dale's cone and added a second dimension. To Dale's 'concrete to abstract dimension' (first hand to third hand) they added a reality dimension (real to modelled). Such classifications are indeed useful but are in need of further thought and application. The essence of the concrete to abstract dimension will suffice for the moment. This idea can be translated into simple terms: doing something for oneself is better than being told about it, and if the 'real' situation is not possible then a close simulation of this reality is 'best'. Experiential learning suggests that the more a learner can experience a situation (ie the more *concrete* it can become), then the better the teaching strategy. It is in games and in particular in simulations that involve role-play that most claim is laid to exploiting experiential teaching/training situations.

QUESTIONS TO CONSIDER

Can the author justify the use of experiential learning?
What characteristics of the learner, the task and the medium does the author's use of simulations and games embody?

Goal-structure

Authors quite often claim that their simulation or game is *competitive* in nature. Indeed, simple classifications of games emphasise the competitive nature of such exercises. For example, 'A game is a contest, usually among player opponents, operating under rules to gain an objective' (Cruickshank and Mager, 1976). Goodman (1973), in a better classification of terms, again emphasises the competitive nature of such exercises. Many examples are to be found in the papers presented at this conference. In Chapter 2 (Training) several authors highlight the competitive nature of simulations and suggest that to model reality requires risk. Individual games in the papers highlight competition; two examples will indicate the assumptions. In LAG (McAleese and Hare), learning to explain, in language teaching, is accomplished in a competitive fashion. Students compete in a game where time is their master and success is accomplished using a panel to 'guess' explanations. Another example, SPACE QUEST (Doherty), uses a board game with competing teams to assist in learning mathematics.

Educational goals can be classified and it is this classification that suggests some further questions for the reader. Goals can be co-operative, competitive or individualistic (Johnson and Johnson, 1974). Co-operative learning implies that the learner shares with colleagues or peers the learning experience. The goals of separate individuals are linked together. Competitive learning implies the opposite. 'The goals of separate individuals are linked together so that there is a negative correlation between their goal attainments' (Johnson and Johnson, 1974). An individualist situation is where the goals of individuals are independent of each other. Whether or not an individual accomplishes a goal has no bearing upon others accomplishments. Strong evidence exists suggesting that co-operative goals are superior to competitive goals (Johnson and Johnson, 1974; Ryan and Wheeler, 1977). Further, competitive goals may result in damage to the learner's self-concept and self-attitudes. There are, of course, contrary views and there is little doubt that learners can experience an increase in goal motivation or drive, something that is essential for *meaningful learning* (Ausubel and Johnson, 1968). The questions that the reader should ask relate more to the wider social implications of competitive play. It is foolish to look only at the restricted microcosm of the classroom or training room. What goes on in schools not only models (simulates) reality *but it causes it*. Too often it is assumed that competitive-aggressive teaching methods are acceptable as they are restricted in their influence and achieve learning goals. There is, some would argue, enough competition in the organisation of society, and further reinforcing of the aggressiveness in teaching is both unnecessary and wrong. One would have to agree that while competitiveness may be essential in reality (life outside classrooms) innovators in schools have a wider responsibility than simply achieving short-term school goals — society may need a lead.

QUESTIONS TO CONSIDER

How far should game designers incorporate competitive goals to model the competitive nature of 'reality'?
Assuming that competitive goals are an accepted part of social organisation, do teachers/trainers not have a responsibility to change the existing state of affairs, as opposed to reinforcing it?
Where there is no true difference between goals, how do innovators choose their goal structure?

Learning transfer

One or two authors in this collection give a cursory examination to the nature of learning or training transfer, yet as a topic it merits closer examination. In one direction it seems easy to simulate reality with a game. One can incorporate risks and details to ensure a close approximation to the real situation. Little attempt is made to map the simulated environment onto reality and identify the application of simulated skills in real settings. The nature of learning transfer is well known. Transfer occurs when a previously learned skill influences the acquisition of another skill at a later time. In simulations this is recast as learning in a simulated situation effecting the learning or performance in reality. Three interaction types of transfer are possible. In *lateral* transfer, the learner applies the skills acquired in training to a similar problem in another context. *Vertical* transfer occurs when the learner generates new skills from previously learned skills. In *parallel* transfer the learner applies the same skills to the same situation in the transfer condition as in the learning (simulated) condition. There are arguments that suggest that there must be psychological fidelity, or identical elements between the simulation and reality, in order to maximise skill transfer. In general there are two types of skill transfer that concern the teacher — parallel and lateral transfer. In arguments that game innovators put forward to justify their tactics, the reader should be looking for evidence that simulated learning can be identified in subsequent situations. In general, this problem has not been solved. There are few if any examples of true transfer being identified in learners' behaviour or further learning in the post-simulated situation.

QUESTIONS TO CONSIDER

Has the author considered the subsequent learning transfer of skills?
Does the evaluation of the innovation take transfer into account?
How might such simulated skills be identified and monitored in real situations?

As was suggested, the papers in this book represent only a small sample of the total concerns of innovators in simulations and games. Likewise the questions asked here represent a sample of the critical concerns that readers should have. In looking for ideas, games or rationales that transfer from one situation to another, readers should reassess the uniqueness of simulations, the implicit goals and evidence of potential transferability of skills. Likewise they should not forget that one of the key features in the success of innovators may not necessarily be technique adopted but the effect of the 'teacher-interventionist' (Roebuck) on the learning outcomes.

Notes

1. Papers for a conference are selected from those offered by participants and those individuals asked to make keynote addresses. Apart from short abstracts, the conference organisers have no detailed evidence upon which to act and provide a wide range of views and topics. Edited conference papers are therefore a biased sample from the possible totality of papers that represent the concerns of authors and, further, of what is considered by authors and others to be important.
2. It is not entirely satisfactory to call games and simulations a 'medium' or even 'media'. The term is used in the sense that the teaching/training strategies used in a game or simulation are content-free and therefore akin to a technological medium (eg tape recorder).
3. No doubt it would be possible to trace such a dimension back through Rousseau, Pestalozzi, Froebel to Comenius!

References

Adams, J (1910) *Exposition and Illustration in Teaching.* Macmillan, New York.

Ausubel, D P and Johnson, F G (1968) *School Learning: An Introduction to Educational Psychology.* Holt, Rinehart and Winston, London.

Cruickshank, D R and Mager, G M (1976) Toward theory building in the field of instructional games and simulations. *Programmed Learning & Educational Technology,* 13, 3, 2-9.

Dale, E (1954) *Audio-Visual Methods in Teaching.* Dryden Press, New York.

Duke, R D (1974) *Gaming: the Future's Language.* Wiley, New York.

Goodman, F L (1973) Gaming and simulation. In Travers, R M W (ed) *Second Handbook of Research on Teaching.* Rand McNally, New York.

Heidt, E (1978) Classification of media. In Unwin, D and McAleese, R *Encyclopaedia of Educational Media Communications and Technology.* Macmillan (in press).

Johnson, D W and Johnson, R T (1974) Instructional goal structure: cooperative, competitive or individualistic. *Review of Educational Research,* 44, 2, 213-240.

Ryan, F L and Wheeler, R D (1977) The effects of cooperative and competitive background experiences of students on the play of a simulation game. *Journal of Educational Research,* 70, 295-299.

Salomon, G and Clark, R E (1977) Re-examining the methodology of research on media and technology in education. *Review of Educational Research,* 47, 1, 99-120.

Shirts, R G (1976) Simulation games: an analysis of the last decade. *Programmed Learning & Educational Technology,* 13, 3, 37-41.

Taylor, L C (1976) Educational materials: their development, supply, use and management. In *Materials for Learning and Teaching.* Commonwealth Secretariat, London.

Teather, D C B (1973) The Society for Academic Gaming and Simulation in Education and Training. *Programmed Learning & Educational Technology,* 10, 4, 223.

Chapter 2: Training

This chapter shows the diversity and the strength of simulations and games in the context of training. The next chapter (Chapter 3) deals with professional education and although it is an artificial and perhaps misleading distinction, training may be equated with the shop floor or the rank and file, whereas professional education is equated with executive or management grades. (This classification is seen, for example, in the Department of Employment's *Professional* and Executive Register and schemes such as the *Training* Services Agency and *Training* Within Industry.) In some ways *ends* are clearer in this training than in education (schools, colleges and universities) and therefore *means* can be more precise, and less conventional teaching techniques may be adopted. Nicholson, in the keynote paper, starts the ball rolling by identifying the gap between reality (industry) and conventional training by suggesting the role that simulations can play. Simulations are identified by other authors as *means* in the armed services (Air Force), the police, the offshore oil industry and in the operation of government policies. As well as discussing the use of simulations, McNaughton gives a most useful introduction to some of the general problems in the offshore oil exploration industry. Of special note is the paper by Humphreys ('The prototype fast reactor training simulator') which describes in some detail the working of a very complex simulator in the nuclear reactor industry. It is a fascinating study of how real such simulators can be. A recurring theme is the simulation of reality and, in some cases, the emphasis on disaster and risk, adding, it is suggested, that essential element needed in simulating reality. Smythe concludes the chapter with a useful set of guide-lines on the commercial exploitation of games. Again strict criteria are set that indicate the clear-sighted view of trainers in industry and the armed forces.

Keynote paper:
Games and simulations: a bridge between industry and the academic world

J R Nicholson, *Press and Journal, Aberdeen*

C P Snow identified a gap between two cultures in the 1950s. There is a gap between the developed and the underdeveloped countries. Further there is a gap between the real world (industry) and the academic world. This paper argues that the most useful role which academic games or simulations can play is to bridge the industry–academic gap. Games permit participants to become familiar with numbers and with academic disciplines and can prepare the trainee for the real world.

We live in an age of gaps. There is the generation gap. There is the gap between the developed and underdeveloped countries — the groups which are now called the north and south countries. In British society perhaps the most talked-of gap in the past 20 years or so is that which was identified by the novelist and scientist C P Snow, the gap between science and the arts. As a novelist and a scientist himself, Snow was particularly well placed to identify and define this.

We have not heard a great deal about this gap in recent years. I think there are two reasons for this. One is that, to the extent that it existed, a great deal was done to close it, especially in the academic world, between the late 1950s and the late 1960s, with the development of so many new mixed degree courses and a general expansion which took place in higher education.

However, my second explanation for why the 'Snow-gap' has melted is perhaps more significant. In retrospect, the decade from the late 1950s to the late 1960s was one of considerable prosperity and real growth in living standards for this country. The terms of trade were operating in our favour at the beginning of the period. This position enabled the Conservative government of the day to win the general election in 1959 on the slogan 'You have never had it so good'. For most of the period inflation was well below five per cent, and unemployment below the half-million mark. As you all know, these circumstances dramatically changed in the early 1970s, and particularly from October 1973, when the OPEC countries quadrupled the price of oil at a stroke.

Since then the minds of most thinking people have been focused on economic problems and their social consequences rather than artistic or cultural issues. But in this new situation, it may be that a new gap has opened up, or rather widened. That is the gap between the academic world, and industry and commerce.

I have no doubt that both sides are unfair to each other. Academics possibly think that people in business are excessively motivated at times by short-term profit considerations, and, if they have any philosophical framework at all in which they operate, it probably relates to some theorist, long since dead. The businessman, on the other hand, may feel that the academics are comfortably sheltered by personal taste, experience, and perhaps tenure from the rigours of the real world, which they do not properly comprehend. Probably there is an element of half-truth in my summary of both views.

What I have no doubt about, however, is the importance of both industry and the academic world working hard and constantly at improving communications with each other in such a way that the gaps can be narrowed and bridged. I have no doubt that in general terms the work of a society like SAGSET and its members can play an important role in bridging this gap and in helping both industry and the institutions of higher education to identify the kind of exposure to academic disciplines which will best suit the requirements of the economy, while educating industry to a better informed view of the kind of people and talents they can expect to recruit from the institutions. More specifically and without question, there are a number of solid benefits which participants, both students and executives in business, receive from playing academic games and simulation exercises.

First, playing these games and exercises increases the familiarity of the participants with what otherwise might seem to be, especially to those people who are nervous about their numeracy, frightening tools. Not very long ago this could even have meant the use of a slide rule. Now, of course, it would mean the use of a computer and the interpretation of a print-out, even the layout and type-face of which can be unfamiliar and disturbing to people not used to such materials.

Next, playing the games can also help increase, albeit on a general or superficial basis, a familiarity with other people's disciplines. It is good for the accountant, the engineer and the salesman to get together 'off-line' in this sort of environment. Again, aside from the absorption of some information about other disciplines, there is also benefit in working alongside representatives of these disciplines. A further refinement of this point, of course, is the benefit of having to work together in a group, as a co-equal member, or as the group's chairman or reporter, with all the limitations and checks and balances which this imposes on people in determining how far they can push their own line and when and in what circumstances there is a need to compromise.

The benefits I have so far mentioned, of course, would be derived from most group exercises. Two further benefits can apply to particular projects. One is the fact that a project can be used as a kind of compact course for the assimilation of knowledge in a desirable area. As some of you may know, the newspaper for which I work, *The Press and Journal*, has been associated over the past four years with Robert Gordon's Institute of Technology and the Institute of Offshore Petroleum in the running of the BRUCE OIL MANAGEMENT GAME. Over the years we have seen a number of companies entering teams at least partly with a view to enabling their executives to take in at least a smattering of knowledge about the development of an offshore oil field. Secondly, at its most sophisticated level, the project can be used to prepare participants for a similar situation which they might meet with in the real world. These projects are obviously of value.

In these brief remarks I have touched on the general role which I feel academic games and business simulation exercises can play, and some of their specific benefits. I would like to close by indulging in two special pleas. You might feel that they are inherently, and indeed mutually, contradictory, but I hope they are not.

Many people share the view that one of the things which has gone wrong with British society in the past 25 years, or perhaps a much longer period, is a lessening of our capacity to take risks. In the past few years there has been an attraction for many people to go into, not just the public sector of the economy, which obviously can be productive, but the administrative area within the public sector on the grounds that that was where 'security' lay. Sadly, there are many teachers or potential teachers, for instance, who, in the past two years, have discovered the hard way that this is not so.

Again we have often invented and brought through to the research stage important innovations in various branches of technology, but failed at the critical point of the quantum jump from research and pilot production to full production. Even in areas where we have seemed to be prepared to take gigantic risks, most obviously the development and production of Concorde, the real motive, in fact, has been a desire to maintain jobs in a physical location or in a particular industry or both, after a sharper appreciation of both the expenditure and the opportunity costs would have suggested that these resources would be better deployed elsewhere. My appeal to you then is that so far as you can (and I realise the danger is that you could devalue some of your games and exercises to a level at which they are equated with LUDO or MONOPOLY) you should build in elements of risk to your models with rewards for successful risk-taking, and financial or other punishments for taking the cautious route which in business, as sometimes in life, can often in the long run be the least secure course of the lot.

Finally, and I certainly do not mean by this point to significantly devalue all that I have said so far, it has to be recognised that the best training for hardened, experienced decision-taking is experience of taking hard decisions under pressure. Games and simulation exercises are manifestly useful tools to better equip individuals for taking hard decisions, but participation in them is not a substitute for performing in a business environment. You all know the old joke about Harvard MBAs being prepared only for the job of company president when they leave university.

I am sure that SAGSET has an important role to play in the further and disciplined development of business games and academic simulation exercises, and I thank you for the invitation to address you this morning.

The prototype fast reactor training simulator

P D Humphreys, *Dounreay Experimental Reactor Establishment, Caithness*

A description of the principal features of the fast reactor is given, including the novel central control room. The simulator hardware is briefly described with an account of the facilities available to the instructor. A summary of the main sections of the mathematical model is followed by an account of the use of the simulator as a training device, and as an operational tool. The paper concludes with some observations on experience with the simulator to date and highlights some modifications to the system that may overcome some of the limitations of the existing simulator.

Introduction

The Prototype Fast Reactor (PFR), located at Dounreay in Caithness, is essentially a prototype for future commercial fast reactor power stations. Its 250MWE output will be fed into the North of Scotland Hydro-Electric Board grid system.

The PFR simulator was commissioned in June 1973 to coincide with the beginning of the PFR commissioning programme. Its purpose was to provide a training facility for the staff who would run the PFR. In addition to this primary function it was to be used as an operational tool, for developing operational techniques and studying the PFR's performance under varying plant conditions.

The PFR plant

The principal items of plant function as follows: The 900 tons of sodium primary coolant are pumped upwards through the reactor core by three primary pumps, then flow radially outwards to three pairs of intermediate heat exchangers (IHXs) where they give up their heat to the secondary circuits.

There are three secondary circuits each containing a pair of IHXs. Secondary sodium is pumped through the IHXs to the superheater (SH) and reheater (RH), the flow being divided between the two. The flows from these recombine to pass through the evaporator and return via the secondary pump to the IHXs.

The steam and water side of the plant is conventional. Feed water, from the condenser, is pumped via the generator cooling system and condensate polishing plant through four direct contact feed heaters to the de-aerator. The single steam-driven boiler feed pump pumps feed water from the de-aerator through three high-pressure feed heaters to the steam drums, and water is circulated through the evaporator by the boiler circulating pump. Saturated steam from the drums flows through the superheater to the high-pressure stage of the main turbine. After expansion in the HP cylinder the steam passes through the reheater, and then through the intermediate and low-pressure cylinders of the turbine to the condenser.

To reduce wastage of feed water during start-up etc, the station is equipped with a high-pressure steam dump system. Steam can be passed via de-superheating stages from the superheater or steam drums to the condenser, regulated by automatic HP and LP dump control systems.

The control room differs from more conventional designs in that the usual indicators and recorders are largely replaced by a dual computer system providing the data processing and display function. Information required for plant operation is displayed on five CRTs grouped around the control desk. In addition there are two printers — one outputs the station log every eight hours; the second, the station reporter, outputs information on alarms etc and allows the operators to communicate with the computers. The computer system also includes three direct digital control (DDC) loops controlling steam temperature (reactor power or core outlet temperature), steam pressure (primary and secondary pump speeds) and main boiler feed pump speed.

The simulator

The trainee operator interacts with the simulator model via a replica of the plant operator's control desk. All the principal controls on the desk are included in the simulation; less important controls, though not currently active, are wired into the interface system for future use. In addition to the control desk, part of the control room mimic panel covering generator synchronisation is simulated on a separate panel. For reasons of computing economy, analogue drum level controllers similar to those on the plant are used. The functions of the station reporter and log printer are combined into a single operator's printer. Ambient environmental conditions are not included in the simulation.

The simulator is controlled from an instructor's console linked to the control desk by telephone. Items of plant included in the simulation but not controlled from the control desk are operated from the instructor's console. The console is equipped with a small CRT display and graph plotter and an instructor's printer. Ten preselected variables can be simultaneously recorded during a simulation, being available for redisplay on the CRT as hard copy, paper tape or the graph plotter.

As well as simulation monitoring, the instructor can inject a series of faults into the system. Nine hundred and ninety-nine are available — some are static faults and others are in the form of drifts.

Simulation runs are started from one of nine initial conditions. These are stored on the system disc store. Eight are loaded by paper tape, the ninth by storing any current steady state during a simulator run. This ninth initial condition can be dumped off disc onto paper tape and may be reloaded as one of the eight standards, thus allowing an extensive library of initial conditions to be built up.

In addition to different starting conditions, the instructor can select differing sets of model constants representing, for example, different amounts of core burn-up.

The model

The simulator model is based on a number of earlier models written to study various aspects of the performance of PFR components. It covers all the main areas of the plant, including the generator and synchronisation equipment. Only two of the three secondary circuits are independently modelled. These are termed the A and B systems. The A system is modelled as a double size unit simulating circuits 1 and 3, the B system being a normal size simulation of circuit 2. The simulation appears to the operator as a three-circuit system. The model is written on a modular basis to facilitate modification and extension. The following brief description outlines its extent and limitations.

Reactor and nucleonic instrumentation: A point neutron kinetics model with two delayed neutron groups is used. A source term is included for modelling shut-down conditions, and fission product heating is also included. A single section thermodynamic model is used, separate breeder sections being omitted.

Primary sodium flow: Primary flow is dealt with in two parts: flow through reactor and pumps, and flow through the IHXs. With the exception of the static head driving sodium flow through the IHXs, static and thermal heads are neglected. Pressure drops in pump pipework are lumped in with the pump characteristic, other pressure drops being assumed proportional to flow. IHX isolation valves are only modelled on the B system. The two intermediate heat exchangers in each secondary circuit are modelled as a single unit.

Intermediate heat exchangers (IHXs): The IHXs are represented using a 'steady state follower' model. The steady state inlet conditions are computed and modified by a suitable transfer function to determine outlet conditions.

Mixing and delays in primary circuit: The effects of mixing and transport delays in the primary sodium are modelled. The primary sodium is divided into two areas: that which takes part in the primary circulation and that which is stagnant. The circulation circuit is further divided into two regions, core outlet to IHX inlet and IHX outlet to core inlet.

Control and shut-off rods: The average position of the five control rods is used to compute reactivity from a worth/position function, shut-off rods being modelled in the same way.

Reactor trips: Generally only trips generated from simulated variables are included, all principal reactor trips being available.

Subassembly outlet temperature map: This section generates individual subassembly outlet temperatures for display purposes, the values being calculated from the temperature of the single channel thermodynamic model.

High-pressure steam dump: This section of the model deals with steam flows between all the HP steam volumes and not just the dump. For simplicity, high-pressure steam pipework volumes are lumped into two steam volumes, the turbine stop valve (TSV) volume and the dump volume. Steam flows are modelled as being functions of the pressures in these and the steam drum volume only. All valves with the exception of the HP dump control and isolation valves have zero stroking times.

Secondary sodium flow: Secondary sodium flow is modelled as a function of secondary pump pressure plus a thermal pressure head component proportional to the differential between evaporator and IHX outlet temperatures. The secondary sodium isolation and cold sodium bypass valves are also modelled. Three transport delays are modelled: IHX outlet to SH and RH inlet, SH and RH outlet to evaporator inlet, and pump to IHX inlet. A mixing term is included in the SH and RH to evaporator delay.

Superheaters: The superheater simulation is based on a three-section finite difference model. Four mesh points are used in the spacial terms, and algebraic expressions are used to represent the steam side of the superheater.

Reheaters: The modelling is essentially the same as for the superheater with the exception that the specific heat of steam is taken as constant and the sodium inlet temperature is a weighted mean of pump and IHX outlet temperature.

Steam drum and recirculation loop: The recirculation loop is divided into four sections — the downcomer, the evaporator, the riser and the steam drum. Generally downcomer flow is treated as constant and evaporator bypass and circulating pump heating are included in the modelling. The evaporator model is a steady state follower, all heat transfer coefficients being assumed independent of flow and the water side temperature being saturation temperature.

The transport and mixing delays in the riser are represented as a simple time constant. The drum model is based on mass balance equations for water and steam spaces and enthalpy balance for the water space. The model includes a term to allow pipe warming take-off. Flashing of steam from bulk water and a representation of drum and loop metalwork thermal capacities are also included.

HP steam space between superheater outlet and turbine valves: The pipework is treated as a lumped mixing volume, for temperature modelling the steam is assumed to be an incompressible fluid of constant specific heat. Steam flow from the TSV volume to the turbine assumes the turbine stop valve, throttle valve and HP cylinder to be a single above critical ratio nozzle, flow being directly proportional to throttle position. The governor, pressure unloading gear and superheater safety valves are also included in this section.

Feedwater enthalpy: Three feed heaters are modelled, high pressure feed heater 8, feed heaters 6 and 7 combined and the de-aerator. DC heater 4 is included with the de-aerator. HP feed heaters are modelled by a steady state follower. The modelling of the de-aerator includes heating from HP dump steam, main boiler feed pump exhaust and auxiliary feed pump recirculation.

Flow of water in feed line: The emergency, auxiliary and main feed pumps are all modelled using quadratic flow-speed-pressure head characteristics. The main boiler feed pump takes steam from the superheater (live) and from cold reheat (bled). These are modelled as mixing in a fictitious steam volume before entering the turbine. The turbine is modelled as an above critical ratio nozzle, feed regulator valves being modelled as having a largely exponential characteristic.

The turbo generator set: This section contains equations representing the mechanical torque produced by the steam and expressions for the various electrical parameters. The machine model is based on the Park two-axis representation. The exported power split between 125 and 275kv lines is also simulated.

The intermediate-pressure steam space: The IP steam space between the HP cylinder outlet and the interceptor valve is modelled as two regions representing pipe volumes before and after the reheater. The two volumes are connected by a flow resistance. This resistance is a function of the movement of the various valves included in the model. Steam temperature at the HP cylinder outlet is modelled as directly proportional to the temperature drop from the inlet. The pressure-density-temperature equation assumes the steam to be a perfect gas.

Operating experience

Following the commissioning of the simulator a basic training course was organised for the PFR operations staff. Operators were taken in groups of three or four and, over a period of five days, followed a course based on the following format:

The first day was mainly taken up with familiarisation with the controls and plant response. Trainees not already familiar with the display system had an opportunity to become so. Having become familiar with the plant the trainees went into a 'cold start' procedure. On PFR a cold start is any start-up taking place more than ten hours after a turbine trip. The trainees then began de-aerator warming and drum filling. The drum water is then warmed by the boiler circulating pump before commissioning the evaporators. With the evaporators commissioned and the dump system operating the reactor is taken critical, and reactor outlet temperature is increased to give the potential superheat required for commissioning the superheater. After superheater commissioning, the main boiler feed pump is brought into service. Steam temperature is further increased to match the turbine casing temperature and the turbine is commissioned. The reheaters are brought into service when the steam conditions at the reheater inlet are suitable. Turbine power is increased until steam conditions permit commissioning of the HP feed heaters and bypassing of the reheater pressure sustaining valve.

During the remaining period trainees carry out hot start and controlled shut-down procedures, manoeuvre the plant at power in manual, and practise manual control of drum level and the main boiler feed pump turbine. Some fault condition recovery may be practised towards the end of the course depending on the trainee's ability.

The basic training course is the only course currently available for operations staff, however, instruction on the simulator is an integral part of the fast reactor technology courses run by the Dounreay Fast Reactor Training Centre.

The simulator has been used extensively in its roles of operational tool and plant response analyser (PRA). It has been found particularly useful in predicting plant performance under the various constraints associated with plant commissioning and non-standard operating conditions. It has also proved useful for carrying out dummy runs on commissioning experiments such as control rod drop tests and the like. Since all the major control loops are modelled, initial settings for plant controller commissioning have been determined by simulation, thus avoiding deliberately perturbing the actual plant excessively — this aspect being particularly useful in drum level controller commissioning.

A series of programs have been written for the PRA mode. The three main programs are data logging and analysis, transfer function analysis and a software reactivity meter. The data logging and reactivity meter programs are in regular use.

Using the simulator as an operational tool has highlighted areas in the modelling that have not been sufficiently detailed. In particular, remodelling has been carried out on the main boiler feed pump, with the inclusion of leak-off and an improved efficiency equation. The turbine modelling has been greatly extended as large departures from normal operating condition produced unacceptable inaccuracies in the HP cylinder outlet conditions. It was also found that six delayed neutron groups were required to provide an adequate simulation for rod dropping experiments. Apart from these exceptions the modelling has proved very satisfactory.

The specification for the simulator allowed for 20 per cent spare core storage, and 20 per cent spare computing time to be available. This, and the modular format of the model, makes model development straightforward.

The assembler language that the model is written in includes comprehensive comments alongside the coding; this has proved invaluable in manipulating and understanding the software. The spare core storage capacity is currently distributed throughout the model, a small section of spare core between each module. The intention is to allow individual modules to be modified and reassembled in isolation. In practice this has not worked out as intended, and would be more convenient treated as a single block of store at the end of the model.

In retrospect, certain facilities not available on the PFR simulator would be well worth considering for future designs. With the limited number of initial conditions available on the simulator, training time can be lost by having to start again from scratch following a plant trip. The lost time can be reduced by manually storing current steady states using the initial condition 9 facility previously described but this has a disruptive effect on the training aspect of a simulation. It might be useful, therefore, to have an option to select automatic storage of current steady states, say, every five minutes during a simulation. On re-initialisation the pre-trip situation on the plant may be discussed with the trainees and suitable corrective action taken. A further useful facility would be the ability to override all the plant trips — at present this is only available on reactor trips. Such a facility would be of considerable value for training and operation use.

Future development

The simulator is likely to be extensively used as an operational tool for some time to come, but it is expected that its usefulness in this role will decline. As the final commissioning phase of PFR nears completion, more emphasis will be placed on the operator training side. A more advanced refresher training scheme is currently being prepared; it is hoped to integrate this as a regular programme into the day-to-day running of the plant. Feedback from plant operators will be employed in structuring the programme. In general, however, emphasis will be on recovery from plant failure situations, practising emergency procedures, interpretation of instrument readings and alarms etc. The general aim of the training scheme is to improve operator efficiency which should lead to improved reliability of the human aspects of safety systems and a reduction in outages caused by operator error.

Future developments of the model software will be concentrated on modifications based on data received as part of a general model verification programme for PFR and will largely consist of adjustments to model constants. Modelling of the hydrogen detection system for the steam generators is also being considered as operator response to indications of sodium-water reactions cannot, at present, be included in training schemes.

Using simulators in an integrated learning programme

John D Smith, *Royal Air Force, RAF Leeming*

This paper gives a brief description of flying training in general and an account of the stages of training for a pilot who is selected to fly a multi-engined aircraft. The paper describes the RAF's systems approach and the training design used as it has evolved with reference to simulators. An account of the nature and function of three synthetic training devices is given. It concludes with a summary of progress during the first training course.

Background

This paper describes the design of a training programme to enable pilots to fly multi-engined aircraft. It gives the background to the problems of multi-engine pilot training, outlines the training policy upon which the design was based and shows how the selective employment of simulators enables the air crew to achieve safe and effective flying standards with a parsimonious number of actual flying hours.

Flying training in the RAF can be broken down into four stages: basic flying training, advanced flying training, operational conversion and squadron training. This is a simplification of a complex process which ignores such things as instructor or refresher training. Following basic flying training pilots are streamed to fast jet, multi-engine or helicopter flying.

During his basic flying training a pilot is taught to fly a simple, single-engined aircraft, the *Jet Provost*. When selected to fly multi-engined aircraft he has to learn many new skills. There is an enormous difference between solo flying in a *Jet Provost* and becoming a pilot crew member of such aircraft as the *Hercules* or the *Nimrod*. The need to bridge the gap is obvious; how it should be bridged is less so. One way to train pilots to fly large aeroplanes would be to send them directly to the operational units where they would learn by on-the-job training. Attractive as this may seem, it is very expensive and would mean the withdrawal of operational aircraft for training purposes. It would also require scattered groups of specialist instructors and a larger standardisation unit than we have at present.

Analysis shows that multi-engined aircraft have a number of common handling techniques. By creating a training unit using a multi-engined aircraft which is smaller and less costly than the operational ones, pilots can be taught the techniques in a compact, standard, cost-effective training situation with a concentration of specialist instructors. This intermediate stage of flying is called advanced flying training because it follows the basic course.

For many years the aircraft used by the RAF to train pilots in the multi-engine role was the *Varsity*. Inevitably this long-serving air-frame had to be replaced and the aircraft selected as the replacement was the Handley-Page *Jetstream*. The *Jetstream* is a twin-engined aircraft now parented by the Scottish Aviation Division of British Aerospace.

The aircraft was introduced into RAF service in 1973 at which time it seemed possible to continue training along the well-established *Varsity* pattern simply making allowances for its more complicated avionics. This pattern was one in which students were given a ground school phase of training followed, since there was no *Varsity* simulator, by the flying phase in which each student flew 70 hours in the aircraft.

In 1974, just as the first *Jetstream* course was ending, two unrelated events resulted in the *Jetstream* being withdrawn. The first was an engineering problem and the second was a severe defence cut. Even though the engineering problem was resolved the aircraft were put in storage and the supply of multi-engine trained pilots was maintained by using those who became available as some squadrons were disbanded and training others on civilian flying courses. The supply of experienced pilots was obviously limited and as the civilian flying courses were not ideal for military pilots, a resumption of service courses was decided upon and *Jetstream* was reintroduced in 1976.

Within two weeks of the decision to reintroduce *Jetstream* a Project Team was formed of two pilots with *Jetstream* experience and an Education Officer as the Training Design Adviser. Four main tasks had to be accomplished: the aircraft had to be brought back into service, an advanced flying training course had to be designed, a refresher course for experienced pilots was required and training had to be given to pilots selected as *Jetstream* instructors. These four tasks are interrelated but it is convenient for our present purpose to regard the training design as separate from the others.

In June 1973 the RAF adopted what can be called a systems approach to training; this dictated the *Jetstream* course design. The new course was based on behavioural objectives which were statements of pilot performance. There were the inevitable constraints, the most significant ones being cost and time, both of which affected our approach. The overall aim was to get students to fly the aircraft as soon as they had sufficient skill and knowledge. Additionally, we had to take account of the simulators which were available. In 1973 the *Jetstream* had a COCKPIT PROCEDURES TRAINER and an INSTRUMENT TRAINER to enable students to practise routine drills and procedures. Subsequently a DYNAMIC SIMULATOR was built which reached Leeming in December 1976. This provided us with the opportunity to reduce the number of flying hours without lowering the final training standard.

The training system

Systems approach savants will be asking about job analysis and the associated inventory of activities. Our tasking required us to have the course and its related documents in print within six months. It was therefore decided to use such training inventories as had been made when the *Jetstream* first flew and augment these with the experience of the team's pilots. In calculating how many flying hours per student were required an initial proposal of 40 was seen to be inadequate; the present 45 hours flying plus ten per cent for flexibility is probably about right so long as there are no snags with the simulator.

The real core of our task was the writing of over 900 behavioural objectives, 250,000 words in six training documents, 15 ground and four flying tests, and designing more than 30 forms. As part of this process we wrote objectives for the COCKPIT PROCEDURES TRAINER, the INSTRUMENT TRAINER and the DYNAMIC SIMULATOR.

An integrated learning programme was produced which aimed at eliminating the 'play-pen' system in which all students stay in ground school for a statutory period of time, then move *en bloc* to simulator training and, only after this, are they allowed aboard the aircraft. The present design integrated ground school, synthetic and flying aspects of training with the intention of creating a logical learning sequence and allowing students to fly as soon as is possible. Such a sequence of training can only be established when all the objectives have been written and are divided into logically sequenced instructional units.

There are seven *critical points* in the course; these are the latest points at which a student must demonstrate that he has acquired the necessary skills and knowledge to fly a particular sortie. If a student fails a test or exercise before a critical point then he has to be retested or the exercise successfully flown before he can continue beyond the critical point.

Although the term 'simulator' has been used for these learning aids it is probably more correct to call them Synthetic Training Aids and reserve the term simulator for the equipment which has a full flight deck and movement. The aids are, however, a continuum of degrees of simulation, the most simple being the COCKPIT PROCEDURES TRAINER. As its name implies, this trainer is designed to allow students to carry out procedural checks of instruments and switches. The learning is routine and has an associated verbal patter. The trainer, built by Scottish Aviation, has sufficient equipment to allow two students to locate and operate switches on a challenge and response basis. As one student calls out the action from Flight Reference Cards the other takes the appropriate action. The roles are then reversed. Such training can be tedious and time-consuming, but the environment of the procedures trainer maintains motivation by its degree of reality and is available at any time. There are no motion or sound cues, the only visual cues are the limited internal representation of the cockpit, and apart from switches moving and knobs turning there is minimal engine instrument response.

The second stage in simulation is the *Jetstream* INSTRUMENT TRAINER, a computer-controlled system built by the Redifen Company in 1973 and used when the *Jetstream* first entered service. It is interesting to note that the behavioural objectives written for this trainer in 1973 have, with some modifications, been incorporated into the present syllabus. The INSTRUMENT TRAINER is more representational of the aircraft than the PROCEDURES TRAINER although lacking the head panel of switches, external visual reference and movement. When a sortie is flown the instruments respond to the controls and a track is traced out which can be analysed by student and instructor after the exercise. The reaction to movement of the controls is limited but the INSTRUMENT TRAINER is of tremendous value from the learner's point of view because he can use it on his own and repeat any manoeuvre which gives him problems. It is not a testing environment since the only report raised at this stage is a note of completion of a particular exercise. This note is made by the simulator operator, not a flying instructor. There are nine INSTRUMENT TRAINER exercises which take 12 hours to complete. With the exception of the first sortie these exercises are programmed in two blocks, one prior to instrument flying, the other just before the high-low-high sortie.

The most sophisticated aid is the *Jetstream* DYNAMIC SIMULATOR. This simulator was built by the Link Miles Division of Singer (UK) Ltd. Because of uncertainties about the location of *Jetstream* the simulator had an itinerant existence before being brought to Leeming at the end of 1976. It is a computer-aided learning environment which closely resembles the *Jetstream* flight deck. It has full controls, switches and sound and motion response, the only major omission being external vision. Control response is not absolutely representational — this highlights one of the oldest problems in the simulator world. Experienced *Jetstream* pilots tend to be critical of the simulator's performance whereas students who are building on their inventory of sensory experience find the simulator to be invaluable. This is typical of simulation in which the degree of reality has to be estimated against the training objectives, generally resulting in a financial trade-off. It is, for example, impossible to justify the cost of a visual system if the training objectives do not indicate it to be essential.

Each student flies 21 simulator sorties of 1½ hours' duration. Time, with the exception of one airways trip, is the same as for actual flights; all airborne manoeuvres are practised in the simulator before flight and a flying instructor is present recording student progress and using the time for demonstration and directed instruction. The objectives and simulator exercises were written before the simulator was installed at Leeming. This sequence, which we believe to be correct, is unusual because simulators have been with us long before the RAF adopted a systems approach. By specifying performance, standards and conditions it is hoped to eliminate some of the abuses of simulation such as putting pilots through simulated exercises without finding out whether the pilots need the exercises or using the simulator as a 'trapping' device in which problems are injected at such a rate as to guarantee mission failure and produce an alienated student.

The DYNAMIC SIMULATOR is the fulcrum of *Jetstream* training, providing an important transition from ground to air in both physical and mental respects. The exercises are flown by students and instructor with the instructor recording the sortie in exactly the same way as for a flying exercise, omitting only the overall assessment. The student is told about his performance and is given a copy of the exercise report. From the student's point of view this system has two main advantages: the student gets immediate knowledge of results to which he can refer later, and he becomes accustomed to the assessment process as an integral part of training.

Unlike earlier training systems the *Jetstream* course has no distinct phases. The synthetic trainers are used as soon as possible and as late as necessary. All flying tests are first practised in the simulator within the limitations of the equipment. If a test is failed in the air then weaknesses can be identified and further practice can be given in the simulator before retesting. The simulator is a reasonable guarantee of safe flying performance and it ensures that high standards are not only achieved but also, through repetitive training, maintained.

The setting of standards for both simulator and flying sorties is the most difficult and emotive part of course design. We chose to follow the path established by the RAF's initial course design team in 1972. We made changes where specific *Jetstream* limitations required them or where problems had been identified on similar training courses. Simulator and flying exercises are divided into a series of actions, each having six levels of performance (with the exception of the observation of aircraft limits which tends to be obvious). In order to make sure that each instructor uses the same levels, a word picture is provided; thus, when a student carries out a steep turn the instructor is able to grade it according to its description. For example level 2 is expressed as:

> The student required some assistance to complete this item/exercise or to avoid critical errors. He knew the technique/procedure but needs more practice to reach an acceptable standard.

Level 3 is:

> The student performed this item/exercise without assistance and with only occasional lapses into non-critical errors. He is fit to practise this item solo (if the syllabus allows).

It can be seen that the first time a student carries out a sortie either in the simulator or in the air he will normally reach levels 1 to 3 and as he gains in confidence and experience this will rise to levels 3 to 6. One of the problems of this criterion-referenced system is to persuade both instructors and students of the logic of starting at the bottom. There is a culturally induced norm-referenced desire to reflect performance, even in the early stages, as 'average' and indicate this by recording levels 3 or 4. Our intention is that at level 3 a student is capable of practising the item on his own — fit solo, by level 4 he has reached the pass grade for the course and with level 5 he has achieved the anticipated course average.

Evaluation

It is far too soon to make any evaluation of the course except in the very raw sense that target dates have been met, instructors are using the system without much difficulty and the students, who have all been interviewed by the project team, say they are satisfied so far. The value of *Jetstream* training will only show when the present students are flying in operational squadrons in 1979. In this description of the course much has, of necessity, been omitted, no mention has been made of learning packages and the sequence of flying exercises has been assumed to be correct, but in day-to-day terms we depend very largely on the DYNAMIC SIMULATOR which is our critical path in course design.

Simulation of offshore activities

Blyth McNaughton, *Robert Gordon's Institute of Technology, Aberdeen*

This paper initially considers the broad philosophy of simulation as applied in offshore activities related to oil and gas exploration and production. Three prime aspects of this are stressed, namely:
  Infrequent and extremely dangerous phenomena which, when they occur in real life, are a hazard to plant and personnel and as such require simulation to permit training in their control. Examples outlined in this area will include well blowout control simulation and fire fighting/damage control simulation.
  The abandonment of offshore installation requires particular simulation by using actual equipment in contrived situations. Training in the use of totally enclosed life boats and life rafts will be reviewed and helicopter abandonment simulation will be considered.
  The training of operators for controlling offshore production plant presents a particular challenge and current thinking and proposed simulation methods will be included.
The nature of existing simulators is outlined and the need for other types and methods is suggested. The paper concludes by considering various simulations.

Introduction

Why simulate when at best a counterfeit of reality only is achieved? When there is a requirement to develop personal skills or plant for demanding and hazardous situations then some form of simulation technique will permit their development efficiently and safely. Simulation is particularly worth while when training plant operatives if the plant is complex and costly and any error in judgement by inexperienced trainees could result in danger to personnel and plant. The attendant pressures of an operational situation are not conducive to constructive learning. Simulations have been made for many centuries from the crude but effective jousting and personal combat simulators to the multi-million-dollar complexes used to train astronauts.

The Link trainer method of instructing aircraft pilots represents one of the first high-technology simulators used for training.

The main areas for simulator applications are:
— research and development where the quality of reproduction must be high,
— education and training where, depending on the application, the demand for fidelity can be less severe,
— testing of plant and procedures.

Simulation can be achieved in a variety of ways which include:
— actual plant and equipment used in simulated situations,
— electrical and/or mechanical analogues,

— use of digital computer models,
— physical models of systems.

Offshore oil and gas operations, because of their complexity, cost and awkward locations lend themselves to a wide use of all forms of simulation. As the supporting technology advances, more demands are placed on men and systems requiring effective education and training. Some simulation methods are already well established and practised by the oil industry. These have been modified from onshore procedures to reproduce the new offshore situations. But new techniques and difficult environmental conditions require new approaches and offer a wide range of possible simulation opportunities.

This paper outlines a selection of some of the existing or proposed simulations for training in:

— control of infrequent and extremely hazardous phenomena,
— safety and survival procedures,
— control and operation of oil and gas production plant.

Infrequent and extremely hazardous phenomena

There are two great dangers which prevail while exploring or producing hydrocarbons:

— well blowout, and
— fire.

Fire may result as a consequence of a well blowout but on the other hand it might be initiated by other occurrences. Should such events take place then personnel trained and familiar with control procedures should be able to react, and restore the situation to normal. Unfortunately, when using technological systems we sometimes react rather irrationally, particularly in difficult situations. Adequate education and training will not guarantee rationality but do give the trainee confidence that if established procedures are undertaken, danger can be averted.

WELL CONTROL SIMULATION

A blowout is the uncontrolled flow of gas or oil from an underground hydrocarbon formation and can occur at any time when the formation fluid pressure is higher than the hydrostatic pressure produced by the drilling mud in the well. A threatened blowout is called a *kick*.

Because of their unpredictability, kicks have always been a major headache for the oil industry. With the increase in deep offshore drilling and the serious pollution risk which a blowout can cause, even greater care must be taken in prevention and control of such phenomena.

In the early days of drilling, *mud* was an unsophisticated fluid introduced primarily to remove the rock cuttings from the hole. Present-day mud is an extremely complex mixture of solids, liquids and chemicals which is varied according to the particular well-bore problem. However, the principle functions of the mud remain:

— transporting rock cuttings to the surface, and
— controlling the formation pressure.

There are two types of kick, water and gas, the latter being the most difficult to control and the most dangerous when out of control. Formation fluid enters the well-bore and a 'bubble' will ascend the hole expanding on its way towards the surface. The expanding bubble causes drilling mud to be intermittently pushed out of the hole and a series of kicks takes place which, if left uncontrolled, will develop into a full-scale blowout.

A blowout can occur for a number of reasons, some of which are:
— mud weight is too low,
— failure to keep the hole full of mud as the drill pipe is removed,
— swabbing effect caused by running the drill pipe in or out of the hole too quickly,
— loss of mud because flow is in formation (lost circulation).

Successful control is dependent on early detection and vigilance is essential. The warning signs of a kick include:
— mud volume increase in surface storage tanks,
— sudden increase in drilling rate,
— appearance of gas or water in mud returns,
— reduction in delivery pressure of the drilling mud,
— reduction in the 'apparent' weight of the drill pipe combination.

It is essential that diagnosis is made quickly and correctly. Since delay reduces the chance of controlling the well, unnecessary shut-down of drilling operations is a cardinal sin. When convinced that a blowout is threatened a predetermined sequence of operations must be initiated:
— stop the drilling mud pump,
— close the blowout preventer valves (BOP). These are a set of high-pressure valves hydraulically operated and located on top of the well casing. This operation will close the well in completely, resulting in a pressure rise in the drill pipe and the casing,
— record the volume of mud displaced by the kick,
— record the drill pipe and casing pressures.

Immediate steps must now be taken to restore the pressure balance in the well by pumping in heavier mud through the drill pipe. The weight of the 'kill-mud' is determined from standard calculations involving the volume of mud displaced and the drill pipe and casing pressures. As the heavier mud is introduced to the well, control by a choke-valve allows the slow, careful ascent of the bubble to the surface. A number of accepted kill procedures have been established with a basic principle of maintaining constant pressure opposite the reservoir. This pressure must be the minimum required to dominate the reservoir, otherwise the formation could be damaged. To successfully recognise and control a well kick demands great skill and patience, and to develop such expertise some form of simulation is vital.

An electrical analogue which provides such simulation consists of panels which provide dynamical representation of the:
— driller's controls,
— choke-valve operation,
— blowout preventer configuration and operation,
— progress of the kill-mud and bubble.

In the USA some universities and companies have test wells which simulate kicks by introducing a quantity of nitrogen gas at depth. Such wells are able to reproduce more realistic flow conditions and thereby duplicate the kick behaviour more precisely. The time required to complete a well control exercise on a 10,000-foot test well could be in the region of three to four hours, and this restricts the trainee throughput. A simulator can allow trainees to practise drilling, experience a kick, circulate the kill-mud removing the intruding water or gas, and restore the pressure balance in a quarter of the real time. The process can be 'frozen' at any stage allowing additional instruction and clarification of difficulties to be made.

Although the multi-component non-Newtonian nature of the flow prevents perfect reproduction by simulators, their use allows greater throughput of trainees, thus ensuring that a greater number of rig personnel are exposed to at least the very elementary aspects of blowout control. Existing simulators are capable of providing more advanced training by introducing a variety of difficulties superimposed upon the basic blowout occurrence. Well control procedures should be rehearsed frequently and refresher training should be an essential part of any training schedule. Training which allows the use of a test well and an analogue simulator has the greatest potential for success.

FIRE CONTROL SIMULATION

Fire on a platform could be the consequence of a well blowout and could progress rapidly until the only policy is to abandon the platform. It is more likely that initially less disastrous fires could be initiated, as are many onshore industrial fires, through plant and equipment malfunction or careless handling and storage of combustible materials. In any event it is essential to have a well-trained fire team able to tackle all classes of fires with confidence. In fire control training it is especially important to permit trainees to become familiar with actual systems and equipment. They should be allowed to operate such equipment in conditions which simulate the snags and confusions of real fire conditions. When crude oil or natural gas burns, large quantities of black dense smoke are produced making movement in confined spaces difficult and dangerous. In the simulation of offshore fires the layout of the plant and the geometry of a platform module should be duplicated. Trainees should be instructed on the use of breathing apparatus and should develop confidence in working with it on.

Real fire conditions are soon to be simulated at the Fire Training Centre located at Montrose and operated for the oil industry by the Petroleum Industry Training Board. All the latest fire-fighting aids will be used in training. Different types of oil and gas and plant fires will be simulated in steel mock-ups representing standard platform configurations. Such simulation will provide the trainee with basic fire-fighting skills, develop the team concept and ensure effective fire control.

Safety and survival procedure

When technology fails and this failure causes loss of life, then deep feelings are stirred and controversy rages as to whether the safety systems are adequate or whether lives could have been saved had survival procedures been properly undertaken. All offshore operations carry an element of risk to human life and health. Operating companies recognising this risk have installed survival systems and procedures to ensure the survival of personnel while on the platform or in transit by helicopter.

ABANDONMENT OF AN INSTALLATION

Reasons for abandoning an offshore installation might include:
— well blowout with or without fire,
— structural failure of the installation caused by severe weather or impact by
 another vessel,
— failure of plant and equipment causing explosion, fire or the release of
 toxic gases.

All platforms are provided with a primary survival system consisting of totally enclosed lifeboats and a secondary system of self-inflatable life-rafts. Twice as many as might be required are supplied to allow for damage or the occasion when a craft might be lowered without a full complement.

The principle requirements of a survival craft should include:
— total enclosure to provide protection for the occupant from the harsh sea
 and weather conditions,
— adequate life support systems and supplies for five days,
— good sea worthiness in severe storm conditions including self-righting
 capabilities,
— easy and rapid embarkation hatches,
— safe and rapid movement away from the platform, perhaps through an area
 of burning oil or toxic gases, requiring a positive pressure within the craft
 to prevent gas entry,
— ability to be recovered back onto the platform.

Primary system: A variety of totally enclosed lifeboats are available and each possesses more or less the above capabilities. The boats are constructed in reinforced plastic with fire-resistant additives. Water spray systems covering the whole of the craft are a vital requirement. Each boat can carry 50 persons, who wear safety straps during the lowering sequence. The drop from the davits to the sea can be anything from 50 to 100 feet.

Secondary system: Since the last war, the self-inflating life-raft has become a familiar item of marine survival equipment. The life-raft with 25-person capacity now provides a secondary survival system on offshore installations.

Manufactured from lightweight rubber-coated nylon fabric, the raft consists of two circular buoyancy tubes, each capable of supporting the raft plus complement, and a canopy supported by an arch. Sheets covering the entrance and an inflatable floor provide protection from the weather and sea. Life-rafts are stowed in glass-reinforced plastic capsules to protect them from the elements. There are two possible methods of launching:
— secure to installation with painter and throw the capsule into the sea. A
 tug of the painter inflates the raft which is reached by a Jacob's ladder,
 scrambling nets or knotted rope, or
— avoid the use of descent ladders etc by using a single arm davit to lower the
 inflated raft and complement.

However, life-rafts do not provide protection against fire and toxic gases. Lack of an engine prevents them travelling quickly out of danger and, depending on the wind and currents, they can be swept into a dangerous location.

Training of personnel in the use of survival systems in simulated conditions increases their chances of survival should a real emergency occur.

The main objects of such training should be to:

- familiarise trainees with all aspects of survival equipment and its use,
- develop confidence in operating systems under simulated conditions,
- illustrate aspects of personal survival.

The Offshore Safety and Survival Unit of Robert Gordon's Institute of Technology is in the forefront of this type of simulated training. Courses at the unit provide each trainee with practical instruction in clearing away, launching, steering and recovery of totally enclosed lifeboats. Man overboard and foul weather recovery procedures are undertaken. In addition the use of the lifeboat equipment and steering by compass in different sea states is practised. Inflatable life-raft launching, dry and wet boarding, and righting capsized raft procedures are undertaken in a training pool. Complementing these 'hands-on' simulations are a series of demonstrations and lectures which include: theory of power boat handling, platform crew drills and weekly inspections of survival systems, platform emergency evacuation procedures, lifejacket drills, firing of pyrotechnics, medical aspects of survival at sea, the use of radio aids and helicopter escape, search and rescue.

ESCAPE FROM A DITCHED HELICOPTER

Considering the magnitude of operations and the large number of helicopter movements to offshore installations (250,000+ passengers per year from the UK) from both British and Norwegian bases, the safety record of the principal helicopter operators is most commendable. In the last five years there have been six accidents and only three resulted in fatalities. The percentage of survival in any accident is high provided the people involved do not panic and have been properly instructed in emergency procedures. There appears to be no agreed policy relating to the extent and nature of training required by passengers intending to travel offshore by air. Naval procedures, as practised at the Royal Naval helicopter 'dunker' located at HMS Vernon, Portsmouth, appear too severe for civilian purposes and less traumatic training procedures are advisable to provide the trainee with an opportunity to gradually develop confidence in his ability to react in emergency situations.

Currently there are six different types of helicopters operating to offshore installations and with their own particular configuration of doors, windows and emergency hatches. To ensure completely adequate training in 'wet' escape from all types would be complex and expensive. However, familiarisation with escape procedures and establishing confidence in the trainee is possible using a helicopter escape survival simulator within a training pool. Should a helicopter be forced down in the sea, the crew and passengers (who will be wearing survival suits) will be required to disembark into self-inflated life-rafts. Consequent on the manner of ditching and the sea state the fuselage will normally remain upright and afloat, allowing this drill to be successfully accomplished. All doors and emergency hatches will have been opened prior to ditching and as a result the sea will flood the cabin, probably to a depth of one foot, but under instruction from the cabin crew, orderly exit will be achieved.

Should the ditch be other than 'normal' and the sea state stormy, the fuselage could adopt a variety of attitudes and levels of submersion which might require the occupants to take a breath of air and swim under water to reach the escape hatch before reaching the surface and the life-raft.

An escape simulator should be capable of fulfilling *three* basic functions if all

requirements, including the most extreme condition of ditching, are to be reproduced:
- — 180° rotation about the cabin longitudinal axis in both directions, simulating the condition of an immobile helicopter floating on the sea surface being rotated about its centre of gravity due to wave and/or wind action on the fuselage side,
- — variable pitch angle of at least 20° to the horizontal nose down, corresponding to the attitude adopted by a capsized helicopter due to a buoyancy difference between nose and tail. (The magnitude of the pitch angle is a function of the type of helicopter and the position of its payload),
- — variable vertical movement of approximately seven feet, to provide different levels of submersion.

Control and operation of oil and gas production plant

The use of scale models in the research and development of complex fluid flow systems is an accepted design method. In recent years, greater use has been made of digital and analogue computers in studying system behaviour. It is considered worth while to spend time and capital in perfecting the system and predicting its operation characteristics, particularly in response to varying flow conditions.

It must be accepted that in simulating plant and processes by any of these methods discrepancies will occur. The scale difference between a model and a full-sized plant can change the flow conditions quite significantly and give errors in predicted performance. With computers, the main limitation is the ability to establish a sufficiently representative set of mathematical equations to describe the flow which can be operated efficiently within the capacity of existing computers. Thus the simulation of flow systems which involve heat, mass and momentum transfer will at best only provide qualitative reproduction and offer broad guide-lines of full-scale performance. However, such reproduction can be sufficiently accurate to be used in the training of plant operators before they are ready to use the real thing. The principles of such simulation would be to challenge the trainee with a sequence of normal and abnormal events and determine his response in comparison with established procedures.

The control and production of oil and gas is influenced by the physical properties of the reservoir. A typical reservoir will normally contain gas, gas-oil mixture, oil, and salt water. These constituents will be found in varying proportions in most reservoirs. When a well is in production an oil-gas-water mixture reaches the production platform where the separation plant frees the oil from dissolved gas and water before transportation by tanker or subsea pipeline. The separated gas must be freed of any remaining oil, water and carbon dioxide, and hydrogen sulphide removed.

When all the necessary plant involved in separation, treatment and pumping is assembled, the production platform represents a concentration of complex interacting engineering systems. If added to this complexity are the facts that, first, no two reservoirs contain precisely the same proportion of constituents, and second, companies prefer their own particular ergonomic layout of control room consoles, then the enormous problem of devising a universal production process simulator can be appreciated.

There is a need to provide training in the operation of oil and gas production systems and undoubtedly there exist opportunities for applying simulation methods to provide hands-on experience.

Three simulation methods which seem appropriate are:
— use of full-scale plant in simulated conditions,
— use of digital and analogue computers,
— use of model plant and components.

On-the-job training using the platform plant is difficult and dangerous with inexperienced trainees, but to provide a plant complex which would simulate every permutation would be extremely expensive.

Analogue process simulators with static mimic boards are available and are used for training in the chemical process industry, but as yet these units have not been extended to simulate offshore production systems.

Digital computers are better able to cope with the complex fluid flow equations and remain the best prospect when their output is used to drive an analogue mimic board representing the control console. On the other hand, working models of individual and combination subsystems are an attractive and a much less costly proposition. Subsystem models are being developed at Robert Gordon's Institute of Technology which could, in addition to providing operator training, permit a fundamental study of the heat, mass and momentum transfers. This study should establish more representative fluid flow equations for use with digital computer simulations. The subsystems under study are oil and gas separation and gas dehydration.

An oil and gas separator is a pressure vessel which, by virtue of its design, is capable of separating the effluent from producing wells into the principle constituents of oil, gas and water. Depending upon the particular reservoir conditions and the proportion of constituents present, a number of separation stages in series may be necessary.

The separated gas will contain water droplets and a little oil and is circulated through a series of absorption dehydrators. The main components of a dehydrator are the absorption column, surge tank, reboiler and still column. Glycol has proved the most effective gas dehydrator because it is highly hydroscopic, stable to heat and chemical decomposition and readily available at reasonable cost.

Both simulators operate under pressure and are fully instrumented to record salient temperatures, pressures and constituent flow rates which can be varied and measured. At present a two-component flow of air and water is being studied but it is intended to ultimately have multi-component flow with the simulators in series.

Conclusion

From the examples considered it should be apparent that simulation of offshore activities is of concern and interest to operating companies.

A number of important considerations make the onshore simulation of such activities attractive. Such considerations include:
— the hostile sea environment and remoteness of platform locations,
— the complexity and cost of plant and installations,
— the need for effective and efficient training in safety,
— the possibility of refresher training to maintain peak response to crisis situations.

Whenever or wherever hands-on experience is possible, then this is to be preferred and this method of simulation is particularly effective when real equipment is used in contrived situations. But the simulator in its various representations of reality constitutes an admirable substitute.

The simulation of disaster and uncertainty

I C Hendry, *Robert Gordon's Institute of Technology, Aberdeen*

Experience in designing the BRUCE OIL MANAGEMENT GAME is called upon to help answer the question of how much uncertainty can be tolerated in a management game. In real life, if complete disaster occurs and results in throwing the project being managed into turmoil, eg the Flixborough and Seveso disasters, the situation has to be managed somehow. In a game the occurrence of a complete disaster will tend to throw all players back to square one which is undesirable on grounds of economic use of educational time. At the other extreme a completely deterministic situation, no matter how complex, obviously lacks realism; the question 'how much uncertainty should be injected?' arises.

In the BRUCE OIL MANAGEMENT GAME a large number of decision points were created, and at many opportunites were taken, to inject uncertainty in the interests of producing realism. A few of the areas where it is desirable to be uncertain are oil price, production capability, transport availability (weather), and refinery throughput. The designers had to decide a level of uncertainty which would keep the game interesting for the players without causing frustration or introducing bias.

Introduction

This paper aims to raise the question 'How far should one build disaster and/or uncertainty into a game in the cause of producing realism?' It would appear that some degree of uncertainty can add excitement; it is postulated that complete disaster would have to be followed by a need to retrace one's footsteps over ground already covered; by its very nature, therefore, through its need for repetition, disaster must make inefficient use of good educational time; when this aspect is considered along with the extreme rarity of disaster in real life the incentive to create a disaster situation is small.

General types of systems

To appreciate the need for uncertainty in simulation exercises we can identify two general types of system:

(a) strictly controlled deterministic systems, and
(b) loosely controlled systems with uncertain outcome.

In category (a) examples arise in science and engineering where the experimenter uses models controlled by well-defined parameters; he varies the parameters within sensible limits and obtains a prediction of the expected outcome. Such models are used to design complicated items like chemical plant, oil refineries, nuclear reactors etc. The designers are confident about predicting results and rely (perhaps unwittingly) on the work of generations of scientists and engineers who have provided accurate measurements of the physical properties of materials and devised the best working models.

The key feature in engineering situations is the ability to exercise control in the real situation and thereby achieve the desired results. A word of caution is necessary, however, because uncertainty does exist in predicting the performance of many real-life science and engineering situations — very often where end-effects or the existence of sharp corners complicate matters.

In category (b) examples are found in the socio-economic field. The key feature is lack of control of the real situation, hence reduced confidence in predicting the outcome. The real-life situation demands a monitoring of the changes taking place so that one can respond to suit one's needs. Normally one has control over only a small part of the whole, hence a high degree of uncertainty exists.

The art of modelling

In all modelling the tendency is to over-simplify in order to achieve a working model. Minimisation of over-simplification must therefore be a key objective. We all want realism but when we fall short we invoke 'educational licence' where we ask to be forgiven our shortcomings in the interests of furthering education. A good educationalist will want to put over a small number of easily assimilated ideas which will be of value in understanding the more complex problems. Against the background of the above general points I would like to discuss the evolution of the model for the BRUCE OIL MANAGEMENT GAME.

Modelling the BRUCE OIL MANAGEMENT GAME

1. GENERAL DESCRIPTION

The game aims to allow players to experience the problems of managing the finances of a large oil company operating in the North Sea; players are required to run the company for 12 years by simulating decision-taking for six two-year periods. Once every three weeks each team is required to communicate to the administrators its decisions for the next two years of company operation; based on these decisions Company Statements are produced summarising the financial position of the company and are used to show the company's progress.

The game is not completely deterministic and progress is determined in part by a team's interaction with the model. The learning process is maintained throughout the game — the extent of a player's own gain in knowledge depends on his starting level.

2. MAIN FEATURES

In focusing on the North Sea operations the essential features which have to be included are shown overleaf:

		Typical capital outlay £m
Explore		200
Establish facilities for:	production	300
	transportation	100
	refining	250

		Typical annual cost £m
Operate facilities for:	production	60
	transportation	10
	refining	50

These are the activities which are a drain on the players' finances; the sources of income are as follows:

		Typical price £/barrel
Sales of oil	crude	6
	refined	7

Viewed at this level one could imagine a fairly simple game should be possible but Table 1 shows how, merely by keeping the choice at each decision stage to the selection of one from two, the game would have $2^8 = 256$ outcomes.

3. GAME DEVELOPMENT

We have never seriously considered the simple game postulated in Table 1 but, I think, the bald presentation of the table leads one to appreciate that it would be a very unattractive game with no feeling of realism about it despite the large number of choices suggested. ('Large' in this context is measured relative to a single person's ability to comprehend.) At best, however, one can see that there is a basis for an exercise (not a game) which would be fairly extensive but could be offered to interested parties to assist in gaining confidence in assessing projects and could include calculation of royalties, petroleum revenue tax and corporation tax.

In practice the game was not designed by sitting down and saying '256 options seems a bit tame but one million options on offer must be more exciting.' Indeed we had no thoughts along these lines at all; we considered each decision level in turn and ultimately agreed what was reasonable.

'Reasonable' meant meeting two requirements:

(a) it had to result in a sensible scenario for the players,
(b) it had to create modelling and computing problems which could be handled in a six-month time-scale.

Feature number	Feature	Choices to offer	
		Simple case	Actual case
1	Explore	1	1
2	Refinery site	2	5
	Capital expenditure		
3	oilfield	2	15 x 6
4	transport	2	2 x 4 x 6
5	refinery	2	4
	Operating costs		
6	oilfield	2	fixed by 3
7	transport	2	fixed by 4
8	refinery	2	fixed by 5
	Price	2	
9	crude		6*
10	refined		fixed by 2*
11	Quantity of oil	1	as requested**
	Other features		
	Limited use of established UK refineries		6
	Gas processing		4
	Marginal field take-over		2
	Total	$2^8 = 256$	0.5×10^6 24.9×10^6

* uncertainty built in, also variable with time

** oil deliveries checked to see that processing plant and transport limits are not being exceeded; in addition plant and transport capability is uncertain to a sensible extent

Table 1. *The complexity of the BRUCE OIL MANAGEMENT GAME*

In the end we landed up with the type of game summarised in Table 1 as the actual game where the number of options is apparently of the order of several million but the choices are not clear-cut since a considerable amount of uncertainty exists. Teams are forced to borrow and invest money as appropriate and must estimate income and expenditure including taxes and royalties at least two years ahead. When this is added to the clinical analysis of Table 1, it all adds up to a satisfactory simulation of oilfield management.

Uncertainty

The question of how much uncertainty to include was always in the forefront as the designers created the model for the computer. It was known from experience that uncertainty would be the life blood of the game, saving it from the inevitable loss of interest which would be bound to develop in a highly deterministic game.

Suggestions were put forward that we should include oil platform collapse or oil refinery destruction in a Flixborough type explosion, and although these events could have been engineered into the game they were considered undesirable on the grounds of inefficient use of educational time and the unlikelihood of being encountered in real life.

In the game as it exists we have moderate uncertainty in selected areas, for example:

oilfield production	say ± 7%
oilfield dry up	a function of player's strategy
weather at sea, operating days	say ± 10%
refinery capacity	say ± 7%
price of crude	say ± 10%
price of refined	say ± 10%

Summary

Our experience with the BRUCE OIL MANAGEMENT GAME has confirmed the need for uncertainty to maintain interest. Each year over the past four years we have found ways of improving our presentation. There is a temptation to increase the amount of uncertainty in some of the areas but there is a restriction that the unskilled managers should still finish up with less chance of winning the game than the skilled managers.

It has been interesting to observe how the satisfaction and enjoyment in playing the game does not depend on being expert in the field. Many players start with little or no knowledge and finish up a lot wiser. Of course, we are pleased to find that in the main games for businessmen it is the experts who win through into the final and we find from talking to them how much thought and calculation was expended in the process.

Acknowledgements

The assistance of the following in designing the BRUCE OIL MANAGEMENT GAME is gratefully acknowledged: Mr R G Angus, Dr G L Riddington and Mr P Strachan of Robert Gordon's Institute of Technology, and Mr D Brown, formerly of the Aberdeen *Press and Journal.*

The BRUCE OIL MANAGEMENT GAME Committee was chaired by Professor N H Langton and included Dr E Addinall, Dr H I Ellington, Mr I R Ellis, Mr B McNaughton and Mr E T Parham of Robert Gordon's Institute of Technology, Mr R Nicholson and Mr P Farrall of the Press and Journal *and Mr P Elgar of the Institute of Petroleum.*

Police action at an unusual incident

J McKelvie, *Scottish Police College, Tulliallan, Kincardine*

This paper describes a computer-based simulation used in the training of senior police officers. The incident on which the simulation was based occurred in reality and the computer version of the simulation supersedes a paper version. The simulation calls for decision-making by the players in a situation where a hole appears in a road and subsequent subsidence and flooding endangers property and life. The paper discusses the computerisation of a successful paper simulation and a possible over-reliance on computers.

Introduction

Although many excellent decision-making and problem-solving simulations have been used in the training of senior police officers in Scotland it has always been difficult to ensure that the individual student derived maximum benefit. This was mainly due to the fact that, like all courses for senior management whether it be in the police or any other profession, much was gained from the exchange of experiences between the members of the course. This invariably meant that group exercises were the mainstay of senior training and unfortunately there was often a tendency for the more vociferous members to dominate.

In view of this it was felt that the possibilities of computer-assisted simulations should be considered. As a test, it was decided to prepare a simulation based on police action at an unusual incident and thus create a basic program that could be developed for a variety of applications.

The reason that this type of exercise was chosen was that it involves all the problems associated with any serious situation which calls for snap decisions and clear logical thinking involving:

optimum use of available manpower resources, call out of requisite essential services, public safety measures, short-term police action in relation to traffic control, long-term police action in relation to traffic control and public safety, and the security of property made vulnerable due to enforced evacuation.

In order not to go overboard for a comparatively new medium the simulation is based on an exercise that has stood the test of time and the results validated both from past experience and current use.

It goes without saying that there are a large number of computer games and simulations but many are primarily concerned with an introduction to, and familiarisation with, computer facilities and operated or based on mathematical formulas with a reasonably correct answer. However, as there are many grey areas in the decision-making process during a major incident, eg the manning of various junctions for traffic control, a student can quite easily choose a different pattern from the suggested solution and still obtain the same end result. This, together with other decisions of a like nature, would make it very difficult to allow for all the various answers on computer. This had been one major argument for avoiding the computer for simulations of this nature. The simulation described indicates that it is possible to computerise any police decision-making or problem-solving exercise.

The simulation

The incident chosen is based on the actual police action taken when a sewer collapsed in Bolton, Lancashire, in October 1957. As a result a large number of houses were evacuated and many were rendered structurally unsafe. After the incident logs of this occurrence were obtained, a paper simulation was prepared and used in courses for potential senior officers. This had been tested for a considerable time and had proved a very successful exercise. In view of this a few minor alterations were made and a new paper simulation was introduced with a view to validating its worth as a potential exercise for the computer.

As a paper simulation, it falls readily into four phases and as a result the computer simulation has been programmed accordingly. The aims of the simulation are:

1. to give students practice in the principles of police organisation necessary to deal with unusual incidents,
2. to increase their general awareness of the problems faced by the officer in charge at an unusual incident, and
3. to develop the student's decision-making ability.

The objective is to enable students to demonstrate their decision-making abilities during each phase of police activity at an unusual incident. In specific terms the student is to:

☐ *Phase 1:* appraise the situation and indicate the correct initial action to be taken;

☐ *Phase 2:* (a) list in order of priority the essential services to be called out, (b) list the services to be altered/informed, (c) decide on the optimum use of the police resources made immediately available to him; (d) identify the most suitable area for setting up an incident post, (e) select the appropriate traffic diversion points and take the necessary action;

☐ *Phase 3:* (a) decide on any further action he would take to safeguard the welfare of the community, (b) specify his plan to ensure the least disruption to road traffic movement, (c) list the police requirements for prolonged action;

☐ *Phase 4:* plan for return to normal traffic flow and withdrawal of services.

Why computerise a successful paper simulation?

As the objectives encourage decision-making and problem-solving by the students in a situation where real conditions cannot operate, a simulation representing reality is an obvious choice. Although this could be achieved quite efficiently by a paper exercise with the students in a group it was felt that computer-assisted learning would be more of an individual decision-making achievement for the student. The paper simulation certainly lent itself to an exchange of experiences prior to making decisions but there was often a tendency for the more dominant members to take control of the decision-making process as the exercise evolved. It was felt that in order to overcome this, if the paper simulation was given to the students as an individual exercise, this would immediately lend itself to the examination situation and would lose much of its appeal, and the student would fail to recognise any similarity with reality. The computer simulation, on the other hand, is an individual exercise which gives a feeling of realism. Under normal operational conditions the inspector in charge during the initial stages of an unusual incident makes most decisions as a result of information passed to him either by telephone or personal radio. In the larger forces (eg Strathclyde) the officer in charge of the force control room uses a computer visual display unit to assist in initiating the action at the outset. There is no doubt that the immediate response required in answer to problems posed by computer simulation is as close as one can hope to get to real conditions.

Therefore, a computer simulation was considered as the obvious choice. In order to add a touch of realism, charts, maps and photographs were given to the student as these items would be available to the officer in charge attending major incidents.

Assessing student performance

As there are a large number of grey areas in the decision-making process during a major incident, for example, manning various junctions for traffic control, a student can quite easily choose a different pattern from the suggested selection and still obtain the same end result. In view of this the only apparent assessing device that could be used with any degree of accuracy was to get the students to discuss the solutions to the various problems with their colleagues when all had completed the computer simulation, and observe their reactions. This also allowed for an exchange of experience between the members of the course, which is essential in all training at senior police level.

In order to achieve this the final phase of the simulation was conducted as a group exercise and an individual score written into the computer program. The score is not an assessment device in its own right but is used to create discussion, ie, there is no doubt that a student who scores 60 will most certainly be motivated to defend his decisions against colleagues whose total score is 90.

This result was certainly achieved in the discussions following the various evaluation runs and a reasonable assessment of each student's decision-making ability was easily obtained. It is envisaged that after the exercise has been used a reasonable number of times the scoring can be made sophisticated and would be used as an assessment device.

Danger of over-reliance on the computer

Throughout each trial run, and once the exercise was operational, the danger of over-reliance on the computer came to light, as shown by the fact that students who had been dominant and controversial contributors in other group discussions tended to accept the answers given by the computer as being 100 per cent correct. When they were challenged on this point they all said that they were convinced that the computer worked out the answers based on the previous decisions that they had made together with the general information provided.

Beyond training

Drew Mackie, *Percy Johnson Marshall & Associates, Edinburgh*

The paper discusses the use of gaming as a tool for the evaluation and testing of government policies in several fields. Examples are given of the use of the technique as a training tool for officials and policy makers at short conferences and at longer residential courses. The COMMUNITY LAND ACT TRAINING SIMULATION is described and its gradual conversion from a training tool to a policy prediction device is examined. The author's experience as a free-lance designer of simulations is drawn upon to further indicate the way in which 'training' simulations may become usable tools in practice, particularly in those disciplines — such as architecture and planning — where the distinction between training and in-practice learning is difficult if not impossible to define. Finally, a fusion of gaming and the Delphi technique is discussed as a possible method of bringing together expertise in order to game through national policies (such as those for the revitalisation of the inner cities) or to postulate future scenarios in fields as diverse as ecological impact studies or foreign affairs.

Introduction

Some of you may be wondering why this paper appears in the conference at all. Its subject is not the use of games in teaching or training nor are the exercises it describes readily transferable into those fields. It will not deal with theoretical ways of measuring the relation of this and that nor will it attempt to justify the use of games in an academic or theoretical way. This is a paper written by a games *player* — who is also a designer and has in his time been a teacher — but whose main concern is gaming in action as a practical, useful tool in the approach to real-life problems in the field; who, quite frankly, has grown a little tired of the theoretical side of gaming — of the tendency of many concerned to stress game theory, of the facility of game *playing* being compared to the amount of literature which appears on the subject. This is, therefore, not so much a statement from the navigators of the gaming ship but more a whistle up the speaking tube from the engine room.

For I believe passionately that games are much more than tools for teaching and training — that there is a whole area of activity into which gaming is now moving which is full of promise precisely because gaming is not a highly theoretical activity and because it can operate in fields where 'numericists' fear to tread. This paper is a personal account of such games — games which have moved 'beyond training'.

Of course the idea of using games as tools in decision-making is not new. The military and business communities have been doing it for years. However, the general extension of gaming into fields of planning and policy-making is the innovation which I wish to discuss and the general question which I wish to ask is: 'can gaming be used as a specific technique in practice rather than as a general training tool?'

Three games

The first game in which I was involved which gave indications that this might be so was a game appropriately enough developed while I was teaching at the School of Architecture at Robert Gordon's here in Aberdeen. This was a game called SODIT (the SCOTTISH OIL DEVELOPMENT INVESTIGATIONS TOOL) — designed as a conversation piece for a two-day conference on the impact of oil development on coastal settlements held at the School of Architecture in 1971. The purpose of the game was to lead to discussions of the oil industry between groups of people whose knowledge varied widely — oil men who did not know the culture of the villages, protest groups who knew little of the structure or operation of the oil industry, politicians who may have known nothing of either. The game was used to put them through situations which could then be discussed. The remarkable thing was that the game, although crude and prepared by students with relatively little knowledge of planning or the oil industry, produced results which predicted many of the infrastructural and social problems which now afflict the settlements of the east coast — and was predicted at a time when the opinion of experts ran in quite a contrary direction. So the idea gradually emerged that a SODIT-like game just might be of some use in real planning.

A couple of years later, while working as a free-lance consultant in Edinburgh, I was asked if it might be possible to design a game to assist in the planning of an overseas tourist project by a leading firm of architects and planners. They had a particular problem in that the team that they had put together to handle this project had found it difficult to come together in design sessions. Although the senior staff wanted full involvement in the process by the whole design team, they found that meetings revolved around their own pronouncements while the junior staff went to sleep! It seemed to me that the problem was largely one of role. Each member of the team was an architect or planner or both. Criticism of project development meant criticism of another's professional role. The game had somehow to break this down.

The solution, therefore, was to give the team a variety of roles and to run these through a rather simple development planning game. This allowed the policies developed by the team leaders to be criticised in terms of their consequences for the 'peasant farmer', the rich landowner, the hotel developer, etc. Thus each role *had* to respond to policy and this response was not construed as a personal attack on the proposer but as a response natural to that role. The method made sure that the interests of various groups were reflected in policies and that potential conflicts in the administration of this large government project were identified. Because of the results of the game, the policy and plan are substantially modified. Unfortunately the project did not go ahead — an outcome not predicted by the game!

However, this exercise demonstrated that gaming can be a *technique* — that at the practical end we are talking about the invention of one-off games to test specific policies rather than the more normal academic exercise of using general games to illustrate processes.

A point must be made here. Writers on the use of games in teaching and training have stressed the encouragement of imaginative solutions. The sort of games which I am dealing with have a quite different purpose and that is the *testing* of policy by demonstrating consequences. Generally the problem we have to face at this level is too many conflicting imaginative ideas which require some sort of tool for their resolutions. Most of the people with whom you are dealing have no shortage of ideas — the problem is somehow to sort out the crackpots from the brilliant! This can be done to some extent by forcing them through the artificial hot-house of the game and rigorously criticising the result.

In fact in most of these games you do not model the structures which you are trying to test. Rather you prepare an environment within which the policies are tested and which generates and demonstrates their consequences. This gaming is essentially a pragmatic technique in the old sense of the word — that is it evaluates policies in terms of their practical consequences in which, according to Charles Sanders Pierce, consist the total meaning of any action or concept. But enough philosophising — back to the boilers!

A game which has relevance to this general line of argument is called RATPAK (Recreation and Tourism Planning Advice Kit). This was commissioned by the Dartington Amenity Research Trust to examine the policy responses of major tourist and recreation bodies in Scotland to likely changes in the national financial climate. As this was a relatively simple policy game I will use it to illustrate some of the methods and problems of this sort of project.

RATPAK was prepared for use by a small team of researchers in order to determine what sort of information might be required in their liaison with local authorities and national agencies in the preparations of regional plans. The game was to be played over a two-day period during which all the researchers would take part together with one of their field advisers. During the two days a range of about six possible national scenarios were to be examined ranging from the doubling of the price of petrol to the total reorganisation of one of the national agencies. The game had to explore the reactions to such situations by the agencies involved in terms of responsibility and finance for recreational and tourist activities. Because of the short time available for play, the game had to be extremely simple and yet to cater for a bewilderingly complex series of possible actions. Also, the contract time for its preparations was only a fortnight from start to finish including the final presentation — no time for rehearsing or experimentation. In fact, I like to compress the time available for the design of games — to quote Dr Johnson 'nothing concentrates the mind as wonderfully ...' In the event the gaming model adopted was similar to the game of TOTOPOLY — the old racing game in which on one board you set up all the preconditions for a race — training, starting prices, etc — and then play through the race itself on a different board. RATPAK works by putting the players through a resource allocations game in which they set their responsibilities and finance, trading where necessary in order to cover the field. A development game is then played in a fictional region of Scotland where the consequences of agency policy and organisation are displayed. RATPAK worked reasonably well except for two points. First, the researchers themselves were reluctant to accept the results of the game because its numerical basis was slight — and these particular researchers had a highly numerical background. They did, however, feel the game was useful in talking through the possible consequences of action. Second, the sponsors of the research study viewed the whole exercise as 'just a game' and were reluctant to carry it further. This reaction to the word 'game' in such situations is very common, especially with government organisations who are reluctant to be portrayed as playing games at the public's expense.

There are, I think, three lessons to be drawn from this exercise. The first is that you must impress your client constantly that hard probabilistic results are not obtainable from the method. The other is that you must, as far as possible, have backing for a game from the highest level within the organisation for which you are working if the results are to be taken seriously. Lastly, you must either call the exercise a 'simulation' or mount a campaign for acceptance of the word 'game' as a description of this type of activity. I favour the second approach which, although it poses many problems, does not in the long term produce confusion with more mathematical techniques and which will, I hope, establish gaming as an accepted technique in its own right.

Another contract which may be of some interest here is a simple game used to assist in the design of a golf course. The problem was to design a golf course which was as playable for beginners as it was for professionals. The game was developed to test a design which existed only on paper. The method used was a simple targeting device which allowed a player to gauge the length of shot depending on the club chosen. The degree of slice or hook was also built into the game, together with the amount of roll according to the ground contour or weather conditions. Given this tool it was possible to play a round of golf on the paper course and after several rounds it became obvious that several holes on the course favoured highly skilled golfers and penalised beginners unduly. The design was then modified. Unfortunately, it took about twice as long to play a round of simulated golf as it would take to play a normal round.

The COMMUNITY LAND ACT GAME

In 1975 I was asked to design a game which would be used for training local government officers in the uses of the Community Land Act. The firm which commissioned this exercise was fast becoming an expert consultancy in this field and I was supposed to provide the gaming expertise. The first task was to divert the firm from its initial efforts in game design, which consisted of running the participants through a series of procedural mazes like rats in a behaviourist's box. I persuaded them to think in terms of the legislative environment within which the act would work and to concentrate on building a model of that against which the new legislation could be tested. The first runs of this game indicated considerable discrepancies between the simulation of the act's operations and the prediction of the government on the workings of the act. Try as we might we could not get the results which reflected the aims of government policy. Was the game totally wrong? We eventually came to believe the game outcome to be totally possible and it is gratifying to observe that, 18 months after these game runs, the real situation is conforming very closely to the simulation. It is not my intention to go into the details of the COMMUNITY LAND ACT GAME and its results — the subject can bore the pants off even the most seasoned listener. Suffice it to say that the game proved to be a most effective tool for predicting the *possible* consequences of the act. And here I must rush up on deck to make a quick navigational point. Because no one should imagine I am claiming that games can be used for detailed and precise predictions – rather I am drawn to the conclusion that games are good at pointing to the *possibilities* inherent in a situation. The probability of specific outcomes is not, in my opinion, an aspect which games can handle and more precise numerical methods are perhaps more appropriate if this is required.

Meanwhile back amongst the pistons the COMMUNITY LAND ACT GAME proved to be a most valuable pointer to the use of games as policy generators and testers and we began to ask ourselves whether it might not be possible to apply the technique to many other areas of policy. With this in mind we approached the Department of the Environment suggesting that a game might be useful in gauging the effects of the change of policy away from the new towns and towards the inner cities. At first we had some trouble selling this idea to the department but eventually we were able to persuade them that such a game might be useful as a policy generator and evaluator. As a result we are now engaged in the design of an INNER CITIES GAME which will guide the policy planners of the Inner Cities Directorate of the Department of the Environment.

This game has posed some very interesting technical problems in its construction. Firstly, it was to be played by a very limited number of people, a small group of policy researchers and civil servants. This fact has been crucial in determining the character of the game. In general small games are much more difficult to design than large ones. A 50-player game such as SODIT develops its own momentum very easily and can be sustained on a minimum framework of rules. A nine-player game requires a more rigid rule structure and probably requires more of its actions to be mechanically determined rather than being left to the discretion of the players.

Another problem has been play testing. Usually on a gaming contract such as this I like to have a roughly playable game ready about a week after starting work. Until you have this you have nothing to test, no way of knowing whether the 'flavour' of the game is correct. Thereafter, the task is one of rigorous play testing. In the case of the INNER CITIES GAME, we would not use the people for whom the game is designed as playtesters – their time is too valuable to involve them until the game is working as a useful tool. We are, therefore, using students of the Royal College of Art in London to test the basic mechanics of the game.

However, it is interesting to note that the process of game design has already thrown up a series of questions as to how specific areas of policy are to be handled, and by involving the client in answering these he has already derived some benefit from the game. The point to be made here is that the process of game construction can often be as valuable in turning up anomalies in policy as the actual game itself. This is because you require rather precise working answers to questions – vague assertions of interest are of no use.

The future

Where do policy games go from here? There are several possible directions which we are exploring at the moment, but primarily I am interested in broadening the areas in which such games may be used. One possibility for which we are seeking sponsorship is an AFRICA GAME – a game which would explore economic, political and perhaps military developments in Africa over the next five or ten years. The idea here is to use a game as a focus for a series of seminars in which experts in African affairs would play through possible future events and particularly the effects of varying initiatives by the major powers.

On a more light-hearted note we have also developed a simulation of a *coup d'état* (the most common form of change of government in the world) which can be used in a fairly serious way to explore the problems of big-power interventions in the politics of a small state or alternatively as a more entertaining exploration of reactions of players to a code of behaviour based entirely on lying, cheating and nastiness!

To handle the development of possible marketing of such games we have formed a company (Warthog Games), and it is intended that this will be used to offer services of serious game design as well as producing its own series of games. Areas being researched at the moment are the political and economic development of an independent Scotland and the consequences of the run-down of oil energy during the next 20 years. The idea is to develop these serious policy games while at the same time producing them as aids to teaching in a simpler form.

So, I suppose after all that there is some relevance to the general theme of the conference — the adaptations of policy games so that they can be used to illustrate and teach. In conclusion, then, it would seem that there is much future in the use of policy games which can be used as a practical tool for the exploration of policy options. There is also, I hope, a considerable future for the 'contract game' if the game is prepared for a specific problem and for a specific client. There is every sign that interest is growing in the use of games in the way I have described and that their serious use in policy planning may become more widespread. It looks as though there may be much work ahead for us stokers!

The commercial exploitation of games and simulations

M E Smythe, *Institution of Electrical Engineers, London*

This paper deals with the way games can be exploited to promote an idea as well as to make money. The first part of the paper discusses the objective of using games to demonstrate a particular career, ie electrical engineering. The second part deals with the use of the disciplines that are normally associated with marketing a project, to ensure that the game achieves a penetration that is necessary to satisfy the primary objective.

How are games born?

Based on a limited experience of educational games it seems clear that they get written for one of two reasons. First, someone 'thinks it is a good idea' and sets about producing the article to meet a need that he, as the author, feels exists. Second, it is commissioned by somebody with a requirement who uses the game designer to help satisfy a need.

At present this Society (SAGSET) appears to deal with the first case rather than the second. This is hardly surprising because the members are mostly enthusiasts, writing articles and making their material available for use by others with a similar need. This also applies to those people who write computer programs to help solve problems and lodge them in a library for use by others in similar areas of work — normally pure research.

Different types of games

'Good idea' project: If we examine this first group of activities one can conclude that they are both *amateur* and *nice*. These comments should not be taken as derisory, but factual. The people concerned nearly all have a high level of competence and are working for the right motives. However, they may not be able to give their product long life and breadth of scope. The usable life of their product is normally limited to the time in which they have an interest in the subject and usually fades once they move on to other work.

Games designed for a job: The next main area is connected to those organisations who have a domestic requirement. This often shows up as a tricky training problem or a difficult educational problem which cannot adequately be solved by chalk and talk routines or other conventional methods. Consequently, a game or simulation can bring to bear other factors which will channel the concentration of the pupils or trainees in the way required. In this case the client can get the game designer's help in designing a product which is tailored to his requirements. As it is purpose-designed it tends to become highly stylised and, as it achieves a degree of polish, it gets expensive. The people concerned with it understand their product but it is very difficult for others to become fully conversant with it unless they have come from a similar background.

Games for 'profit': Another group who will commission games are those who require them for use outside their domestic environment, either for financial gain or for some less obvious motives. The large game suppliers are possibly the very best example of the first category. The Institute of Electrical Engineers, I believe, falls into the second, and it is worth while considering why it exists. Apart from the main objectives as set out in its Royal Charter, namely: to promote general advancement of electrical science and engineering and their applications; to facilitate the exchange of information and ideas on these subjects by means of meetings, exhibitions, publications and the establishment of libraries; to give financial assistance for the promotion of inventions and research; it also has an obligation to show the people outside the profession what the function of professional electrical engineers should be, and to bring to the attention of younger people the scope of electrical engineering. Consequently, games can be used as one of a series of activities designed to show what electrical engineering has to offer as a possible career for future generations.

THE POWER STATION GAME (designed by Ellington *et al* in Aberdeen) is being played competitively during this conference. It is a prime example of a way in which a game can be exploited. We take a group of young, intelligent people and we make them think about electricity generation for two days. Admittedly it could be claimed that they deal with the problems in a rather superficial way, but they are not sheltered from the magnitude of the problems which concern the profession. They are made to face up to the social and amenity considerations and to realise how much pressure there is to depart from the very best technical solution. They learn that other professions impinge on electrical engineering and they see how other disciplines, for example geography and accountancy, fit into the equation.

This is our aim. It should be the aim of anybody who is exploiting games for a lobbying process, as opposed to a purely financial one. In our case electricity generation happens to account for about 20 per cent of our membership and in consequence it is a natural subject for our first venture into this field. Our next area will be broadcasting which employs about six per cent of our members.

Product design

When a project is commissioned it needs to be both robust and polished. Robust, because it will be played under the direction of (we hope) many people, mainly school teachers or lecturers, with varying skills and degrees of competence. They need to be able to cope with it and get worthwhile results from it, without feeling as though they want to give up. They should not have to approach the suppliers for help and guidance. Polished, because it has to show an area of electrical engineering in the very best light and because purchasers must be maintained in a state of high readiness for the next game. If our games are successful they need to be good and if they are good they will either teach or add to a pupil's education. In this company it is not really necessary to enter into a discussion on the difference between these two words. These requirements demonstrate the need for authors to meet the demands of the market place. To meet my requirements of 'robust and polished' the product has to be tested, not in the laboratory, ie, in the author's own environment, but at 'arm's length'. The author and the exploiter have to get it right because purchasers can reasonably expect to get value for their money.

The demands now meet financial exploitation and lobbying. When the dominant requirement is to promote an idea there is a strong temptation to give the game away. Before doing so, two likely reactions must be considered. First, group one: 'It's free, I'll have it' or at the other end of the spectrum, group two: 'Can't be any good, they sell everything else!'

So a market price should be charged. If it transpires that it is not value for money despite all the testing, people will complain, especially if the supplier is somebody like ourselves. Sales will fall and it will be clear that the product has failed.

Define the market

One of the decisions to be made between the salesman, the author and the promoter is how to define the market. There are three main possibilities, although, of course, the boundaries between the three can be blurred. First, the highly specialised, for example, firemen or aircraft pilots. Second the general users, say A-level children. Third, a mass market where it is necessary to believe you have found a new MONOPOLY or MASTERMIND.

Penetrating the market and achieving the sales becomes more risky and difficult the higher up you go. If the market is defined as a small group of people in a highly specialised area, it is possible to approach them almost individually. The value of the product will be known, its potential sales and the cost should also be judged precisely, and if the sums work out wrong the project either needs to be dropped or funded from elsewhere.

Switching to the other end of the spectrum it is necessary to get to the retail outlets or interest a well-known distributor so that he will take up the product. Should mass advertising become necessary a deep market penetration may result but a new magnitude of costs is now entered.

Tune the product

If the product is to be sold it has to be right. At this point the person who is in control of the sales activity has, in many ways, the dominant point of view; it must be respected. If it is not, it must be rejected only with the full realisation that the project could well fail as a result. Too many schemes fail simply because it is a good idea first and a saleable commodity second.

To achieve success it is essential that a product satisfies the following requirements. It must be:

- robust,
- polished,
- technically sound,
- aimed properly at the desired market,
- accepted by the marketing people,

— properly priced, and
— properly packaged.

All of the above are essential regardless of whether the exploitation is financially based or whether it is lobbying, or promoting an idea, or any other purpose. When it comes to penetrating the market, the technique will vary according to whether it is the first venture by the organisation in that particular field or whether it is a follow-up.

Launching a new product

For the first game one is naturally starting from scratch and it requires a skilled advertising campaign, which need not necessarily be large. It is also essential that such cash as is available is used wisely. When agreeing the promotion campaign, which includes advertising, determine the general style (or styles) that will be used. Is it to be aggressive and brash, top-end, learned, etc? In planning the promotion it is necessary to counterbalance advertisements in journals and newspapers, articles in learned journals and trade and subscription magazines, press conferences, interviews with the media, coverage by reporters in diaries and information distribution leaflets produced by a wide variety of organisations. As a further complication the requirements of overseas markets should be considered if the overseas market is going to be part of the general area of exploitation.

Regardless of how dull the subject, somehow or other it is necessary to create interest and to try to inject an element of charisma at some stage along the line. This can be very hard as it involves the use of a good logo and/or good packaging and everything must remain respectable.

As if the above limitations are not enough, one must always keep in mind that you may wish to promote another game or simulation in the same area of the market, and this demands that whatever is done is honest. If it is not honest (and here again it is not enough just to avoid being dishonest) it will be remembered. Consequently, your next product would suffer sales resistance.

In most cases it is very hard to determine the likely level of interest in the first product. If the interest is going to be limited or, worse still, non-existent, no one is likely to buy. Consequently, while it is not always true, it is better to regard lack of purchasing as lack of interest and vice versa, unless there are very good reasons for deciding otherwise.

Second and subsequent projects are much easier. For a start, the purchasers of the first product make excellent prospects for the next and the effectiveness of each promotional activity tried on earlier schemes will have been demonstrated.

When producing the first package the various parties involved in the production and publication of the package should reach a properly documented understanding about who does what and who gets what. If this cannot be achieved at the time when the parties all wish to proceed, trouble is being stored for later, because any negotiation that has to take place against a background of difficulty is much less likely to arrive at a reasonable solution. Similarly, if each party knows what its aims are at the time the project is started it should not change part-way through and become jealous of what other parties may achieve.

Conclusions

Selling games and books is very competitive. Few products make substantial profits and it is not an area for starry-eyed optimism. However, if the proper tactics are adopted and warning signs are heeded it is possible to achieve realistic objectives.

FALA: a board game for leadership training

John P Gillingham, *Army School of Instructional Technology, Beaconsfield*
and Graeme W Fraser, *RAF Newton*

This paper introduces the FALA game in the external context of leadership training in the RAF. A statement of the training problem is given, and the objectives are formulated. The rationale is then given for the choice of a game as an appropriate learning strategy in leadership training. The paper gives a brief description of the initial design and an account of subsequent evaluation. It concludes with some alternative designs and strategies for its adaptation as a transferable leadership game with a potentially wide application.

Introduction

The FALA game was initially produced as part of a course design exercise, while the authors were on a post-graduate course at Sussex University. While it is not, on this occasion, necessary to go into the full details of the design of the course, perhaps a brief introduction giving the external context, the perceived training problem and the training objectives particularly relevant to the choice of a game will serve as a background to a subsequent description. We will then give our rationale for the choice of a game as an appropriate learning strategy.

The external context

Leadership training given in the RAF is based on the FUNCTIONAL APPROACH TO LEADERSHIP ANALYSIS (FALA) devised by John Adair (Adair, 1968). This leadership model distinguishes functions and needs related to three areas, namely: task, team and individual. The functions include, for example, making a plan, setting standards, giving status. These are directly related to needs in this way: making a plan (task needs), setting standards (team needs), giving status (individual needs). The model devised by Adair enables decisions to be analysed in relation to the three overlapping needs.

The training problem

It was felt that all too often the young officers who are posted to the directing staff of the OCTU are not only new to the officer training role but are utterly innocent of any instructional qualifications and experience especially in leadership training. The new staff require pre-employment training, particularly in leadership instruction.

The objectives and choice of a game

After an analysis of the problem, objectives were formulated, amongst which were the following, which are relevant to the selection of a game as an appropriate strategy:

— 'Students will accept FALA as a tool for analysing and instructing in leadership behaviour.'
— 'Students will demonstrate a sound knowledge and comprehension of FALA.'

The specific enabling objectives for the game were: students should

(a) 'be aware of the difficulty in teaching leadership',
(b) 'select FALA as an instructional tool',
(c) 'state the interrelated needs of task, group and individual',
(d) 'comprehend the interrelated needs of task, group and individual'.

Goodman (1973) states that to turn learning into a game is to formalise the exercise in a precise way. In a simulation game the player may often be required, as he will be here, to make the moves allowed by the game rules according to the principles which would guide a particular individual in his role as 'leader' in the real situation. Thus a player, to conform to the game rules, must consider the principles of the leadership role as he has learned about it, in a way which is formalised by the game rules. In this way, the implications of the highly general, patterned sequence of actions, which is the learned role, are rendered precise by the restrictions of the move rules. Or, it might be said: 'A game is essentially a simplified slice of reality. Its structure reflects a real world process' (Gordon, 1972).

Leadership involves making specific choices from a range of choices. In real life the range of choices is not as precisely defined as it is by the game rules; this is what makes the two situations only somewhat similar rather than the same. But, as Gordon puts it: 'In playing games students tend to develop feelings of effectiveness and control because the actions they take in the game produce results.'

The game can formalise learning about a role by making precise what is otherwise defined in only a rather general way. A person playing a role in a game must nevertheless compare the choices he is aware of in terms of his understanding of the role of, in this case, leader; that is, with those choices which would be open to him in a real situation. In the game: 'the rewards or penalties do not carry over into real life [but] the experience the player gains does carry over' (Livingston and Stoll, 1973).

If, as has been suggested, learning in the game itself is a function of what the player has learned prior to the game, it is possible, or indeed likely, that it may also affect what happens after the game, in our case in the *real* exercise situation. It is also likely that a player may learn part of the lesson of the application of FALA after the game itself in a post-game debriefing. The|instructor may be able to demonstrate the usefulness of some aspects of the approach if it has not been fully appreciated by the player in his own playing of the game. It may also be true that the player's reflections on the functional approach will continue after the debriefing, and thus learning may be considered to be continuing.

A student who had doubts about the effectiveness of FALA as a learning tool might be convinced of its value in the game situation, as Livingston and Stoll have found evidence in recent research that not only can 'simulation games increase the student's knowledge in terms and concepts of specific facts . . . they can change the student's attitudes to things which are simulated in the game' (Livingston and Stoll, 1973). Further, as Gordon has indicated, 'Games provide an excellent vehicle [for] educators [who] wish to develop problem-solving and decision-making abilities in their students' (Gordon, 1972).

Thus, from many viewpoints, the game is a useful aid to learning. Goodman refers to a series of definitions which can prove useful to those interested in games and learning. In defining a game it is argued that it is only such when there are at least two players (Von Neumann and Morgenstern, 1947; Rapoport, 1966). Nevertheless, the designer can remedy this by incorporating a 'dummy' which makes specific choices that affect the play of the player or players. The dummy, however, can and often does mirror the personal choices of the designer himself. Rather than use a dummy as an opponent or second player, the designer may decide to provide chance cards or devices to serve as a dummy. Thus the dummy does not make personal choices but only chance choices. In this way, a designer can stay fairly free from introducing his own personal choices into the exercise, yet he can provide for learning which might not take place at all if the behaviour involves only the choices of the potential player. This, therefore, is the approach that the present design favours.

The initial design of the game

There now follows a description of the game and an indication of the way it was used in the initial course design.

1. The instructions for the directing staff:
   It is assumed that the objectives in the preceding topic area have been achieved by the student.

   Introduce the FALA game to the student and give him a brief outline of the rationale for his using a game. Give him the scenario and game rules, procedures and interpretations. The emphasis throughout should be on the accurate use of FALA terms on the decision and report sheets; the game should be presented as the enabling device.

   Give him the board, all the game equipment and a time for completion (40 minutes after commencement). Be available in the event of any explanation or interpretation of the rules being necessary.

   At the conclusion of the game read all his decision and report sheets in the light of his usage and understanding of FALA.

   Discuss with the student his written report and decision sheets and his justification/explanation in FALA terms. Indicate any apparent misunderstanding of FALA terms and negotiate shared meanings on its application to the decisions taken throughout the game.

   Throughout, the discussion should be focused on FALA rather than on the playing of the game. It may be necessary, however, to reconstruct certain points in the game to illustrate and negotiate certain decisions and their meanings.

2. Various playing pieces represent the federal troops. The red one is the leader, the green ones are the troops which are all numbered and have individual

characteristics which are described in the game rules, eg 'Number 3 is physically strong but irresponsible.' The silver piece is the 'highly sensitive, electronic device', and there are very specific rules on its handling and movement. The board has designed into it various constraints:

2.1 Routes are along roads (grey circles), tracks (brown circles) and open country (green circles). Movement along these is at different speeds, simulated by appropriately coloured dice with different scoring values.

2.2 Red circles indicate likely enemy action and if a playing piece lands on one such circle the decision wheel is spun to indicate the man's fate.

2.3 Yellow circles indicate that a chance card must be picked up and the instructions complied with. This can be advantageous or not and serves as a dummy which affects the game situation in a random way.

2.4 Large black numbers on circles indicate that the player should complete a report sheet at this point and state his current situation and the nature of the interrelated needs of his team using FALA terms.

2.5 Woods can be used as hides and certain rules appertain as to how the device and men may be hidden.

2.6 There are specific rules about the formations in which players can move and the distance between them.

2.7 Reserves are provided to replace men lost to enable the game to be played to completion. The colours of the reserves are an indication of the losses sustained; they have the characteristics of the weakest team member.

2.8 The decision cards are the major controlling device and continually change the detailed requirements of the task. They are used in a given sequence and are collected at decision points when decision sheets must be completed by the player. Throughout, the player should use FALA terms and detail the nature of the interrelated needs of his team.

Subsequent evaluation

There is a need for minor redesign of some of the elements and revision of the rules as a result of the evaluation but none involving any major changes in the game. It was generally felt that the game would be more effective and hold interest more if it was played by small syndicates who could negotiate issues and decisions during the game. This could obviate the need for a great deal of the report writing. The very act of report writing prolonged the game for longer than some users felt desirable.

Evaluators saw a number of uses other than the initial one, but there would be a requirement for some adaptation of the game. These are indicated when we consider alternative designs and strategies.

Alternative designs and strategies

The game was initially designed for a very narrow target population and the designers have always been aware that for more general use some adaptation would have to take place.

It is felt generally that a series of scenarios could be written, using the same constraints, but possibly each with a separate series of decision cards or with a larger pack of more generalised decision cards with no fixed sequence. This would lead to greater variation in the game and to greater use of it. The game as it was originally designed was a 'play once' game for each player. These adaptations would undoubtedly make it more like a conventional game and more enjoyable to play as such.

If it were used in a variety of leadership training situations such as problem-solving, giving an appreciation of a problem, as a basis for a briefing or order group, testing for leadership potential etc, it would not necessarily involve such an overt link with Adair's model and consequently the need to make copious written decisions and reports could be avoided. This would also make the game more motivating and shorter in the playing process.

In conclusion we are fully aware of many of the game's limitations, particularly in its initial design, but we feel that with further development it could be a transferable leadership game with many uses and applications.

References

Adair, J (1968) *Training for Leadership*. Macdonald, London.

Goodman, F L (1973) Gaming and simulation. In Travers, R M W (ed) *Second Handbook of Research in Teaching*. Rand McNally, Chicago.

Gordon, A K (1972) *Games for Growth*. SRA Associates.

Livingston, S A and Stoll, C S (1973) *Simulation Games*. Collier-Macmillan, London.

Rapoport, A (1966) *Two-Person Game Theory*. Michigan.

Von Neumann, J and Morgenstern, O (1947) *The Theory of Games and Economic Behavior*. Princeton University Press.

Chapter 3: Professional Education

This chapter, although containing fewest papers, represents a growth area in simulation terms. Of the four papers, three represent the area of management training. There may be some truth in the claim that management trainers were first to see the use of simulations and games (Thomas, 1957). Certainly there were attempts in the 1930s to use games (in America, if not the UK). The American Management Association's GENERAL MANAGEMENT BUSINESS SIMULATION, first used in 1957, was an example of this interest. Cooper, in a wide-ranging and humorous paper, summarises the key points in management game design. Hornby analyses four games used with trainee managers and with pupils in economics classes. Hart, in the keynote paper, maps the economic and management background and develops the needs of management in terms of simulations and games. Rothwell and Davidson take a more 'professional' look at simulations, as they speculate on the application of such techniques to the training of speech therapists.

Reference

Thomas, C J (1957) *The Genesis of Operational Gaming*. Operational Research Society of America.

Keynote paper: Simulation and gaming in management education and training

R T Hart, *Robert Gordon's Institute of Technology, Aberdeen*

This paper attempts to determine an appropriate perspective for the techniques of simulations and games in the field of management education. After considering the current demands on management these are related to possible education and training techniques. The strengths of the main types of simulations and games are outlined and the benefits to participants indicated.

Unlike those who are delivering papers to the conference today I have the freedom, and the responsibility, to use a broad brush on a large canvas. In recognition of this fact I will attempt to reconsider some first principles of management education and training and the particular place that gaming and simulation may occupy in this vital field.

We are being exhorted from all quarters to make education more relevant to the attempts at national economic regeneration. This must encourage many to see national salvation being entwined with management education. There will be those who will seek to gain personal career advancement by novel developments within this sector of education, a perfectly legitimate and commendable form of activity. An obvious and tempting line that might be pursued by such 'thrusters' is to develop the application of gaming and simulation to management education. My initial reaction is to seek to encourage such development, but I am apprehensive that over-enthusiasm may see these techniques elevated to the critical point where they are purveyed as a nostrum.

My main message and plea is that we obtain, and maintain, a proper and appropriate perspective for gaming and simulation as a teaching technique in management education. I therefore wish to draw your attention to a number of facts which may be of assistance in obtaining such a perspective in relation to your own educational activities.

While I do not wish to become enmeshed in a pointless semantic wrangle, it seems necessary to make some definitive statement in respect of management as it is the determining factor in the discussion. I would suggest that we accept one of the classical definitions as our standard:

Management – a social process entailing responsibility for the effective planning and regulation of the operations of an enterprise, in fulfilment of a given purpose or task, such responsibility involving:
(a) the installation and maintenance of proper procedures to ensure adherence to plans, and

(b) the guidance, integration and supervision of the personnel composing the enterprise and carrying out its operations (E F L Brech).

Similarly a definitive statement in respect of gaming and simulation within the management context seems called for. On this score I would offer a definition given by Mrs Pam Sykes, Director of the Centre for Business Simulation: 'a simulation exercise in which an industry model is tested empirically in a competitive situation with feedback'.

Having established some criteria to determine the boundaries of the subject there seems considerable advantage in seeking to establish the main features of the primary components involved. These would appear to be:

(a) the current demands on management,
(b) the main sectors of education and training for management,
(c) the types of instructional techniques appropriate to the main sectors and also subsectors of education and training for management,
(d) a classification of gaming and simulation applicable to management education,
(e) the advantages which participants may obtain from use of gaming and simulation.

The current demands on management could provide the subject for a full conference but I will select only those features which I consider have brought about the most marked changes in the last decade or two. I see these within five main heads as follows:

Increased scale — particularly the increasing impact of the multinational enterprise which transcends national and governmental boundaries.

Increased complexity and sophistication of operations — as evidenced by the tendency for a single corporation to cover a range of diverse products and processes while employing continually advancing technology in all its activities.

Governmental involvement — this has ranged from increasingly detailed legislation covering such matters as employment, redundancy, wages, prices, to actual stake money in the enterprise itself.

Employee aspirations — as this level has risen, so has the demand for greater participation in decision-making and access to information, increasing mobility of management both within and between companies.

Societal pressure — as survival and subsistence levels have been left behind attention has centred on 'the quality of life' and particularly those environmental aspects which may be adversely affected by industrial and commercial activity. Linked with this is a moral/guilt philosophy which confuses the work/endeavour ethic and seems to overlap with, at times, a disproportionate concern for minority groups.

At the same time the major objectives of business enterprise have remained, ie continued expansion and an increasing profitability. The key to achieving these objectives remains the competency of the managers of the enterprise.

When we associate the current demands on management with the substantial investments in research and development (often politically inspired) which pay off with new technologies and products, we cannot be surprised to discover rapid change and the real chance of managerial obsolescence. This produces an all-round demand for management development. On the part of the individual manager it is a means to retain managerial status while on the part of the enterprise it is the means to increase managerial effectiveness and maintain continuity of the managerial work-force. It is now accepted that to increase managerial effectiveness by management development, attention must be given to three main areas of management education, namely, factual knowledge, appropriate attitudes and specific skills. Imparting factual knowledge poses the least number of teaching problems as its content is the relevant store of knowledge in respect of the specific location and environment in which the manager and his enterprise operate. Such knowledge may be classified as economic, political, legal and social and treated at three levels — fact, function and technique. All lend themselves to the classical and traditional teaching methods of lectures, discussions and work assignments, along with the selective infiltration of programmed learning as both a substitute and a complement. The area of appropriate attitudes involves an initial individual stock-take of personal values which have resulted from life experience to date. Particular attention is given to such matters as attitude towards power and authority, degree of self-reliance and confidence, ability to take requisite executive action. The results are placed against the comparatives of the needs for the specific operational location, and the degree of fit determines the action required for modification of attitudes. Such action is based on the provision of additional emotional experience directly linked to controlled introspection usually involving the use of one or more of the sensitivity training techniques. The third area of specific skills is indicative of a level of competence determined by the ability to act, which is largely constrained by the extent to which the individual has had the opportunity to practise. Knowledge and attitudes are insufficient to guarantee the skills and competence. Therefore, by definition, participative methods such as case studies, incident method, role-playing, management laboratories, simulation exercises and group projects are necessary. Each of the methods is highly effective only over a narrow range of skill applications, despite justified claims that they are multi-purpose.

There is a general consensus that a meaningful classification of the most important management skills is as follows. The ability to:

   (i) observe,
  (ii) select pertinent data,
 (iii) diagnose rational and emotional problems,
 (iv) formulate alternative solutions,
  (v) reach decisions,
 (vi) communicate decisions,
(vii) motivate people to act on decisions.

Work at numerous management education and training centres has indicated the relationship between a specific skill and the effectiveness of a particular participative method. This has been well summed up by B Hawrylyshyn, Director of Studies of Centre d'Études Industrielles, Geneva (Figure 1).

Having arrived at the point that games and simulations are most useful in the specific skills area of management education and training and that they are basically concerned with the development of decision-making and problem-solving, it is useful to consider the stages involved and the way the various types

Skill	Most effective method
observe	field studies
select data	incident method
diagnose problems ⌉	
	case method
formulate solutions ⌋	
decisions	simulations
communication	role-playing
motivating	group projects

Figure 1. *The relationship of method to skill (Hawrylyshyn)*

of games stress particular stages. The stages are fivefold:

1. determination of objectives and/or identification of problem,
2. collection and/or analysis of information,
3. definition and/or comparison of alternative courses of action,
4. action, and
5. review including feedback.

We are now able to home in on the most effective contribution that gaming and simulations may make to management education and training, namely in terms of decision-making. Chris Elgood has from his experience as a consultant and management trainer provided a useful categorisation of the main types of exercise which fall within the definition of gaming and simulation and are applicable to management education:

Conventional model-based games: These dominate the field and their creators have provided everything which can happen within them. Their main characteristic is their logical framework of rules which operates on several variables so that a single result is produced. At a more sophisticated level they are constructed to be interacting, the results of one participant affect the results of the others, and progressively provide a multi-result. Constraints are laid on decisions and the passage of time is simulated in an accelerated state. To provide additional reality, forms and procedural rules are used; to avoid an entirely deterministic game, a chance factor may be introduced.

Puzzles: These are based on the assumption that students have sufficient knowledge to arrive at the definite solution to the problem proffered. It involves a continual heuristic process which is repeated until either the solution is reached or the participant exhausts his knowledge and fails. It is almost identical to the process for completing crosswords.

In-tray or in-basket exercises: This is a problem in logical analysis. The participant faces a series of written documents which are considered to be his 'in-basket' at a particular point in time. He has to decide both the priority for attention and the action to be taken.

Mazes: This type of exercise places a premium on experience and judgement as opposed to intellectual imagination. The participant is faced with a stated situation and is required to select one of a number of possible courses of action. This selection creates a new situation requiring a new choice and so on. The emphasis is on being able to cope with conditions of uncertainty.

Inquiry studies: Sometimes termed 'incident method', they are a type of incomplete case study where the participant has sources of information and must ask the correct questions to make progress.

Encounter games: This type of exercise provides experience of unstable and dynamic situations. It simulates the future in general terms, eg there will be new products. It then overlays the generality with a number of incidents requiring appropriate action. It increases awareness and the ability to cope with the unpredictable.

Behavioural games: These are really human laboratory experiments which necessitate role-playing. They can be played either against a fixed standard or simply as interactive games. In both cases they are competitive. They have the main characteristic of provoking a form of behaviour which, while inappropriate to the problem, is recognisable as a norm.

Practical simulations: Completion in this case requires the ability to apply social skills and managerial techniques within a stated operational context. A task is presented to a group and their performance in coping with it is assessed using criteria normally met in commercial situations.

Using this categorisation, Elgood (1976) has developed a ranking table which relates the type of game and its relative power as an instructional device in relation to the major aspects of the decision-making process. This table indicates that firstly, conventional model-based games are an across-the-board instructional device. The puzzle places emphasis on the collection and/or analysis of data and the action and review aspects. The maze places emphasis on the definition/comparison of alternative courses of action and action and review. Secondly, the in-basket exercise ranks with the conventional model-based game as an across-the-board instructional device. Inquiry studies emphasise the collection and/or analysis of information aspects. Encounter games emphasise the definition comparison of alternative courses of action and review. Thirdly, behavioural games emphasise the determination of objectives and action and review. Practical simulations have their emphasis in the definitive comparison of alternative courses of action and action and review.

I have now put down a number of markers which should help obtain a meaningful perspective of the place of gaming and simulation in management education. It is, however, necessary for me to enter a very clear caveat. Games and simulations used within management education are radically different from those in engineering-type simulations. The latter seek to create an exact model of conditions from which the student learns and develops the correct set of responses which can be reproduced in real-life situations. Recall of the definition of management given initially makes it clear that one is concerned with a highly complex area of activity involving factors and forces that are many, varied and incompletely understood. It is therefore not economically possible to include them in a model. To compound the difficulty, it is worth remembering that what is not known cannot be modelled and most management situations have a number of unknowns. The most we can seek from a management game is to provide an extension of the participant's experience and increase his adaptive skill. As yet we have no evidence to prove a relationship between ability in management games and in the real-life practice of management. It is therefore necessary to reject all claims of a play-to-practice correlation for such techniques.

Perhaps this is the area in which profitable serious research might be mounted. In the meantime, enjoy your gaming. It may do you no good but it is unlikely to do you harm.

Reference

Elgood, C (1976) *Handbook of Management Games.* Gower Press, Teakfield Ltd, Farnborough.

But it doesn't really happen like that: a look at business games in management training

Norman Cooper, *Norman Cooper Associates and Skene Onshore Services Ltd, Aberdeen*

Management training needs as much help as it can get and a great deal of help could be found in well-constructed games and simulation exercises. The background to gaming is discussed and some of the basic principles examined in the light of management training needs. With the more urgent requirements of management training increasing daily, it is vital that those responsible for the design of such aids appreciate the real significance of the work and co-operate with management in designing sensible exercises. It is also incumbent upon management to find a way of translating practical experience into a training system.

Origins

Most of my management training took place during a period when business games were simply something one read about in order to answer questions in an examination paper. Certainly management training, such as it was in those dark days, never seemed to find time for adequate games in the management training syllabus which, to my recollection, consisted of a series of boring lectures, the most boring always being kept for immediately after lunch on a warm summer afternoon!

Later management training sessions, however, were more enlightened and, like any convert, I have become one of the greatest disciples of the application of games and simulations to the continuing problem of adequate training for management. Training of management is expensive, especially when one considers the total cost of replacing the manager who leaves for greener fields on returning from a residential course. The idea of being able to invent a game whereby management can be trained without the attendant cost of errors and drops in profitability can only appeal as a very bright possibility on the horizon of anyone responsible for developing and training management.

One problem we face when speaking about games is that the word is easily connected with the idea of entertainment. While this is certainly a valid result, it is not generally the main purpose of game designers. To avoid a misleading association of ideas, therefore, the word 'game' will be used in the context proposed by McKenney, ie 'competitive mental activity wherein opponents compete through the development and implementation of a strategy'.

The development of business games can be traced back for many years, and it is now commonly accepted that chess and other similar board games were used at a very early stage as symbolic equivalents to warfare. I once heard a lecturer explain the derivation of noughts and crosses in relation to business games.

Certainly I have heard rather tongue-in-cheek references to hopscotch as being the original training ground for teaching children, and therefore future management, exactly where they should put their feet to avoid being in it up to the neck!

The greatest step forward from symbolic games to war games took place in 1798 in Germany, with the introduction of the NEU KRIEGSPIEL, the main characteristic of which was that real maps instead of boards were used and from this developed the free KRIEGSPIEL and rigid KRIEGSPIEL games as the two main streams. These games always depended upon the services of an umpire to direct them and his role was to decide what to do when unusual problems arose during play. He was also responsible for the evaluation of the game results and this 'judge and jury' situation inevitably led to umpires being strongly criticised for alleged arbitrariness. Anyone who has umpired a cricket match or refereed a football or rugby match will, of course, be fully aware of the unwritten law which states that they can never be right and that they are always highly biased. As a result, war game designers modified the rules and the consequent movement towards highly structured play led to the development of rigid war games.

The increasing use of modern mathematical apparatus by the military encouraged designers to develop very complex war models which were criticised as being too theoretical and too artificial; this was counteracted by the introduction of real war data in the game so as to make it more objective. I suppose one could look upon this as the first introduction of live ammunition and, in fact, one could probably trace the roots right back to poisoned arrows. The introduction of real war data into a game makes sense but too many people concentrate on the war these days and not enough on the game! A similar criticism can be made when so-called 'real business data' lead to students concentrating on what might be the wrong (in the training sense) aspect of the exercise they are given.

Definitions

The rather haphazard growth of design techniques and the association with management buzz words have produced some odd expressions. The real meaning of 'simulation' is difficult to explain but it is certainly shorter than a full definition of 'game' which might be 'a contest among player opponents operating under rules to gain an objective'. There are, of course, different types of games. A non-academic game is a game primarily for fun with no, or very little, counterpart in life and no preparation for a distinctive part of life. Some critics of management training games suggest that this in fact defines a game devised by an educational establishment or a management consultant. Such games as LUDO and BINGO, for instance, could be described as non-academic games.

Academic games are games primarily for learning purposes, with a counterpart in life, and playing the game is very much like the action of a part of life. Non-simulation games are academic games in which players must know and use clear and agreed upon principles of some academic subject or subjects, and simulation games are academic games in which players are given a simulated environment.

The difficulty is that the definitions themselves produce a great number of problems for anyone studying the subject. It is, for instance, still a matter of contention as to whether games of anagrams – SCRABBLE and the like – are academic games and whether or not MONOPOLY has any decision-making advantages for a future property developer. I have one business colleage who is terrible at MONOPOLY but extremely good as a property developer. There must be a lesson here somewhere. They are, nevertheless, all games primarily for, or based on, learning as opposed to pure games of chance, such as managing a corporate closed company! Anyone who has played MASTERMIND will also understand the importance of making economical decisions by choosing a route selected from some previous information, rather than merely adopting the several-million-to-one possibilities of sticking the pegs in the holes in any order.

I have so far refrained from talking about oil games. There are two reasons for this. First of all, I am probably expected to talk about them and therefore there is a sort of automatic reaction, and secondly, both my children have successfully beaten me at both the games currently available on the market, thus proving that they are of no use at all in developing management!

The availability of high-speed computers has constituted a decisive step in game design but one of the most influential factors is that today's managers tend to consider their problems more and more in a strategic context. This movement towards defining and evaluating different courses of action has also contributed to underlining the similarities between actions in the business game and in the military field and, in turn, has stimulated the development of management games. There are many other connections between business games and military training. The use of simulators in aircraft training has undoubtedly led to fewer crashes and this is a typical example of simulation training providing valuable training benefits. I hope that one day someone will invent a really effective simulator for training in financial matters, thus avoiding a few crashes in those areas. The use of a simulator is a vital ingredient. Firstly, it compresses more events into a shorter time-span and allows the trainee to face selected problems more frequently than would normally occur in the work situation, thus reducing learning time. Secondly, it is cheaper and somewhat less wearing on all concerned, from the superior to the trainee, to the equipment, to the customer and to the profits if mistakes are made in training.

There are many different types of business game, all with different possibilities. They create considerable rivalry between the groups who play them and the resulting atmosphere can provide opportunity for the examination of group behaviour and management practices such as motivation, communication, organisation, budget achievements and the like. They can also show how decisions can be based on wrongly preconceived ideas or reached without much consideration of the facts of the situation — a common fault at all levels of management. Talking of the examination of group behaviour, I know some people who react to certain business games in much the same way as many sober citizens react to motor cars. Once they are involved, they take on a completely new personality. Business games, like motor cars, often given one a chance to examine the Jekyll and Hyde character of a prospective manager before one carries his development too far. Robert Wilson, in his paper on the origins of business games, states that history, including retail history, is littered with the debris of the consequences of decisions arrived at in a blinkered fashion. Often, unfortunately, it is the key critical and major decisions on which much time and effort have been spent that are the most blinkered.

Classification

It would be useful to attempt to classify games into a few main sections.
Functional games are games covering only one function performed within a
simulated company. Company games are games where most of the functions of
the company are simulated but the participants are only concerned with the
internal operations and consequences. Management games involve the simulation
of competing and interacting companies. Society games simulate more general
problems of economics and political warfare. Abstract games are games in which
the basic model is not based upon existing markets or companies; a real situation
is vaguely indicated but never in such detail that a student may readily transfer
his real-life experiences to the game. Specific games are games in which the
model is based upon the real situation in a company or market. There are also,
of course, computer games, often designed by computer manufacturers for
reasons more closely associated with the sales of equipment than with
management training; and I suppose also there are non-computer games which
are in the main not designed by computer manufacturers for equally obvious
reasons!

Any business game designer must work in such a way that he is always
considering the six main points of any design plan:

1. the general design and the selection of the subject,
2. the simulation model,
3. the rules,
4. the teaching staff involved,
5. the evaluation procedure, and
6. the selection of the trainees.

No business game will be satisfactory unless the designer has considered all
these six points and has built them into a total specification which should receive
just as much publicity as the details of the game and the methods of operating.
A well-designed game will provide a focal point for thought and discussion and
establish a common basis for communication between teacher and student. For
example, most managerial decisions are made under conditions of uncertainty
and it is really pointless to devise a business game for management training which
does not include several conditions of uncertainty. The importance of long-range
planning and policy-making is an aspect of management which can be stressed by
devising an appropriate game. It is difficult enough to persuade most managers
of the importance of long-range planning and policy-making and any training
programme which can inculcate this particular discipline to the point where it
almost becomes second nature is very valuable indeed.

Such games would not include stress problems of time for the participants
and the games would be so designed that decisions had an influence on more
than one period — as opposed to a well-designed game for training managers in
problems of *immediate* management which would certainly have a considerable
time pressure element.

Management games

What, then, is a game designed for adequate management training? A game must
be sophisticated enough to hold player interest but not so detailed as to frustrate

response. There must be flexibility also; if basic familiarity of what goes into a gaming situation is needed for it to be effective, it might be better to use it only with experienced employees. If the design of the game is effective and it is played in the correct manner, the participants can extrapolate what they discover to situations in the organisation. This can be accomplished one step removed from the job, multiplying the value since there is no real threat to anyone's livelihood.

Model games, such as those designed like MONOPOLY, can heighten awareness and increase sensitivity in such areas as positive action and equal opportunity. Moral games, such as Bob Merrill's GHETTO, are used by the Federal Reserve Bank in New York to give middle-class people some idea of the problems other segments of society confront. In the game, players are assigned a role, chips and a certain amount of time to get where they are going. Chips carry various weights. It is much more profitable, for instance, to hustle drugs than to do work condoned by society. That seems to me to be a particularly realistic piece of game design.

To take one simple example in the design of business games, continuing inflation alone means frequent and careful alterations to any game which uses money values in its decisions and performance results. If this is not done, then the game itself will not make sense to those who are playing it and managers cannot use their experience and knowledge, because the game will be reflecting circumstances no longer prevailing in their work situations.

A well-designed game has to be surrounded by constraints such as production costs, market trends, seasonal factors, availability of finance, industrial relations, stock-holding costs and so on. Information has to be presented in exactly the same way as in practice, equivalent to hiding a tree in a forest, so that no one can pick out what is important. Throwing one or more unimportant variables into prominence to mislead the game player is a valid exercise, as is saying little about the necessary critical variable and saying it so that its importance may well be overlooked. This, in fact, is what happens in practice and it is good training for anyone who anticipates having to delve into piles of information to reach the one fact which is important.

Generally speaking, games do not teach factual information particularly well. The lecture or the lesson, both maligned (understandably but excessively so) as training techniques in recent years, do this job better. This is why the business game and the lecture and the lesson and the case studies should all be considered as potential tools for inclusion in any training programme, all to be subjected to the queston 'Which mix does the best job?' in teaching the training objectives required.

The selection of the simulation model is an area which gives rise to the greatest difficulty which, in a way, prompted the selection of the title for this paper. 'But it doesn't really happen like that' is an expression which can be heard time and time again at any management training centre. The plain fact is that, as a management consultant, I can tell you that almost invariably it does really happen like that and I do not really mind exactly what we are talking about. The selection of the model for the game is critical and the basis for the selection can be found in real life in almost every direction in which the game designer wishes to look. A careful survey of the financial and business reports in some of our leading newspapers, for instance, will produce a model which most people would scoff at as being entirely impractical. But I recall that once, before travelling to

Australia on a lecture tour, I cut out several interesting facts about various companies from different newspapers for a period of three months. I then selected these for their influence on various factors such as communications, industrial management, financial planning, etc and developed a company with the glorious name of Photosludge. The PHOTOSLUDGE project, which was based on a model photographic company, was so impossible when it was finally produced that I was told by all my associates it could never happen like that. When I eventually took this particular training game on tour in Australia I was continually meeting people who said, 'How did you know what had happened to my company in the last few years?' The harsh realities of bad financial planning, bad budgetary control, bad stock keeping, bad industrial relations, bad communications and bad management training are seldom recognised as being factual in a business game and once again the title of this paper can be heard reverberating around the lecture rooms.

The simulation model can *always* be obtained from a study of real-life situations. Even if certain situations are put together to form the whole, each of the individual situations will be taught and, consequently, the fact that all of them together may not occur to one company at one time is not relevant. Having said this, however, I can think of many companies where everything has happened in a very short space of time, to such an extent that no game designer would include the information on the grounds that he would be afraid of being called fanciful.

Having designed a game and provided a sensible model, the rules of the game have to be carefully drafted. It is no good leaving the lecturer to decide arbitrarily on the various rules as the game goes on. It must be carefully set out as a part of the game, and the extent to which the trainer can help the trainee must be carefully included as a part of the rules.

Random factors, for instance, might well be set out for the trainer to use as he sees fit, but certainly the factors themselves should be set out and the way in which they are to be used, should they be used. Relatively little information should be fed back automatically to the participants and relatively great opportunities should be given to them to buy information. Anyone who has tried to obtain simple information, such as a set of accounts, from auditors who can take up to eighteen months to produce the figures, will realise what good management training this would be.

The rules should not be so complicated that they cannot be understood by all concerned and certainly they should not resemble Acts of Parliament or ED18. The rules must be capable of being properly interpreted by the trainer and understood by the trainee and, while being sufficiently flexible to allow some individual choice on the part of the trainer, they must not be so flexible as to make comparisons between the results of the various trainees difficult.

The staff who use business games in training are clearly very important people. The training director must be able to guide the play to help drive home the message and this means that he must understand the game, the model and the rules. A game is not always a game, and games and simulations should never be taken lightly. Dealing effectively with people is the important dimension in management, and games can help you do that, but only if the climate is relaxed, open and non-threatening, because if a player starts to feel embarrassed about his own performance the purpose of the game is defeated. A similar result, of course, can be obtained in real life by brow-beating and threatening a trainee manager to the point where he does not really care. It is not only in management games that one has to be careful how one approaches the problem of training. At no stage in the conduct of the game should the trainer adopt the attitude of a dictatorial company chairman. In many cases this attitude should be built into the game as a stumbling block for the player to overcome, and to find it existing in the trainer as well as in the game could well be too much for his peace of mind.

The staff who conduct the games are critical. Management games make considerable demands on the time and the number of staff. They also require staff who are not only competent to run the mechanics of the exercise, but who are willing and able to forward the learning process in their allocated group, in observing, guiding and improving the involvement of all participants in the decision-making process. Too many of the staff who conduct management training games do so in a bored manner, expecting stereotyped results from the varied personalities sitting around the table. I often think that a game run on the basis of training the staff who conduct games would be a very interesting exercise, but I do not know who could possibly devise such a Machiavellian scheme. I have been subjected to this sort of training on more than one occasion. Having spent two days and nights working on a problem and producing an answer which, by admission, was entirely acceptable, I was told that it could not be considered. It was not one of the answers which had been expected as a result of observing the operation of the game over the past ten years. You can understand that I was slightly disenchanted not only by business games in general but by that group in particular. I must admit to taking a great deal of pleasure in turning the tables somewhat when I was asked to go back to that centre as a lecturer recently and found that some of my old lecturers were sitting listening to me. That night I sat up very late and devised a special game and I can assure you that it produced some very interesting results. Fortunately for management training in this country, this sort of occurrence is an exception rather than a rule. Although many of the games that are well-known and well-established have by now taken on an extremely dog-eared appearance, there are many colleges and centres of management training which are devising games continually and using staff who bring a completely fresh approach to a game with each body of students who play it. The staff should look at the games which they use at least every six months and should indulge in a considerable amount of self-analysis in order to decide whether or not the game, and the way in which they are playing it, is still relevant.

It is always helpful if those responsible for the use of games have some industrial experience themselves or have taken the trouble of carefully examining the possible response to the game by people in a work situation. I can, for instance, design some fantastic crosswords but I can only just manage the clues in some of the popular daily newspapers. The trainer, therefore, must always try to put himself in the position of the trainee, and must keep asking the question 'Is this what the trainee wants, is it relevant, is it sensible and would I like it if someone were to do it to me?'

The evaluation of the game is, like the construction, very much a matter of personal taste. There are two basic ways in which a game may be evaluated. The objective criteria of the game — for example, market share or group progress — are an economic evaluation. The main problem connected with such evaluation is that the criteria chosen may be inconsistent, so that the team which has the greatest market share is not necessarily also the most profitable. There are a number of criteria that may be used — market share, profit, or rate of return on capital. The first two give the same result, unless the game is designed so that competing companies start off in an equal position. It is important, too, that an early decision be made about all the various evaluation factors which have to be considered such as method of stock valuation and, once made, the decision should carry on from group to group so that valid comparisons can be made. The evaluation procedure refers either to the measurement of the performance of the different simulated companies involved in the game or to the evaluation of the extent to which the game's objectives have been achieved.

Evaluation procedure should essentially be a part of the game itself. We are all aware of the situation where a group of business executives sit up late into the night working on a project and then elect those amongst them to report to the assembled group the following morning. I have always been most doubtful about the effectiveness of this system, although certainly from the training point of view it uses up time and therefore nicely lengthens the course a little. I do not know if there is any real answer to this problem and the type of evaluation will be determined by the type of game, but the evaluation procedure should be written up and should be included in the rules. There should be models on which evaluation can be based and at the same time these models should be flexible enough to allow for the one or two people who will come up with different, but entirely acceptable, answers.

The selection of trainees for management training by this method is as, if not more, vital than the selection of the staff who do the training. The game content and the decisions participants are expected to take must be within their own technical competence. These decisions must stretch, but not go beyond, their analytical skill. In other words, the game must match the participants' potential skills and abilities. Great care must be taken to ensure that the Peter principle, which states that in a hierarchy everyone eventually rises to their level of incompetence, is not brought into practice in this particular case. The games often provide participants with the chance to play a role which they will seldom play in real life and the connection between certain business games and certain television programmes is not difficult to see. Time constraints are very important and a game should not be put into a training programme lightly. The whole game structure and the classification of the type of person who might benefit from that type of game must be carefully examined.

It is, of course, pointless merely to send one's management trainees away to do a business game. Management training, like management consultancy, is often reckoned to be the panacea of all ills and many senior managers shelve their responsibility by filling in an application form for the training course and sending one of their juniors on it. This abnegation of responsibility for management training is endemic in business in this country and, while it has led to an increase in the number of management training centres, it has also led to a decrease in quality. Any senior manager involved in the development of juniors must understand that he cannot expect his work to be done for him by management training centres, and he has to assure himself that the training which he is inflicting on his junior is right and proper not only for the job in question but for the personality of that junior. The training needs of the participants for whom the game is intended must be identified and, from these training needs, training objectives have to be fashioned clearly and precisely. A business game using a model to simulate reality, in order to provide managers with opportunities to make decisions under training conditions similar to those in their workaday world, is a game which is very precious indeed.

Two major elements condition the effectiveness of games:

1. the link between objectives and design,
2. the teaching environment in which the game is used.

It is clear that the growth of management training games during the past few years has led to a great deal of abuse. I have mentioned before the necessity for management to examine the situation carefully before inflicting the training programme on anyone. Equally it must be understood that industry and educators need to maintain a very close link in order to ensure that the game and the training is right and proper. With the more urgent requirements of management training increasing daily, it is vital that those responsible for the design of such aids appreciate the real significance of the work and co-operate with management in designing sensible exercises. It is also incumbent upon management to find a way of translating practical experience into the training situation.

Acknowledgements

To all the authors of the many papers on the subject, many of whom have been quoted and even more mis-quoted.

The use of simulations and games in the teaching of economics to trainee business managers

W B Hornby, *Robert Gordon's Institute of Technology, Aberdeen*

This paper looks at the growth and development of simulations and games in the teaching of economics in general and in the teaching of economics in business studies degrees in particular. A distinction is made between business games and economics games and the relevance of economics games is discussed within the context of business studies degrees. It is argued that simulations and games are a particularly appropriate technique for teaching economics in terms of (a) the students' needs, (b) the nature of the subject, and (c) the objectives of a business studies degree. Finally, four games and simulations, used by the author with trainee business managers, are described. Two are simple non-computer simulations — PERFECT COMPETITION PRICING and OLIGOPOLY PRICING. Two are computer-based and are from the Schools Council project *Computers in the Curriculum*. These are MAXPRO — produced by the author and two colleagues — and BUDGET. Some tentative conclusions on the effectiveness of these games are given based on experience of running these, both in school economics courses and in business studies degree courses.

Introduction

The growth of games and simulations in a variety of subjects in the last few years has been quite dramatic. In economics this growth has been no less dramatic. Pat Noble (1975) recently produced a resource list for SAGSET in which she listed 33 simulations and games which covered such areas as banking and finance (of which there were six games and simulations), development economics (of which there were seven), macroeconomics (eleven games) and microeconomics (nine games and simulations). Randall (1975a) also reported recently a total of 76 computer-based games, simulations and what he calls 'demonstrations'.

The advantages of using games and simulations have been well documented although it has proved difficult to measure precisely their impact on teaching effectiveness. Various business games have been developed, some manual and some computer-based. For example, for a number of years the Institute of Chartered Accountants has run a business game and Esso also has produced two manually operated business games that have been widely used in schools and colleges. Business games, however, have in many cases been drawn up without any specific teaching programme in mind nor have they been designed to assist in the teaching of any specific subject area. The business games have usually been interdisciplinary in nature, involving elements of accounting, marketing and production. They are no less valuable for that. However, the point I would like to make here is that the economics principles involved in such games have often been submerged and it requires some effort to extract these from the mass of other information produced by such business games.

In recent years there have been moves to try to integrate games and simulations into teaching programmes in a more systematic way. Games and simulations have, therefore, become less of an optional extra and much more an essential part of the teaching process. The kind of approach which is developing in economics is to start with a given topic or subject area and to examine how it is being taught at the moment. One then asks what role a game or simulation could play in teaching the given topic more effectively. For example, Randall (1975b) in a project paper for the Schools Council, 'Computers and Economics Education', has made the point that there may be many areas of economics which are not likely to be enhanced by this approach but he adds:

> It might be rash to delineate them in the absence of unambiguous research findings. A more useful approach is to identify some features of economics which suggest that computer-generated material would be an appropriate method of teaching the subject.

This approach is being increasingly used in economics and it has led to the development of specifically economic games and simulations.

The growth and development of economics games and simulations has mirrored the growth and development of economics as a subject in both schools and polytechnics. The development of CNAA degrees in business studies has led to economics forming one of the main core subjects in such degrees. The main structure of such courses has generally had two features which have implications for teaching economics to business management students: firstly, the sandwich element and secondly, the discipline-based courses of the first two years usually give way to interdisciplinary, functionally-based courses, such as marketing or industrial relations, in the final year. This has meant that economics courses in the first two years have generally been concerned with the fundamental economic principles that are seen to have practical relevance in subsequent parts of the course. There is less emphasis therefore on academic disputes between economists on points of theory, as one might find in some courses. Also, the method of teaching is perhaps slightly different. Traditionally, business schools in America and elsewhere have placed emphasis on 'experiential' or action learning through role-playing, case studies and simulations and this method has been thought to be more appropriate to trainee business managers than more traditional teaching methods. The emphasis therefore in economics courses in business studies degrees has been increasingly on 'learning by doing' (Randall, 1975a).

This development is very much in line with developments in economics teaching elsewhere. For example in one fairly recent and influential report on teaching economics it was stated:

> We have given much thought to the extent to which teaching methods that are based on what are commonly known as 'heuristic' principles can usefully be applied to economics (*Report of Joint Committee on the Teaching of Economics in Schools*, 1973).

The report then goes on to detail a variety of teaching methods which may be described as *discovery* methods. Finally, the authors outline two reasons why they consider such methods to be important:

> Firstly, they ensure that economics is seen in action as a means of handling real problems. Secondly, they ensure that students are faced with the problems of

seeing how to set about a piece of economic analysis and the choice of appropriate economic techniques for handling it.

Advocates of games and simulations in the teaching of economics would claim that games and simulations do exactly that. Those involved in teaching economics in higher education cannot fail to be aware of the increasing number of students who have 'A' level or 'H' grade in economics and who have been on the receiving end of these developments in economics teaching in schools. If for no other reason, this in itself should force many institutions offering business studies degrees to look seriously at the way they teach economics. Therefore we cannot fail to be influenced by economics teaching developments elsewhere.

Economists have frequently stressed three features of their subject: firstly, its *scientific nature*, secondly, its *relevance* to solving problems, thirdly, its *realism*. (Indeed it would be strange for them to claim otherwise. I have yet to meet the economist who claims his subject is unscientific, unreal and irrelevant, although I have encountered a few students who hold these views!)

The methodology of economics with its hypotheses, assumptions and predictions is not very easy for the student new to the subject to grasp. It is at a level of abstraction that is somewhat remote for those following introductory courses in economics. Yet this is the aspect which is frequently stressed by authors of introductory textbooks. Hardly a textbook is produced which does not have as its first chapter a discussion of the methodology of the subject.

Perhaps the most difficult methodological problem for teachers of economics to overcome at any level is the *ceteris paribus* assumption frequently made by economists — the idea that when examining the relationship between two variables we assume that all other intervening variables are constant. The development of computer-based simulations enables the student to explore for himself the implications of such an assumption. Students are thus able to use the computer as a kind of laboratory and to experiment and probe in a way that would simply be impossible using conventional teaching methods.

It is often claimed that the use of games adds a sense of realism to a subject. Players are asked to think as managing directors (or as chancellors of the exchequer, although whether many students will wind up as chancellors of the exchequer is doubtful!). The players receive feedback on prices, profits and stock levels. Robinson (1975a) has emphasised the role of games in this respect.

> Students meeting economics for the first time often feel that there is a gulf beween theory and practice. Although they may have a good understanding of the models presented to them and may have considerable expertise in manipulating these models they may nevertheless be unable to relate them to the real world in order to gain a better understanding of the complexities of observed behaviour.

Lee and Entwistle (1975) also acknowledge that the Achilles heel of economics teaching is the alleged unreality and consequential irrelevance of much of what is taught. Games and simulations are thus seen as a way of bridging this gulf between theory and practice, a gulf which, I am sad to say, has been perhaps more noticeable in economics than in some other areas of business education.

Games

The games and simulations described here are ones which have been used by the economists at the School of Business Management Studies in our teaching of economics to first- and second-year undergraduate business studies students. The four are:

1. PERFECT COMPETITION PRICING SIMULATION (Joseph, 1965),
2. OLIGOPOLY PRICING SIMULATION (Joseph, 1965),
3. MAXPRO — a decision-making game based on the theory of the firm (Hornby *et al*, 1978),
4. BUDGET — a macroeconomic policy game (Endall *et al*, 1978).

It is generally acknowledged that one of the most difficult areas to teach in economics is what is called 'the theory of the firm'. The role of theory is very often misunderstood by students. The object of the theory of the firm is to predict how firms in general would react in certain market conditions given certain assumptions about their behaviour. Various market structures are outlined and these may be viewed as being on a spectrum with perfect competition at one end and monopoly at the other. In traditional expositions the extremes are then examined and comparisons are made.

One such extreme is perfect competition. As one lists the assumptions of such a market form it becomes apparent to students that this market structure has its feet firmly planted in mid-air. Consumers do not have perfect knowledge, products are seldom if ever homogeneous. As unrealistic assumption piles on top of unrealistic assumption it is hardly surprising that students tend to write off perfect competition as irrelevant. Yet a consideration of such a market form is important as a bench-mark against which other market forms can be assessed.

How then should one teach perfect competition as an economic concept? Those markets which correspond most closely to it in reality are probably the stock exchange, foreign exchange or commodity markets. Thus one way in which to overcome the problem is to simulate one of these markets prior to a discussion of the concept of perfect competition.

A group of students (the more the merrier, but preferably over 60) is divided into buyers and sellers and identified as such. They are issued with buying and selling cards giving appropriate instructions; one card to each student. These instructions are to buy at not more than, or sell at not less than, a given price for a homogeneous product, for example wheat. They are to act as brokers and to try to obtain the best deal they can. One needs a fairly large room so that players can mingle as on the floor of the stock exchange. Once a buyer and seller agree on a price they then turn in their cards to a controller who records the price at which the bargain is struck on a board or OHP visible to all participants before issuing new buying and selling instructions.

These buying and selling instruction cards may be distributed in the manner shown in Table 1.

This distribution tends to produce a market price of around 180p per bushel. What one observes is that after five or ten minutes when the range of agreed prices is quite wide there is a gradual convergence at or near the market price. This can often occur quite quickly once the market of buyers and sellers realises what the equilibrium price is likely to be. In other words, one can observe a dynamic process in action which is impossible using conventional teaching methods. The controller can then feed in different cards for a different market environment — increased demand or reduced supply.

The use of such an exercise prior to discussion of perfect competition does, in my experience, overcome to a very large extent the charge of being unrealistic levelled at this aspect of the theory of the firm.

Price (p)	Buyers (not more than the price)	Sellers (not less than the price)
280	4	—
260	4	2
240	4	2
220	4	2
200	4	2
180	4	4
160	2	4
140	2	6
120	2	6
100	2	4

Table 1. *Instructions on buying and selling for players*
(PERFECT COMPETITION PRICING SIMULATION) (from Joseph, 1965).

OLIGOPOLY, on the other hand, is a situation where three or four firms dominate a market. In such a situation the firms are likely to be highly interdependent, the actions of one firm having a direct effect on the policies of its rivals. In my experience, it becomes difficult to explore the implications of this market structure on firms' behaviour using conventional teaching methods. The theory of games and games strategy offers a basis for exploring these implications in a simulation of an oligopolistic market which has been developed by Myron Joseph (1965).

There are three firms in this simulation. Each is producing an identical product, they have the same costs of production and more or less equal market shares. Each firm has the choice of fixing prices at a high level of £4 or lower level of £3. A pay-off matrix can then be built up for our three-firm oligopoly market.

Price Combination	Costs = £65 + sales 'times' £ Prices: high (H) = £4 low (L) = £3 Sales and profit combinations of high £4 and low £3								
	Price	Sales	Profit £	Price	Sales	Profit £	Price	Sales	Profit £
HHH	H	30	25	H	30	25	H	30	25
HHL	H	10	−35	H	10	−35	L	80	95
HLL	H	5	−50	L	50	35	L	50	35
LLL	L	36	7	L	36	7	L	36	7

Table 2. *OLIGOPOLY PRICING: pay-off matrix* (From Joseph, 1965).

Students are divided into three-firm markets and asked to fix prices independently for the first decision period. Price wars quickly emerge and eventually prices reach low-price positions in all markets. The controller can then instruct some firms to collude with a view to maximising the joint profits of firms in the industry while others pursue their own independent goal of profit maximisation. A comparison of the pricing process of firms operating under different experimental conditions can be made.

Price combination	Collusion	No collusion	No strategy
HHH	15	0	0
HHL	2	5	5
HLL	2	4	3
LLL	1	11	12
	20	20	20

Table 3. *Pricing policies of different firms (OLIGOPOLY PRICING SIMULATION)*

Students quickly realise that there are now two competing forces influencing their behaviour. Firstly, competitive influences, ie to maximise one's own profit without regard to competitors' reactions. Secondly, co-operative influences, ie to maximise the profits of the industry as a whole. Students experience at first hand the pressures to collude and the futility of price wars. One of the main predictions of oligopolistic theory (viz the stability of prices and the tendency of firms to compete in non-price ways) comes out quite clearly in this simulation.

Developments in the use of the computer in economics games and simulations have been considerable in the last few years. In America, Attiyeh (1970) developed a macroeconomic policy game designed to teach undergraduates certain economic principles about the economy. This has now been developed at Heriot-Watt University into three macroeconomic games of increasing complexity and sophistication. At Reading, Robinson (1974) developed his MACROECONOMIC POLICY GAME. A description and discussion of this game was given at a previous SAGSET conference and an evaluation has been given elsewhere (Robinson, 1975a, 1975b).

At North Staffordshire Polytechnic, Randall (1975a) has developed several on-line computer games and demonstrations. In 1973, the Schools Council *Computers in the Curriculum* project turned its attention to economics. An account of its work in this field is given elsewhere (Lewis and Randall, 1975). At about this time I became involved in their work in this area and developed with two colleagues a computer-based package on the theory of the firm which has been in use at the School of Business Management Studies (Hornby *et al*, 1978).

This unit is called MAXPRO and it attempts to teach the principle of profit maximisation. Students are introduced to the various cost and revenue concepts in a series of pre-computer tasks. They are then given some information about the costs of production of a company involved in the production of shirts called the Maxiprofit Shirt Company. Initially the price of the shirts is exogenously determined (ie determined by the market or controlled by regulation). Students are required to select output levels that will maximise profits. The computer gives feedback on various costs, eg average costs, marginal costs, fixed costs, variable costs; computes profit/loss figures and gives some suitable comment on whether the student is anywhere near the correct output level.

Students have several opportunities at various prices to obtain the profit-maximising output level by trial and error. The whole idea of the unit is that students should have a chance to explore for themselves the relationship between output, costs and profits and to discover for themselves the profit maximisation principle.

The unit then moves on to look at the profit maximisation principle with different cost constraints and with different demand conditions. Finally, the assumption about externally determined prices is relaxed and students are free to set prices or output levels so as to maximise profits. Before each section or mini-program on the computer, students are required to familiarise themselves with the various concepts that will be used in that section by using students' notes provided. After using the computer there are several post-computer exercises, eg constructing the company's cost curves or devising a supply curve for the company at given prices. Students can also choose which section they wish to work on. The basic idea behind this is that it can be used as a self-instruction device. It can also be used to reinforce a conventional treatment of the topic of profit maximisation or it can be used as a remedial programme.

Macroeconomic policy games are designed to teach macroeconomic principles. Although the School of Business Management Studies at Robert Gordon's Institute of Technology, Aberdeen, is not primarily concerned with turning out future chancellors of the exchequer it is clearly important that business management students should appreciate the forces at work in the economy.

BUDGET is a simple macroeconomic game developed in 1975 by the economics group of the Schools Council *Computers in the Curriculum* project. Students form themselves into governments. They have to achieve four objectives, viz stable prices, growth, full employment and equilibrium in the balance of payments. They can vary the rate of tax and government spending subject to certain political constraints. Students thus experience at first hand the problems of reconciling these various goals. Results generated by BUDGET can then be used as a basis for discussion of the relationship between certain key economic objectives (eg price stability and full employment). In this game there is no right answer, only, hopefully, a greater appreciation of the complexities involved in managing an economy.

Evaluation

A full-scale evaluation of these games has yet to be undertaken, but such feedback as we have obtained from students who have used MAXPRO, for example, at Robert Gordon's Institute of Technology and elsewhere, indicates some modest success. The problems of evaluation are, however, formidable. For example, are simulations to be used as well as or instead of traditional methods? I tend to favour the former approach, in which case there would also need to be a proportional increase in student performance to justify the use of a game or simulation. In other words, for a given increase in inputs (ie the games and simulations) there needs to be a more than commensurate increase in output (ie students' performance). In one evaluation of a computer-based economics game (Wing, 1968), the author concluded that on average students attained approximately the same amount of learning with considerably less investment of time and that in terms of learning effectiveness games appeared superior to conventional classroom teaching.

There is a further problem. Business studies degrees are general degrees. Even if it could be shown that economic games and simulations improved performance in learning effectiveness in economics, if additional time is devoted to such things then it may mean less time is devoted to accounts or law. If performance in these other areas deteriorates then it could be argued that games and simulations have added nothing to the overall educational process. This point has been forcefully made by some commentators on games (Robinson, 1975b).

Another approach to evaluation is to draw up a list of criteria for success of a game or simulation and then check off its performance against each item on the list. It has been argued (Garvey, 1971) that any game should do five things:

1. motivate students,
2. change attitudes held by students,
3. enable students to acquire conceptual knowledge and retain it,
4. enable students to gain certain skills and to gain confidence in their use of these skills,
5. provide students with a 'laboratory' so that they can explore various possibilities and comprehend the complexities of certain economic processes.

There is some evidence, albeit informal or anecdotal, that the games and simulations I have described achieve these five objectives. For example, with MAXPRO we have noticed that tutorial papers produced by students who have used the simulation tend to be fuller and more detailed than those who have not. Insofar as this can be taken as a measure of motivation, then MAXPRO appears to be a good motivator.

There is also some evidence that students who have taken part in MAXPRO and BUDGET, for example, tend to perform slightly better on multiple-choice questions in these areas. The samples were very small as were the differences in scores, but the results were suggestive.

In terms of attitude change, one finds, for example, among students who have run BUDGET, a greater sympathy with the problem of managing an economy in such a way as to achieve multiple goals. Students' attitudes to this part of the course also change. This has not been measured in any systematic way, but in terms of the frequency with which students who have used BUDGET answer examination questions in this area against those students who have not used the programme, one can get some idea.

There is always a danger in using simulations that students may mistake the simulation for reality. How realistic should a simulation be? In all four of the examples I have quoted, things have been simplified, indeed possibly over-simplified. However, I would defend this vigorously. It seems to me that there is always a trade-off (to use an economic concept) between realism on the one hand and effectiveness on the other. It simply does not follow that the more realistic simulations are the more effective they become. It seems to me quite acceptable to simplify games in order to emphasise specific teaching points.

Objective empirical evidence on the value of simulation is often difficult to obtain. One has often to rely on subjective impressions. I have given you mine in relation to four economic simulations which I have used in teaching economics to trainee business managers. One commentator attempting to evaluate simulations in general came to the following conclusion:

Although the judgements, findings and hunches are not always supported by empirical evidence there is no room for doubt that simulation possesses some solid advantages for use in education. That it is always successful is obviously not supportable. It is equally obvious, however, that simulation affords some advantages which simply cannot be duplicated by other instructional techniques (Garvey, 1971).

It is my contention that this last aspect of simulation applies with great force in the teaching of economics in general and more particularly in the teaching of economics to trainee business managers.

References

Attiyeh, R E (1970) Policy making in a simulated environment. In Lumsden, K (ed) *Recent Research in Economics*. Prentice-Hall, New York.

Endall, J C, Fox, D W and Green, W (1978) BUDGET. In *Computers in the Curriculum*. Schools Council, London.

Garvey, J (1971) Simulation: a catalogue of judgements, findings and hunches. In Tansey, P (ed) *Educational Aspects of Simulation*. McGraw-Hill, London.

Hornby, W, Holley, D and Still, D (1978) MAXPRO. In *Computers in the Curriculum*. Schools Council, London.

Joseph, M L (1965) Role playing in teaching economics. *American Economic Review*, 55, 556-565.

Lee, N and Entwistle, N (1975) Economics education: educational theory. In Lee, N (ed) *Teaching Economics*. Heinemann, London.

Lewis, J and Randall, K V (1975) Some developments in computer-based materials for economics teaching. *Economics*, 11, 45-46.

Noble, P (1975) *SAGSET Resource List* 3A-3E.

Randall, K V (1975a) *Computers in Economics Project*. North Staffordshire Polytechnic (mimeo).

Randall, K V (1975b) Computers and economics education. *Computers in the Curriculum Project*. Project Paper Number 9. Schools Council, London.

Robinson, J N (1974) The Reading University macroeconomic game. *Economics*, 10, 383-388.

Robinson, J N (1975a) Teaching economics with a game: a progress report. *SAGSET Journal*, 5, 80-85.

Robinson, J N (1975b) The Reading University macroeconomic game: an attempt at evaluation. *Economics*, 12, 144-158.

Wing, R L (1968) Two computer-based economics games for sixth graders. In Boocock, S S and Schild, E O *Simulation Games in Learning*. Sage Publications, Beverley Hills, California.

The use of simulation in the training of speech therapists

S J Rothwell, *Robert Gordon's Institute of Technology, Aberdeen*
and G W Davidson, *Chambers Publishing Company, Edinburgh*

There are currently two routes of entry into the speech therapy profession: diploma courses and degree courses. In addition to the extensive theoretical study of such disciplines as psychology, neurology, and speech pathology and therapeutics, training courses of both types include a large component of practical work, the major part of which consists of clinical training. The aims of this clinical component can be summarised as being to aid the development of the student's self-awareness, to develop in the student full awareness of the communicative handicaps of patients suffering from speech and language disorders, and to assist the student to develop the skills and techniques required in the treatment of such patients.

It is argued in this paper that simulation techniques have an important part to play in the training of speech therapists. Simulation exercises are to be seen as complementing the training received by students in speech therapy clinics, and are intended, like the clinical training, to promote the student's personal growth. By so doing, simulation exercises increase the student's ability to establish interpersonal relationships and develop the student's awareness of the dynamics of the normal functioning and of the breakdown of the communication process.

Simulation exercises appropriate to the training of speech therapists are described and their benefits and drawbacks assessed.

Background

At present, simulation techniques play very little part in the training of speech therapists in the United Kingdom. It is the purpose of this paper to consider, firstly, the benefits which would be derived from the incorporation of simulations into the teaching programmes of speech therapy training schools, secondly, the ways in which such techniques could be integrated into these programmes and thirdly, the type of simulations which would be most appropriate to the training of speech therapists. In particular, we will argue in this paper that there are certain aspects of the overall professional competence required of a speech therapist which can be developed and enhanced more effectively by means of simulations than by any other means.

For the purposes of this paper, we will restrict the concept of simulation to free role-play activities simulating interpersonal interactions in clinical, or other, situations.

Our argument will be developed in three stages. First, we will outline the nature of the work of a speech therapist, and distinguish the various roles which a speech therapist may be called upon to fill in the course of his or her work.

Second, we will describe briefly the training courses currently running in this country which provide an entry into the speech therapy profession, and discuss their effectiveness in training speech therapists to fill the roles which we have outlined. And third, we will consider the ways in which the current training programmes could be improved by the inclusion of role-play simulations.

To begin with, then, we will take a brief look at what it is a speech therapist does. To many people, a speech therapist is, in the words of the 1972 Quirk Report on the Speech Therapy Services, 'little more than "an elocutionist in a white coat"' (Department of Education and Science, 1972). Within the framework of this paper, it is not possible, nor is it necessary, to give anything other than a most superficial indication of the range and complexity of the speech and language disorders with which a speech therapist may be confronted in an everyday clinical situation, but it cannot be too strongly emphasised that to see in a speech therapist little more than an elocutionist is not only to seriously underestimate the personal qualities and academic ability required of a member of the profession, but is also to evidence a considerable misconception of the nature of this work.

The terms 'speech therapy' and 'speech therapist' must not be interpreted too narrowly or too rigidly. There are indeed many people within the profession who feel that the label 'speech therapist' is both inadequate and misleading, in that the term 'speech disorder' can be correctly applied to only some of the impairments presented by patients in clinics, and the term 'therapy' really only applies to one aspect of the speech therapist's work. Under the rubric of 'speech therapist' one can differentiate four distinct but interrelated roles which the speech therapist must be competent to fill. These four roles, which we will discuss briefly in turn, are *diagnostician, clinician, therapist* (in the particular sense in which we will define the term) and *counsellor.*

First, the speech therapist as diagnostician. Unlike many counterparts in the paramedical professions, the speech therapist is not dependent on a medical practitioner for the diagnosis of the disorders presented by patients, nor for the prescription of appropriate courses of treatment. It is the therapist who is responsible for the assessment of patients, the diagnosis of their disorders and the planning of their treatment.

Closely related to the speech therapist's role as diagnostician, and for obvious reasons very dependent upon it, is the role as clinician. As a clinician, it is the function of the speech therapist to treat the speech or language disorder which any patient presents as a specific clinical problem, isolated to some extent from the patient as a person. As a clinician, the speech therapist must devise and implement a treatment programme designed specifically to alleviate, or 'cure', the patient's communicative dysfunction.

There is little doubt that it is in the role of clinician, as one who 'corrects' or 'cures' speech and language impairments, that the speech therapist is best known to the lay public. It is doubtless this very restricted view of the speech therapist's function which has led to the misconception that a speech therapist is nothing more than a sort of paramedical elocutionist. But an equally important aspect of the speech therapist's work, although one which is less obvious to, and less well understood by, the public at large, is the role of therapist proper. It is this role that we consider next.

While it is true that in any clinical situation a person comes to, or is referred to, a speech therapist because of a specific speech or language problem, the particular dysfunction from which a patient is suffering will affect that patient in all parameters of his or her life — work, relationships with the family, and social relationships outside the family circle. While we have suggested that it is the function of the speech therapist as clinician to treat the patient's linguistic dysfunction as an entity in itself, isolated *to a certain extent* from the patient as a person, it is equally important for a speech therapist to view the patient's disorder in its total perspective, to see the patient not just as a syndrome but as an individual. This is particularly important where thinking in terms of a 'cure' for the dysfunction is quite simply unrealistic, as is the case, for example, with patients suffering from certain *acquired* disorders.

A speech therapist will be called upon to treat both patients who present dysfunctions which can be 'cured' and patients with dysfunctions which may, at best, show some very slight improvement through time. As we see this role, it is not the job of a speech therapist to treat the person as a patient, but rather to treat the patient as a person, to be concerned not so much with the patient's linguistic problems but rather with his or her global social and personal problems which have arisen either as a result of the linguistic dysfunction itself or as a result of any concomitant physiological dysfunctions arising from the injury sustained by the patient. Indeed, speech therapists (as *therapists*) will of necessity not only concern themselves with the problems of patients, but also of the patients' families.

The fourth and last role which we will distinguish is that of counsellor. Increasingly nowadays the speech therapist acts as an adviser to patients' parents, to their teachers, and to their husbands or wives, on treatment which they themselves may carry out with the patients, instead of, or in addition to, such treatment which the patients receive in speech therapy clinics. This counselling role of the speech therapist is related to and dependent on his or her ability as a diagnostician, a clinician and a therapist.

We consider these, then, to be the four major roles which a speech therapist is called upon to play in clinical work. It is the function of speech therapy training courses to develop the student speech therapist, personally and academically, to be fully effective in all four capacities, and we will now consider to what extent the current courses fulfil this goal.

Present position

There are currently two routes of entry into the speech therapy profession: by four-year degree course and by three-year diploma course. While the five schools which offer degree courses have considerable freedom to develop these courses along independent lines, all the diploma courses follow a syllabus laid down by the College of Speech Therapists in London, which is not to say, however, that there are no differences of emphasis between the courses run by the various training schools concerned.

TRAINING COURSES

In this brief outline of the speech therapy training courses currently run in the United Kingdom, we will refer only to the diploma courses, but the remarks we shall make are essentially applicable *mutatis mutandis* to the degree courses also.

Speech therapy training courses can be considered as consisting of two major components — a theoretical component and a practical component. The *theoretical-academic* component is designed to provide the student with a thorough knowledge of the wide range of disciplines with which a practising speech therapist must be familiar. The subjects of study laid down by the College of Speech Therapists in 1976 include phonetics and linguistics, psychology, anatomy and physiology, neurology, and speech pathology and therapeutics. Training schools are permitted to add other disciplines to this curriculum if they so wish.

The *practical* component of the diploma courses consists of the students' work in speech therapy clinics. In their second year, students go out into clinics to sit in with experienced therapists, and thus begin to learn how to apply the knowledge they obtain from the academic component of the course by seeing it applied by a therapist in a clinical situation. In their third year, student speech therapists begin to treat their own patients in clinics, under the supervision of experienced speech therapists. In order to be competent in all four of these roles, we would suggest that a speech therapist must have three main attributes: a high level of academic ability, a high level of practical skill, and a high level of personal maturity, insight and awareness. One might say that the first two of these attributes are those which are particularly necessary to the diagnostician and clinician, and the last is that which is especially required of a therapist and counsellor. In reality, of course, it is impossible to make the relationship between the roles and the attributes required for the filling of these roles quite as definite and rigid as we are doing here.

There is little doubt that the present training courses provide a perfectly adequate preparation for the speech therapist as diagnostician and as clinician. Over the three or four years of a course, the student will learn to recognise a wide variety of syndromes, will come to understand the underlying etiologies of these syndromes insofar as they are known, and will be taught the general outlines of appropriate treatment programmes. This information is provided by the academic component.

Of course it would be quite wrong to assume that 'if you give a student a lecture on a certain condition, a number of techniques on how to ameliorate it, and a standard textbook to fall back on, he will be able to function as a therapist' (Byers Brown, 1971). It is, in fact, 'extremely hard for a student to make a transfer from a class lecture to a clinical skill. Information is not enough' (*ibid*). This has long been recognised in speech therapy training schools on this side of the Atlantic, though less so in the United States until recently, and it is this transfer from theory to practice that the practical component of the course is designed to assist, by allowing the students first to see the theoretical principles being put into practice, and then to put them into practice themselves under supervision.

But, as we have already outlined, there is a great deal more to speech therapy than the mere diagnosis and treatment of communicative disorders. A fully effective training course must also assist speech therapy students to develop as therapists and as counsellors, roles which, as we have suggested above, require that a speech therapist has a high degree of personal maturity, of self-awareness, and awareness also of the patient at something more than a purely superficial level. We would argue that the therapeutic, as opposed to clinical, skills which are required in these two roles, and the maturity and insight which they presuppose, cannot be given to students by the staff of the training schools, but must rather be acquired by the students themselves during their training.

One further attribute that a successful speech therapist must possess is confidence, and the speech therapist must not only have self-confidence but must also be able to instil confidence in the patients. This ability to instil confidence in patients, many of whom will be much older than the therapist, is one further skill which student speech therapists must acquire for themselves in the course of the training; it cannot be taught.

As far as the preparation of the student speech therapists for their roles as therapist and counsellor is concerned, one can suggest that the function of the training schools is not dissimilar to the task which Muriel Spark's character, Miss Jean Brodie, set herself in education: it is our purpose 'to put old heads on young shoulders'. This is, as we have suggested, essentially a matter of the student's own personal development, but three or four years is not a great deal of time for a young and relatively immature adolescent to develop into a mature and confident speech therapist. The major function of the training school must be, therefore, to provide each student with the maximum opportunity and optimal environment for this personal development and maturation, and it is our contention that simulations could, and should, play a major part in this area of speech therapy training.

Development

At present, the lectures on psychology and communication which form part of the academic component of the training courses provide the students with some insight into the complex dynamics of interpersonal communication and the social and personal disruptions which arise from a patient's communicative and physical handicaps. In addition, a student will learn by practical experience how to handle patients and their diverse problems, and with experience and practice will come confidence, maturity and awareness. The present writers feel, however, that more could be done to assist this self-development in students during the course of their training, and it is this we see as the major function of role-play simulations. Simulations should be complementary to the current theoretical and practical components of the training courses, and should focus on the student's personal maturation and the development of the student's therapeutic skills.

There are several different types of role-play simulations which could be considered appropriate for this purpose, each one contributing to the development of a particular aspect of the student's overall insight and maturity. These are: firstly, simulations which provide insight into the problems of patients suffering from communicative or physical handicaps. Secondly, simulations which provide insight into syndromes which the student has not encountered in clinical practice. Thirdly, simulations which provide the student with the opportunity to practice coping with situations which might arise in clinics or which have arisen in clinics. Such simulations provide the students with an insight into their own personality, ie they are a means of developing the student's self-awareness. As an example of the first type of role-play simulation, one could envisage the setting-up of a role-play session in which the student had to adopt the role of a stammerer or of an aphasic in a public house, on a bus, in a shop or elsewhere. One could perhaps even demand that the student play this role in a real-life situation, among total strangers. While this might seem to be a relatively trivial form of role play, there is really no other way in which student speech therapists with full command of their faculties could gain insight into the communicative handicaps of the patients and the interpersonal, social and practical problems that these give rise to.

Secondly, one could use role-play sessions to simulate disorders which are rarely met in clinics, and which the students will know only from lectures and textbooks. However, we would still stress that, in our opinion, simulations are to be seen less as a means of developing a student's knowledge than as a means of developing the student's awareness, less as a means of providing the student with facts — which will be provided by the academic component — than as an opportunity for the student to develop skills, confidence and insight.

In addition to simulating syndromes which the student has met only in textbooks, it is possible also to simulate situations which the student has not encountered during clinical practice but wishes to simulate in order to assess his/her reactions to the dynamics involved. As an example, one might note that informing a student that a minimally brain-damaged child may well be hyperactive is of little use in helping the student to cope with a hyperactive brain-damaged child who is running amok in a clinic. A simulation of such a situation will allow students to be aware of, and to come to terms with, their reactions to the situation before it arises, and may therefore assist in their coping with the situation when it does arise.

Furthermore, situation simulations of this third type can be invaluable not only as a means of simulating situations which might arise in clinics, but also in simulating situations which *have* arisen in clinics and which, for one reason or another, the student has been unable to cope with. Such role-play simulations can thus act as a sort of safety valve, allowing the student to express reactions openly which, if allowed to surface in an actual clinical situation, could be profoundly damaging both to the student and to the patient. Role-play simulations will allow the students to develop greater awareness of themselves, of their reactions to certain patients or certain syndromes and other underlying causes of these reactions. If role-play simulations do not help the student to overcome negative reactions, they may at least help in understanding them and in coming to terms with them.

In the film accompanying this paper, we will see one example of a student speech therapist who found herself unable to relate positively to a particular patient. After a carefully constructed role-play session, guided by an experienced psychotherapist, the student was able to understand the dynamics of her relationship with this patient and her reactions to her, and was able to relate to the individual concerned, both as a patient and as a person.

The writers would wish to stress that role-play sessions such as have been outlined in this paper should only be run by a psychotherapist or some other suitably trained and experienced member of staff who is aware of, and able to control, the interpersonal dynamics of the role-play situations. Otherwise the sessions must be kept at a 'safe' and therefore superficial level, or one would run the serious risk of the sessions getting out of hand and being more destructive than constructive. While we are advocating the wider use of simulations in the training of speech therapists, we are in no way suggesting that this could or should be attempted in the absence of suitably trained staff.

Finally, with regard to the integration of simulations into speech therapy training courses, we would wish only to make the following points. Firstly, to be fully effective, simulation sessions should be integrated into a more general course of practical classes which are designed to aid the student's self-awareness and maturation. In the speech therapy training school which provided us with the videotape which accompanies this paper, this course begins in the students' first year, and continues and develops over the three-year training period. Secondly, the role-play sessions should, as far as possible, be linked to the students' practical experience in actual clinical situations.

Conclusion

In concluding this paper, we would note that in its evidence to the Quirk Committee, the Royal College of Psychiatrists stated that speech therapists are at present 'inadequately trained in psychodynamics, family dynamics, and psychotherapy' (Department of Education and Science, 1972). While role-play simulations such as have been outlined in this paper can in no sense be considered as constituting a training in psychotherapy and psychodynamics, it is to be hoped that when speech therapy training schools come to realise the full value of simulations in the training of speech therapists, they will also begin to consider the possible value of role-play sessions as one form of psychotherapy which could be of as much use in the speech therapy clinic itself as in the speech therapy training school. It is, in other words, to be hoped that in the near future speech therapy training schools will not only include role-play sessions as a means of training in therapeutics, but will also provide training in the use of role play as a means of therapy.

Acknowledgements

The writers wish to acknowledge the kind assistance of Mrs E Hodkinson and the staff and students of the Speech Therapy Department, the Central School of Speech and Drama, London, in supplying the videotape which illustrated the paper presented at the Conference.

References

Byers Brown, B (1971) *Speak for Yourself: The Life of a Speech Therapist.* Educational Explorers, Reading.

Department of Education and Science (1972) *Speech Therapy Services.* Her Majesty's Stationery Office, London.

Chapter 4: Education

Perhaps more has been written about the use of simulations and games in education than in any other field. Certainly this chapter contains most papers and reflects the emphasis seen in previous SAGSET conferences. The papers show a range of subjects from chemistry (Zoller and Timor), through language skills (Harvey and Wheeler; McAleese and Hare) and geography (Walker), to mathematics (Doherty) and physics (Addinall and Ellington). Applications are seen at both a secondary and a tertiary level (Dowdeswell and Bailey; Kirkland). Glandon looks at the assumptions behind the use of simulations in the school curriculum and thus bridges both the subject gap and the school-to-university divide. Roebuck, in the keynote paper, focuses more on the teacher in the secondary context and raises serious questions about the quality of knowlege extant on what goes on at the microlevel in simulations. He uses the concept of structured materials to describe simulations and typifies the teacher-innovator as an interventionist. Percival takes up the 'hot potato' of evaluation and, using a variety of studies, indicates some of the methodological weaknesses and solutions. The clear message of the papers that describe games/simulations is a search by the authors for *innovative* solutions to teaching problems. This attempt to innovate (ie use *new* tactics) is common to all game designers.

Keynote paper: Simulation games and the teacher as an adaptive interventionist

Martyn Roebuck, *Scottish Education Department, Edinburgh*

This paper argues the case for treating simulation games as a form of structured material. It is argued that not enough is known at the microlevel of pupil-material interactions and that the *implicit* objectives of teaching materials may be apparent to a rather restricted group. Subtle secrets may not be known to the average user of materials. The paper concludes with the observation that acceptance and utilisation of such materials in schools will come when organisational problems are met and there is a greater understanding of the micro-methodologies of pupil teacher-concept interactions.

Introduction

When we begin with the title we are really being asked to examine not *one* interaction of *one* classroom with *one* game, but very many different interactions. This is an impossible task. The only solution is to take a synoptic view — or is it? Is that not one of the real problems? Should we look across the board at educational methods and media? The broad view tells us very little, because in the long run it is the effect on the individual child which counts. The learning is by actual individuals in real classrooms (or open-plan areas) and not by some average generalised student.

Last weekend was the August Bank Holiday in the lower part of mainland Britain. On Tuesday last week, the *Guardian* said that it was ironical that the Pack Report (1977) should have been published 'in the middle of the school holidays'. When I commented on this I was told, 'Ah, yes, but it is the middle of the school holidays in England!'. Indeed, for 90 per cent of the island population it was so, but the Pack Report is on 'Truancy and indiscipline in schools in Scotland' and the *Scottish* schools were not on holiday at all. It was the beginning of the school year in that part of the country to which the report referred. The relevance of truancy and discipline to the teaching situations in schools *in general* in the UK was not the concern of the Pack Committee; thus it ought not to have been criticised for being inappropriate in its timing for the majority!

Returning to the title; gaming and simulations have a significant contribution to make, but *in general* they have no relevance to schools. The point at issue is that the relevance must be to particular teachers, to their particular pupils at specific times and with certain concepts, principles and applications in mind. This is what I want to explore albeit briefly; the game, the pupil and the teacher.

Simulation games as structured materials

Games and simulations are an aspect of educational technology in that they are devices and means of organising the ways in which learners and media interact. 'Educational technology' is a jargon term which covers this concern for putting pupils into a particular educational context, causing them to react, interact and respond with specific aims in mind, and with finding out what happens.

Games and simulations are a subset of 'structured materials'. In or associated with this set we have books, programmed materials, worksheets, educational broadcasts, assignments, workbooks, audiovisual courses, objective tests, interactive computer software, the Dalton plan and the Keller plan. Whereas programmed texts, books and films, for example, can or do involve media and student interactions, games and simulations share with discussion groups and, perhaps, projects, some emphasis on and use of student-to-student interactions. You may not accept this rather rough grouping but from a practical and school viewpoint simulation games share a lot of characteristics with other packaged resource materials. First, they are pre-structured; second, the teacher has to learn about their content, scope and use. Third, they cost money and take up storage space and fourth, while they may cover several important aspects of the work of a class they may omit important parts of the syllabus. They may also spend too much time on items which are not necessary (in the view of the teacher!).

Simulation games may also share operational characteristics with other structured materials. They are not as widely used as the devisers would *like*. They are not being used in the way the designer would *expect*, or would prefer or want. Let us consider a simple example from a different context. Games are unfamiliar to many teachers; educational broadcasts have been around a long time. In a recent survey 141 secondary schools were questioned about their use of television programmes and 53 stated that they used a particular science series during the autumn 1976 term (38 per cent). It was therefore one of the most popular television broadcast series for secondary schools. It is a biology series with ten programmes on different topics chosen from the GCE/SCE and CSE syllabuses. The topics were verified as key topics by choosing them from responses by several hundred teachers. To accompany the broadcasts there are teachers' notes which give details on the topics which are not readily available elsewhere.

What do we know about the use? One might expect, given that these ten topics covered items from two years' work, and that schools could record the programmes and that schools would show to the classes those programmes which were relevant to the work of that term, that these showings would be supplemented with information from the teachers' notes and from elsewhere. If we examine the figures in greater detail we find 53 schools using the series; of these only 20 used all ten programmes (that is 33 used less than ten); of those using less than ten only 14 used the teachers' notes. So we see that only 14 schools used a selection and with the teachers' notes. That is, only a quarter used the materials in a manner similar to that intended — but we still do not know what happened *in* those 14 schools. Where did the viewing take place? What was the picture like? What happened before the broadcasts? What happened after the broadcasts? Indeed what happened *during* the playback; perhaps the headteacher chose to pass a message over the Tannoy, or perhaps the RAF chose to pass overhead?

Simulation games do not achieve their aims to the same extent as when the authors/designers are in charge of the teaching. The objectives of the materials may not be understood by the teachers and it may not be clear what the objectives of the materials are, and what methodology the teacher should employ. Lastly the teacher's style may not match that anticipated or intended by the designers.

One thing that we seem to be learning about teaching materials is that their *implicit* objectives may be implicit only to a somewhat restricted group. The subtle secrets may not be known at all to the average user of the materials.

The teacher as an adaptive interventionist

In looking at the way pupils learn and teachers teach I make a basic assumption: that the role of the teacher is that of an interventionist. He or she *intervenes* between the learner and his environment in order, hopefully, to facilitate the learning process. The teacher mediates between the resource (the verbalised ideas, or physical materials) and the learner. His (or her) style of teaching is his style of intervening. He may simply intervene by writing a verbal form of an idea on a blackboard and cause pupils to write it down. Interventionists can clearly be negative as well as positive in their effect. The good teacher is one who is able to adjust and alter his mode of intervention to match the learner, the context and the concepts.[1]

Structured materials expect some form of intervention and it will differ between materials. Some types, such as programmed texts, may require a more restricted range of roles for the teacher. Others, including games, could require a range of types of intervention which may not be predetermined in detail. Thus the activities of the teacher cannot be prescribed or set out in guide-lines.

Are the expectations of the materials sufficiently clear to teachers to enable them to recognise their particular functions? What evidence do we have about the ability of the average teacher to take on board these different roles?[2] Recently we have had some research into the extent to which teachers adapt their style to the objectives of the curriculum:

> ... the results counsel a *flexible* approach ... It would appear that the teacher's approach should be varied to match the skills it is desired to develop within the pupils. The evidence from the process part of the research indicates, however, that this is not a universal practice among the sample of teachers observed ...
>
> The tendency is for the style to be consistent, no matter what form the activity takes. Didactic teachers teach practical work didactically. Teachers favouring investigatory methods of learning do [that] sometimes to the exclusion of anything else ... Our experience suggests that the science teachers who claim to vary their style according to the needs of pupils were more often referring to the different ability levels between their sets rather than the variety of objectives subsumed within a particular activity. Even then, altering a style was usually equivalent to changing the pace of delivery rather than to altering the overall lesson strategy (Eggleston *et al*, 1976).

And from a Scottish source (Brown and McIntyre, 1977) an examination of the extent to which the objectives of *Curriculum Paper 7* ('Integrated science in the first two years of secondary schools') were achieved, produced the following results:

> First, in response to questionnaires and interviews less than nine per cent of schools

claimed that they were following the pattern implied in *Curriculum Paper* 7 for 'teaching towards the objectives' of the course. Second, where in *Curriculum Paper* 7 there are implications for pedagogy (eg presenting science as 'integrated'; responding to differences in ability; teaching by 'guided discovery'; teaching towards objectives) there is *little* ground to suppose that they have been incorporated into classroom practice (Brown and McIntyre, 1977).

Macro- and micro-methodologies

I assume that SAGSET is a group of people primarily concerned with methodology, albeit a particular approach to methodology. An association of geography teachers would, I suggest, be more concerned about the *geography* that is taught than about the methodology in a geography context. Clearly there would be an interest and an expertise in methodology as such but the approach would be from the curriculum and content end. All of the examples and comments that I have used so far have been drawn from curriculum examples. They are, I suppose, illustrations of the current belief that when a new curriculum development is adopted, what is adopted is a content rather than the implicit methodology. It suggests that there is an inability on the part of teachers and trainers to comprehend methodology, and thus to take on board methodological changes. If there is this inability then for those like yourselves whose prime concern is with exploiting the methods, as well as the content, there is a double hurdle. Understanding the methodological approach is the first aim, not a second spin-off achieved once the new content orientation has been comprehended.

Gary Shirts (1976) makes an interesting observation:

> If one were to observe the actions and effects of many different games through a one-way mirror, without the benefit of sound or script, it would be very difficult to tell one game from another. Probably *75 per cent* of the games are concerned with basically the same process – one in which the participants are asked to allocate scarce resources within various decision-making modes, and different role and power relationships.

The comment reminded me of the worksheet, of the objective test item and of the programmed text and the similar view which could be expressed about these. Do you remember the programmed text of the 1960s – a string of single sentences with words missing, laid out in a strange format? The secret of the successful programmed text was, and *is*, I believe, in the individual pupil-item interactions, and in the planned cumulative effects of such interactions. It is certainly not primarily in the format. Yet programmed texts were published for reasons which seemed more closely related to the conformity of the format than to the quality of such interactions. Why? Is is because of the ways in which teachers are trained, the ways in which curriculum developments are presented, the manner in which beliefs about the psychology of learning are exemplified? Is it because they leave to much to be *induced*? As a result, methodology is comprehended only at a *macrolevel*, at the level of organisation, of formats, of group sizes, of the number of alternatives in a question; and the comprehension is not at the *microlevel* of concepts, principles and individual student interactions with these parts of the structure of a body of knowledge.

In the same article, referred to above, Gary Shirts comments on the practical problems associated with the take-up or otherwise of simulation games. He seems to assume that some of these problems are peculiar to games. He begins, for example, 'Teachers know and understand how to use a text book, lecture, conduct a discussion and work on projects of various kinds'. This may well be the case at a macro-, organisational level but not at the microlevel. He gives as an example:

> In the game itself, there are mysteries and problems to work through and it is difficult for many teachers to repress their helping instincts while the students grope and struggle in confusion and frustration to solve them. At the end of the game, the temptation is to interpret, explain and lecture on the meaning of the experience rather than helping the students interpret and draw meaning from the experience themselves (Shirts, 1976).

Shirts is talking about *guided discovery*. So were Eggleston (*et al*, 1976) and Brown and McIntyre (1977) in their respective reports. They were referring to teachers who *guide* discovery, for example by dictating the answers to open-ended worksheet items. Eggleston *et al*, in commenting further on their findings, say:

> Each separate curriculum . . . had its own philosophy embodied in a statement of aims — but the common theme developed by all of them was to move away from the teaching of science in school as 'a set of received facts and principles' towards a greater participation of pupils in the exploration of novel ideas. Thus, in terms of Bloom's Taxonomy, emphasis was put on the higher cognitive skills — towards guided discovery. In terms of classroom activities we should expect to find pupils manipulating data to interpret and make inferences from observations. Pupils might be led to develop their own explanations of observed phenomena and to devise experiments to test the consequences of these ideas. Yet, . . . we see that over a quarter of the teachers never encourage the designing of experiments through their questioning, and there were both chemistry and physics teachers who never asked questions on what pupils observed during practical work . . . Our findings suggest therefore that there is considerable dissonance between the curriculum developer's aims and the related practice within the classroom . . . Our study of the classroom suggests that these early developers failed to take into account the consistency of the teacher's approach, irrespective of content change (Eggleston *et al*, 1976).

The article by Shirts identifies some features of the future: firstly, the immediate future for games and simulations will be like the immediate past, the level of take-up will not change dramatically. Secondly, take-up and acceptance is not a sign of strength (there are examples of acceptance: over 95 per cent of schools use some form of school broadcasting; a very high proportion of history teachers use worksheets; but what are the features of the use of these at pupil-concept level?). Thirdly, the main problems are with the uniqueness, where games do not fit time and space expectations, budgets, publishing systems and teaching styles. Lastly, on the plus side, games claim to create opportunities, to have face validity and to be motivating.

I am suggesting that the features that Shirts identifies are mainly *macro* features, and that under these problems which are common with those outlined by Eggleston *et al* and which appear to contribute to the lack of total success of some curriculum changes.

That is the extent of the understanding by the teacher or trainer of his or her role as an adaptive interventionist; and the lack of explicit statements about the reason for designing materials in a particular way with a given structure.

Evaluating the contribution and relevance of games

So far, I have deliberately avoided concerning myself with the quality of the games and simulations which are available. I have seen some which appear to be devices within an acceptable body of content which do little beyond provide extended exercises for pupils, which in this over-emphasis would clearly not normally be acceptable. I would strongly suggest, therefore, that as soon as you begin to try to examine what the actual pupil-pupil-knowledge interactions are in some games, their validity will be highly suspect. In others, the findings will merely reinforce the opinions of their present promulgators, that is, they are effective. Games and simulations cannot be different and I am sure they are not unique in this respect. Glossy worksheets, highly publicised tape-slide sequences, can often turn out to be very shaky when examined on a structure and function basis.

In discussing structured materials in education, methodology is frequently left out. Quite clearly it is a difficult topic. *Curriculum Paper 15* (1976) is an excellent start at looking at structures and aims and materials, but it does not talk about 'how' at a pupil level. Shipman (1974), in his evaluative study *Inside a Curriculum Project* does not refer at all to methodology, certainly not at this microlevel.

Simulation and gaming are methodologies but only at a *macro*level. They are organisational devices for arranging interactions as are class sizes of 30, worksheets, close seating in discussion groups, head-sets and microphones in language laboratories: but they are not stated as such. Neither are there explicit statements as to the particular micro-methodologies which can follow from their use. One would have to conclude that acceptance and utilisation in schools will come only when producers and users recognise that these structured materials constitute a micro-methodology. Secondly, the organisational problems are met (such as the fact that the length of a particular game makes it impossible to use seriously at any time other than in the middle of June). Thirdly, there is an understanding of the micro-methodologies which follow at a pupil-teacher-concept level.

Returning to the title of this presentation, games *do* have a relevance if the functioning is understood and as far as possible is made explicit at the microlevel. The relevant games will be those which can demonstrate the form and effectiveness of their functioning at this level and can communicate the nature of this functioning to potential users.

At a recent conference the evaluation of a game in chemistry was described. The potential of the material was expounded at length. The designs of the individual items were shown on close-up slides and the ways in which they incorporated new chemical ideas were ingenious and commendable. The game had been evaluated with a class over a period of weeks and pre-testing and post-testing revealed gains on the part of the students who stayed the course. What we were not told was to what the gains could be attributed. In other words, how did the game interact with the students? That would have revealed important detail, not least about why out of the twenty-five who began playing the game only five were around at the end to be post-tested!

Notes

1. The teacher as interventionist has elsewhere been described as the teacher as a mediator in the learning process. This is not the same as the American term 'mediated teacher'. That is a teacher who carries an overhead projector in his back pocket!
2. The evidence quoted is published by others; however, I have little if any evidence of my own which contradicts the conclusions here stated.

References

Brown, S and McIntyre, D (1977) *Factors Influencing the Effectiveness of Innovations*, Technical Report (mimeo). University of Stirling.

Curriculum Paper 7 (1967) *Science for General Education.* Her Majesty's Stationery Office, Edinburgh.

Curriculum Paper 15 (1976) *The Social Subjects in Secondary Schools.* Her Majesty's Stationery Office, Edinburgh.

Eggleston, J F, Galton, M J and Jones, M E (1976) *Processes and Products of Science Teaching.* Schools Council/Macmillan, London.

The Pack Report (1977) *Truancy and Indiscipline in Schools in Scotland.* Her Majesty's Stationery Office, Edinburgh.

Shipman, M D (1974) *Inside a Curriculum Project.* Methuen, London.

Shirts, R G (1976) Simulation games: an analysis of the last decade. *Programmed Learning & Educational Technology*, 13, 3, 39-41.

Simulation in the teaching of a first-year ecology course

Wilfrid Dowdeswell and Caroline Bailey, *Bath University*

Ecology is an increasingly important component of university biology courses. It is essentially a practically based subject and for its effective study students must become well acquainted with natural populations of plants and animals. However, first-year university classes tend to be large and for organisational reasons ecology may have to be taught in mid-winter. Such considerations tend to preclude visits by students to suitable ecological environments. If the teaching of the subject is to retain its practical emphasis, it is necessary to devise appropriate laboratory alternatives. The first-year ecology course at Bath University is based on a series of simulations which have necessitated the development of appropriate experiments accompanied by new kinds of printed materials, and also a close co-ordination of the lecture and laboratory programmes. The new scheme has been subjected to full evaluation, particularly the extent to which students are able to translate their thinking from simulation to reality. The approach could have important applications in the teaching of ecology to sixth forms of schools, particularly in urban areas.

Introduction

Some of the greatest changes in human outlook during the last ten years or so have derived from a gradual awakening of our environment consciousness. Such concepts as the finite nature of resources, the process of recycling, and environmental change are now widely accepted although their precise significance may not always be fully appreciated. Against this background, ecology — the study of living organisms in relation to one another and to their environment — has made great advances and has become an important component of biology courses at all levels. By its very nature, ecology is a difficult subject both to teach and to learn since most of the problems it poses are multivariate, the precise role of the different variables often being unknown or incompletely understood. Bearing in mind the importance of the subject and the manifest problems it presents in teaching, it is somewhat surprising how little appears to have been achieved by way of developing new approaches since the last symposium of the British Ecological Society on the subject more than a decade ago (Lambert, 1967).

As has been pointed out elsewhere (Dowdeswell and Potter, 1974, 1975), the sort of problems outlined above are exacerbated in the teaching of ecology at first-year university level. Thus the numbers of students may be so large as to preclude visits to natural habitats, either for purely organisational reasons or because of the degree of destruction that they could cause. Again, the total time available for a single subject in the first year is bound to be strictly limited, while circumstances may require that it be taught at a time which is unsuitable for fieldwork. On the other hand, it is important that first-year students should be exposed to such a course, and that they should see ecology as an integrated and practically orientated subject with a wide relevance to other areas of biology and to their everyday lives. For some it will be their only experience of ecology at tertiary level; for others the course will provide the foundation for more advanced studies of animal and plant ecology later on.

Course aims

The course which has been developed at Bath University takes place during the spring term and is timetabled for a duration of ten weeks, provision being made for two one-hour lecture/discussion sessions and a three-hour laboratory/practical period each week. The number of students taking the course is about 50, but at some universities such as Glasgow the numbers can reach as many as 450. Any course at this level and of such limited duration will inevitably be somewhat fragmentary. This need not matter provided the aims have been clearly thought out in advance and the work based upon them. From the course at Bath it is hoped that the student will acquire:

(a) a broad approach to the subject bearing in mind that for some this will be their only experience of ecology at university level,
(b) an appreciation through experience of practical work and the use of second-hand information, of certain basic ecological ideas,
(c) a familiarity with certain ecological skills such as the measurement of the physical environment, the construction of models in biological investigation, the use of sampling procedures and certain statistical methods of analysis,
(d) an appreciation of the interdisciplinary nature of the subject and its importance for the understanding of kindred subjects such as physiology and genetics (Dowdeswell, 1971),
(e) an idea of the methods used in ecological research based on actual examples used as case histories (Hardisty and Potter, 1971; Day and Dowdeswell, 1968),
(f) some appreciation of the relation of the subject to man, and the influence of human activities on the environment and on natural populations of plants and animals.

Although the course was designed primarily for first-year university students it will be seen that its aims are not all that far removed from those of a comparable school sixth-form curriculum. Moreover, the problems facing schools, particularly those situated in urban surroundings, are in many respects similar to those of universities outlined earlier.

Methods of teaching

In the teaching of ecology there is no perfect substitute for the real thing. Ideally, students should visit at least one natural habitat and study it at first hand. However, bearing in mind the constraints mentioned earlier, this may well not be possible in the context of a first-year university ecology course. The problem, then, is to devise a suitable alternative. There are various possibilities:

(a) to defer the teaching of ecology until the second or a subsequent year when numbers are smaller. This is the solution favoured by some universities but in the present context it is unacceptable since it fails to satisfy aim (a) above;

(b) to provide a first-year course based entirely upon lectures and problems using second-hand data. This solution is also popular but fails to meet aims (b) and (c);

(c) to devise a course of integrated lectures and practical work, the latter conducted entirely in the laboratory, the exercises being simulations of real ecological situations. In theory at least, this is a solution which should satisfy all the course aims, and it is the one we have adopted at Bath University.

As Bligh has pointed out (Bligh *et al*, 1975), like laboratory practical work, simulation is a principle of teaching which has been employed for centuries. It involves the use of models which are simplified versions of reality and although widely applied, they appear to have been subjected to little rigorous investigation as a teaching tool. In the teaching of ecology using simulations the basic ecological ideas will often be unfamiliar to students, with the result that they may find considerable difficulty in translating their thinking from a micro to a macro context. Great care, therefore, has to be taken in setting up the practical work and in the preparation of hand-out materials to facilitate this transfer and to ensure in the end that it really has taken place. As we shall see, it is perfectly possible to investigate habitat preferences and spatial distribution in a population of flour beetles inhabiting a dish six inches in diameter, using rigorous quantitative methods. But to a student this is far removed from, say, a population of caddis-fly larvae in a river where precisely the same methods of study apply and similar ecological principles obtain. Simulation and reality must somehow be dovetailed one into the other.

Design of the course

In addition to the educational aims summarised earlier, there were certain organisational aims which we considered it essential to achieve if the course was to be a functional entity within the constraints of time, space, laboratory staff and material resources likely to be available in the kind of biology department where the course might be used. These organisational aims were (a) to enable large numbers of students to be taught simultaneously, (b) to provide a course which was easily set up, using equipment that was readily available or cheaply constructed, and (c) the living material to be used must be readily obtainable and easily maintained.

As explained earlier, in its present form the practical part of the course consists of ten three-hour laboratory sessions. Each is a separate unit covering a particular aspect of ecology and, although distinct from one another, they form a reasonably logical sequence. Moreover, they possess an inherent flexibility in that material can be omitted, combined or added according to requirements.

Unit 1: The species concept is based on samples of snail shells, the students being required to deduce how many species are represented and to give the reasons for their conclusions.

Unit 2: Spatial distribution involves the use of populations of flour beetles *(Tribolium confusum)* in small dishes. Students are required to analyse their distribution and habitat preferences in the three alternative media available — flour, crushed oats and sawdust, using simple sampling techniques and statistical methods of analysis.

Unit 3: Population growth makes use of populations of the vinegar eelworm *(Anguilla aceti)* grown in tubes to different ages. Again, sampling and counting (using home-made sampling chambers) involve rigorous quantitative treatment.

Unit 4: Population structure makes use of artificial flour beetle populations of two different ages (young and old), the students making a comparison of the proportions of the developmental stages in each.

Unit 5: Estimation of population size makes use of cultures of the flour beetle *Tribolium confusum* in dishes, the size of the population being determined by the process of mark, release and recapture. Estimated numbers can then be compared with those actually present.

Unit 6: Population interactions involves a study of the distribution of the small organisms colonising different parts of the body of the freshwater shrimp, *Gammaras pulex*. The students are required to deduce the relationships of the different colonists with their host.

Unit 7: Ecological genetics simulates in small plastic boxes a natural situation in which slugs feed on cyanogenic and acyanogenic forms of clover *(Trifolium repens)*. The purpose of the exercise is to determine the extent to which food preference and differential plant selection is occurring.

Unit 8: Primary production is concerned with the measurement of production by pond organisms, both plant and animal, as judged by oxygen production. The standing crop is also estimated by counting the organisms in samples of pond water.

Unit 9: Community change introduces the concept of succession. Here again, this is simulated in samples of pond water, the parameter used being the number of species and the ratio of the different plant pigments present.

Unit 10: Applied ecology emphasises pollution which is simulated by a study of pure cultures of algae such as *Chlorella*, and the effects of herbicides or pollutants such as detergents at different concentrations upon them.

The purpose of each unit is not to introduce a new organism but a different ecological principle — presented as the simulation of a real situation. The students are then required to translate their thinking from a micro- to a macro-context. As has been illustrated so well by the Open University (Varley, 1974), the preparation of such ecological material requires great care. The printed matter provided for our students at the beginning of each unit is divided into three parts.

1. *Practical instructions:* These include the rationale of the practical and its ecological significance, together with an explanation of how a simulated ecological situation relates to reality. Instructions for conducting the

laboratory work are provided together with suggestions regarding methods of data presentation and analysis.

2. *Extension work:* This consists of a problem based on a real situation which is set out in some detail and demands the same ecological approach for its solution as that required for the simulation. The students are required to complete this work during the laboratory period and the results are discussed together with those of the practical exercise. In this way it is hoped that students will appreciate the relevance of the simulated situation in a real context. In addition, the students gain experience of coping with more complex and complete data, and obtain an insight into the time and effort required for the collection of ecological research data.

3. *Back-up material:* This is an optional section that the students can complete as they wish, in their own time. It consists of one long or several shorter ecological problems, usually based on research papers, involving the same principles but extending into wider fields of both plant and animal ecology. The purpose of this material is to broaden the students' outlook and they can also use it as a means of checking their grasp of ecological principles and methods.

As indicated earlier, the practical sessions are paralleled by two lectures a week. The lecturer is free to approach the lectures in any way preferred using the practicals as an introduction or as a reinforcement. The role of the lecture is simply to expand the selected topics while introducing new ones and to illustrate both with different and varied examples. This provides for great flexibility in that the lectures can be presented satisfactorily by individuals with widely differing ecological interests.

Evaluation

In evaluating the course we have attempted to determine the extent to which the educational and organisational aims have been achieved. Our approach has represented a blend of the experimental, involving the use of quantitative parameters such as the results of student assessment, and the illuminative, being also concerned with broader issues and outcomes of a more subjective kind (Munro, 1977).

A pilot study of the course in embryo stage was carried out in 1976 involving 45 students and a sequence of eight lectures and four laboratory sessions. The approach was rather informal and the information collected was largely subjective. However, from this preliminary enquiry certain tentative conclusions emerged:

(a) in general the course appeared to be well received by the students. Personal communication indicated that they found it stimulating and different from anything they had attempted before;

(b) students who had previous experience of ecology, usually obtained on Field Studies Council courses, did not appear to object to the apparently retrograde step of taking ecology into the laboratory;

(c) the practicals tried were reliable and feasible;

(d) the level of treatment was about right.

By the following year, a generous grant by Esso had enabled us to complete the practical exercise and the student materials in readiness for a full-scale evaluation in the spring term of 1977. Owing to various technical difficulties the course had to be reduced to ten lectures and five laboratory periods (units 1–7, numbers 1 and 2, 3 and 4 being combined).

Evaluation consisted of the following:

1. *Information* obtained from students as a result of: (a) pre- and post-tests, (b) questionnaires on practical sessions given to samples of students, (c) questionnaires on lectures, (d) personal observation of practical sessions by at least one member of staff (usually two were present), (e) free-comment sheets given to the students at the end of the course, (f) students' practical notebooks, and (g) students' examination answers.
2. *Comment sheets* completed by members of staff involved in the lectures and laboratory sessions.
3. *Questionnaires* completed by the laboratory staff involved.

Analysis of the pre-tests showed, rather surprisingly, that many of the students were unfamiliar with the topics included in the course in spite of the fact that these are all to be found in GCE A-level biology syllabuses. As was to be expected, the post-tests showed that this knowledge had considerably improved.

The questionnaires given to the students in the practical sessions related to the ease or difficulty of each section, time taken, amount of background information provided, level of supervision required and interest. These yielded interesting results which allowed refinements to be made to the worksheets; they also indicated areas of difficulty or confusion. In general the interest level was high for each of the sessions.

The questionnaires covering the lectures also provided useful information on content and student reactions to specific topics. Generally, the lectures were well received but, inevitably, some were more acceptable than others. It is significant that there was sometimes a disparity between lectures regarded as successful by lecturers and those found acceptable by students. Personal observations in the laboratory helped to identify students who were persistently unreceptive and provided an opportunity to question them regarding their attitudes. Bearing in mind the diversity of student backgrounds it was gratifying to find such a high level of student acceptance of this unfamiliar approach to ecology teaching. Students' practical notebooks were duly marked, largely to ensure that they had an accurate record of their work. The books had limited value as evaluation material due to the fact that the whole class had participated in the discussions during the practical periods. The individual comprehension of each student could not therefore be measured by this means. The questionnaire completed by the laboratory staff showed that no particular problems were encountered in the setting up of the course. Evidently, the technicians found the unorthodox approach a welcome departure from tradition.

In conclusion, the evaluation showed that, organisationally, the simulation approach was feasible requiring only as much or even less preliminary preparation than other comparable first-year classes. All practicals worked although suggestions for minor adjustments were made. The students showed a high level of interest and mostly enjoyed the course. From data at present being analysed, the indications are that the transfer of knowledge was high. But the ultimate measure of the success of the course will come when some of the students find themselves faced with real ecological problems in the field.

References

Bligh, D *et al* (1975) *Teaching Students.* Exeter University Teaching Services.

Day, J C L and Dowdeswell, W H (1968) Natural selection in *Cepaea* on Portland Bill. *Heredity,* 23, 169-188.

Dowdeswell, W H (1971) Ecological genetics and biology teaching. In Creed, E R (ed) *Ecological Genetics and Evolution.* Blackwell, London.

Dowdeswell, W H and Potter, I C (1974) An approach to ecology teaching at university level. *Journal of Biological Education,* 8, 46-51.

Dowdeswell, W H and Potter, I C (1975) Ecology in the university first year? *Journal of Biological Education,* 9, 247-250.

Hardisty, M W and Potter, I C (1971) The behaviour, ecology and growth of larval lampreys. *The Biology of Lampreys,* 1, 85-125. Academic Press.

Lambert, J M (ed) (1967) *The Teaching of Ecology,* British Ecological Society Symposium Number 7. Blackwell, London.

Munro, R G (1977) *Innovation: Success or Failure?* Hodder and Stoughton, London.

Varley, M E (ed) (1974) *Ecology Units 1—16,* The Open University, Milton Keynes.

Managing innovation:
simulations for potential innovators

G H Kirkland, *Jordanhill College of Education, Glasgow*

This paper describes two simulations, developed for the Jordanhill College of Education Diploma in Educational Technology. They concern the way in which change is managed in a school and a further education situation, being designed to give educational technologists the chance to apply the management skills already learned to a typical set of circumstances. The first part of each simulation is print-based with a supporting audiotape and is designed as an assessable exercise. The user has to consider all of the factors involved in introducing a particular innovation and arrive at a solution for implementing it. In the second part, each participant is allocated a certain role in the school or college and is required to further the views held (or deduced to be held) by that character in the ensuing encounters with other participants. Thus some of those involved in the simulation will be attempting to encourage the innovation, while others will be doing their best to thwart it. The school-based simulation, LANGBRAE HIGH SCHOOL, is concerned with the headmaster's desire to introduce a measure of resource-based learning into the curriculum. The further education one, NEWHILL COLLEGE, deals with a number of problems facing the head of the Learning Resources Unit in the college in trying to bring about changes in teaching and learning methods in the college.

Introduction

The two simulations outlined in this paper were developed as part of the Jordanhill College of Education Diploma in Educational Technology. It is appropriate, therefore, to set them in the context of the course since this was a major influence both on their content and on the way in which they were structured and used.

The diploma in educational technology is a CNAA diploma designed to train educational technologists for posts in schools, colleges, universities and education authorities. The course derived from a need expressed by a variety of educational institutions for staff trained to develop and run resource centres, to direct educational technology units or to assume responsibility for local education authority resource provision. Because of the problem of applicants obtaining release for an extended period to attend a residential course, the diploma was designed on a four-term distance teaching basis, involving short, intermittent periods of attendance at Jordanhill, interspersed with spare time study at home, on Open University lines. This has now been extended to six terms so that all the periods of attendance are out of school and college term times. College sessions are arranged for weekend and holiday periods.

116

The content of the course is 'parcelled up' into instructional units or 'modules', each of which is designed to occupy a student for five hours and to be completed in the course of a week. With a five-hour day when the students are in college, the total timetabled hours for the course become base modules (132.5 hours) and college contact (320.0 hours), giving a total of 452.5 hours.

The course has been divided up into three main areas:

Theoretical studies: the psychology of communication, objectives, curriculum methods, assessment and evaluation and the systems approach.

Management studies: the management of resource centres, contract and copyright, budgeting and purchasing and the management of innovation.

Practical studies: the production and application of materials in fields such as reprography, photography, tape-slide, film and television.

The background to the simulations

The simulations dealt with in this paper form part of the section of the course on management of innovation. This section is timetabled halfway through the management studies part of the course and draws together threads from a number of earlier parts. The three modules preceding the simulations are concerned with: 1. general stragedies for handling and implementing innovation or change within an educational institution, and the practical problems which such approaches may present (covered by means of case study material); 2. the existing organisations and structures which have some responsibility to foster and aid innovation (the Central Committee on the Curriculum [CCC], the inspectorate, advisers, etc); 3. the variety of roles which an educational technologist might fulfil in acting as a 'change agent' in an educational establishment.

The simulations are designed with two main purposes in mind. Firstly, to put the student into a realistic situation in which he has to make decisions based on the earlier content of the course and on his own experience. Secondly, to give the student an opportunity, through a role-playing development of the simulation, to follow through these decisions and to practise the handling of the personal interactions with other people affected by these decisions.

Content

Two different simulations were produced. The first of these, LANGBRAE HIGH SCHOOL, is concerned with the problems of introducing a measure of resource-based independent learning to a junior high school in the east of Scotland. The second, NEWHILL COLLEGE, deals with four situations in which the co-ordinator of resource services in a central Scotland college of further education finds himself.

Each of these was designed in two parts. In the first part, the situation is set by means of print information supplemented, where appropriate, by audiotape. The problem to be solved is presented here and the student asked to produce a solution or series of solutions to it, either in written form on its own, or with the assistance of other media. These solutions form one of the assessable exercises

117

for the course. This part of the exercise is carried out by the student at his home base, and should occupy two-and-a-half to three hours.

During the following in-college session, a further two-and-a-half hours is devoted to a role-playing development of the exercise in which students are allocated roles in the simulation and asked to explore the implications of the suggested changes and the way in which the personalities on the staff would influence these proposals. A description of the simulations, at this point, will clarify the essential features.

LANGBRAE HIGH SCHOOL

General objectives

At the end of this module, [the student is told] you should be able to:

(1) make a critical assessment of the way in which an innovation has been 'managed',
(2) produce a plan to further this innovation, taking into account the objectives of the innovation, the constraints of manpower and accommodation, and the problems of dissemination of the innovation,
(3) relate the strategies outlined in 2 above to the problems detailed in your assessment of the situation in 1 above.

The school is situated in Markwell, a town of some 94,000 inhabitants in the east of Scotland. This is a town in which there has been a considerable diversification of industry since the war, resulting in unemployment statistics which are still among the lowest in the country and well below the Scottish average.

The school was built in 1973 to accommodate 1,340 pupils. It is a junior high school, taking pupils up to SIV. They can transfer to a senior high at the end of SII or SIV if their performance merits it. The present roll is 1,252. Details of the catchment area, its social mix, plans of the school, and the timetables for four of the first-year classes are all provided. There is a total of 61 teaching staff in the school, assisted by a qualified librarian, five office staff, five school technicians and an auxiliary. Background details of career and attitudes are provided for the headmaster, depute head and two assistant heads, along with some of the staff in the English and social subjects departments (the two departments involved in the innovation).

The headmaster wishes to experiment with the introduction of some independent learning techniques, preferably based on resources, including audiovisual resources. He is anxious to set up some organisation structure which would facilitate this development in one subject and with one selected group of pupils. He has already floated this idea with some of the heads of department. From these initial approaches, he has some idea of likely reactions. He now wants to take his ideas a step further, and let other heads of departments hear about them. Accordingly, at the end of a meeting of heads of department, he outlines his philosophy on independent resource-based learning techniques.

Summary of headmaster's statement

As a subscriber to the views of Piaget, the headmaster feels the children must have concrete experiences first. He wishes to provide as much motivation as possible for the slow learners and smooth the transition from primary school by employing more discovery methods. To this end, he would like to explore different methods of communication in some of the courses, methods which would emphasise the vital art of acquiring information for oneself. He suggests the introduction of some individualised learning in the first-year social subjects course, producing materials which would enable the pupils to undertake a study of the local area. He would like to involve the English department, seeing them as occupying a key role in the communications methods employed. To produce the necessary suitable print materials, slides, tapes, etc, he envisages one or more persons on the staff spending part of their week solely on the production of these resources. He goes on to suggest the possible time allocation, the proportion of the pupils to be involved and the kind of teaching methods he would like to employ, including team teaching, seeing this as a way of introducing the staff to methods which involve interdepartmental co-operation. He promises to prepare a written plan of the scheme and invites written reactions from heads of department so that he can take these into account in his planning.

The print material of the simulation then includes the memo which the headmaster sends round his heads of department. This outlines his aim and the 'chain of command' which he intends to set up. It details the job specifications for the subject principal teachers, the person responsible for co-ordinating the production of the materials (an assistant principal teacher), the librarian and the support staff (secretaries, technician and auxiliary). He announces his intention to form a small *ad hoc* committee chaired by the assistant head teacher (curriculum) in order to draw up detailed plans for the project. Also included is a confidential memo from the headmaster to the assistant head teacher (curriculum) giving details of the membership of the committee and its remit. The attitudes of some of the staff to the idea are recorded on audiotape. These have been overheard or picked up in conversation in the staff room and range from 'Och, it's a bit gimmicky!' to 'I'm quite excited with the idea really. It's a pity that only the better pupils are going to try it. I'm sure it would be successful with the less able too . . .' Finally, details of the type and extent of the audiovisual provision in the school are provided, along with its location.

The instructions given to the student are as follows:

(1) Write a critical assessment of the way in which the innovatory plan for introducing a measure of independent learning at Langbrae High School has been 'managed', up to and including the memo of 22/11/76 from the Headmaster to the AHT (Curriculum). Consider, for example, where you would place the management technique on each of the scales of authoritarian . . . democratic; systematic . . . opportunist; unilateral . . . consultative.

(2) Produce your own 'ideal' version of the plan called for in the Headmaster's memo of 22/11/76, under the headings of Staff, Accommodation, Production Schedule and Communications.

(3) Indicate the ways in which your 'ideal' plan would meet any problems or difficulties arising from the way in which the innovation has been 'managed' up till 22/11/76. Pay particular attention to strategies you would use for ensuring good communication and dealing with apathetic or hostile members of staff.

The role-playing exercise

Students are each allocated a role as a member of the sub-committee. Depending on the number of students available, the committee consists of as many as possible of the following list:

assistant head teacher (curriculum) — chairman
programme co-ordinator (APT) — secretary
headmaster
librarian
principal teacher of English
principal teacher of social subjects.

The committee is instructed as follows:

You should be prepared to modify your 'ideal' plan in the light of what you can deduce about your 'character', 'attitudes' and 'philosophy' from the information given in the text. Other course members will assume the other roles. You will require to put forward and argue your plans to a meeting of the 'Committee'. The principal teacher of English will not be able to attend this meeting, so that you will have a committee of five. The aim of the committee will be to produce the final version of the plans for the project — a version which takes account of the feelings of the committee and the staff as a whole.

NEWHILL COLLEGE

General objectives

By the end of this exercise, course members should have:

(1) decided upon and implemented the best course of action to further an innovation stemming from the periphery of the college (an unpromoted member of staff),
(2) identified an opportunity for innovating arising from casual conversation, and devised a means of furthering it,
(3) dealt with a particular set of problems arising from a recently initiated piece of innovation,
(4) assessed the problems of disseminating information about ongoing innovations to the rest of the college and produced a plan for overcoming these, as far as possible.

Newhill College of Further Education was established in 1951 in buildings vacated by a technical school. Over the years it has grown in size and, in fact, is still expanding. As a result, the campus is now a scattered one with a new urban motorway cutting across part of it, making communication among buildings difficult. It is situated in central Scotland and has a potential catchment area of 112,000 inhabitants. Nearby is a flourishing industrial complex with a considerable commerce element — accountancy, banking, law, insurance, etc. It provides a very extensive range of courses of all types, with a total of some 6,500 students.

The participants in the simulation are asked to approach it in the role of the co-ordinator of resource services. To this end, details are provided of the facilities offered by resource services in the college. These include:

production services	— design, photography, printing and duplication, sound and television
sales service	— bulk purchase of consumable materials
equipment loans service	— including maintenance
information	— catalogues of non-book materials within the college and from other sources
training	— in equipment handling and materials production for staff of the college.

Information on some of the 143 members of staff is provided. Each of these brief profiles outlines the previous career of the member of staff and his attitudes to innovation in teaching methodology. Finally, the role of the co-ordinator of resource services is defined, although no information on his attitudes, philosophy and so on is given, since these have to come from the student.

The exercise is divided into four case studies, each presenting a problem for the co-ordinator to solve.

Case 1 concerns the accountancy department. The study is presented in the form of a number of memos between the co-ordinator and Mr Duffield, a member of the accountancy department. He is running a course which involves his students in working through case study material on industrial relations during the extensive periods when they are not in college. His problem is to obtain sufficient quantities of the large number of required books for his students. A passing reference to the possibilities of microfilm has given him the idea of transferring all the case studies to microfilm or microfiche and sending these out to his students who would be supplied with cheap, portable microfiche readers. The co-ordinator of resource services provides some information on equipment and costs. However, Mr Duffield's head of department is not particularly enthusiastic for three reasons:

- he is not sure that it is the easiest and most effective way of solving the problem,
- he thinks it is too costly,
- and he is worried about copyright problems.

The student's problem is first of all to produce evidence to persuade the head of department of his best course of action (not necessarily using microfiche) and prepare a case to present to a forthcoming finance committee meeting for approval.

Case 2 is in the form of an overheard conversation between the co-ordinator and a lecturer in charge of science technician courses. During the conversation, in which the lecturer is arranging some instruction for the technicians in the handling and maintenance of audiovisual equipment, the lecturer mentions in passing (among other things) a problem he is having with some self-instructional materials prepared some time ago by the resource services unit. The task set in this case is to identify the problem contained in the conversation, write to the lecturer suggesting a possible solution and work out a tactic for presenting a case to the head of department concerned. Because of this particular head of department's rather traditional views on the methods used in his department and his determination not to make changes in his department before he retires in a few years' time, this case has to be carefully argued and justified and couched in such terms as to make the most effective approach to the head of department.

Case 3 is initiated by a memo from the head of the physics department who is keen to make more use of audiovisual techniques in his department. He has one lecturer with some free time and proposes his secondment for part of each week to the resource services unit in order to prepare audiovisual materials for the physics courses. Some six months later, we find the head of department considering, due to some pressure from the enthusiastic seconded lecturer, the possibility of introducing a measure of independent learning into his courses. He would like some assurances about the effectiveness of such a move, some guidance on how the management problems could be overcome and some ideas on the setting up of a resource room to be used as a teacher workshop. One of his problems is that of dealing with the attitudes of the rest of the staff in his department. These range from the apathetic to the openly hostile on this issue, the staff themselves varying between highly competent and just keeping one's head above water.

The student, as co-ordinator of resources, has to aim to have a fair measure of independent resource-based learning in the physics department by the end of the following session, with most of the staff of the department committed to it.

Case 4 consists of a memo from the principal of the college, mentioning that he has heard, from a variety of sources, of the innovatory work going on in, and in conjunction with, the resource services unit. He would like to find some way of disseminating information about this work and other work of a similar innovatory nature to the rest of the college. Accordingly, he is offering the co-ordinator a sum of £500 a year to finance any ideas for such an information service.

The student's problem is to draw up a report to the principal outlining his proposals, the reasons for this choice and the approximate cost of implementing them.

The role-playing exercise

Only two of the case studies really lend themselves to role-playing, namely, cases 1 and 3.

Case 1 is carried out by allocating students to the roles of co-ordinator of resources, the head of the accountancy department and the lecturer in charge of the industrial relations courses. The rest of the students play the roles of the members of the finance committee. After an initial policy meeting among the three principal role-players, they put their case to the finance committee and try to obtain funds to implement the innovation.

Case 3 role-playing can simulate a staff meeting in the physics department in which the suggestions for the introduction of independent learning and the establishment of a resource workroom are put forward. The roles of head of the physics department, the seconded lecturer and the co-ordinator of resources are obvious ones to allocate, with the rest of the students taking up the roles of the rest of the physics department staff, adopting, if possible, a range of attitudes to change before starting and trying to stick to those throughout. This meeting requires careful handling by the head of department and co-ordinator, particularly if some of the other participants adopt traditional, deeply entrenched attitudes.

Conclusions

A number of alternative ways of achieving the objectives of the simulation were considered at the outset. A lecture by an outside speaker, himself involved in innovatory work, followed by a discussion, has the advantage of providing first-hand experience and information, but limits the involvement of the students, particularly the less dominant in the group. Neither does it allow students to take part in decision-making and the process of following through the effects of these decisions. The same arguments would apply to carefully constructed case studies where the process of innovation has been carried through and some or all of its effects can be seen. Visits to suitable educational establishments are another possibility. However, the process of innovation is such that it is not easy to gain an appreciation of its workings or progress from a single visit or even a few visits.

In fact, all three of the above techniques are employed at various places in the course in dealing with topics which have an element of the management of innovation within them. The cumulative effect of these techniques combined with the simulations seems to be an effective way of tackling an area which is difficult to deal with because of its widespread nature and the variety of its implications.

In retrospect, the division of each simulation into two parts has had the following advantages:

The exercise gives practice in thinking through some typical situations with which the student is likely to be faced in the future. It allows time for the student to consider all the possibilities without the normal pressures of time and the responsibility for the consequences of the decisions made. It requires the student to draw on the content of most of the previous parts of the course and on his own previous experience in education. Lastly, it forces the student to set down his ideas in print and to be able to justify them.

The role-playing directs the student to consider carefully a strategy for handling the personal relationships which are so important in furthering any innovation. It requires the student to adopt the views and attitudes of his role (often opposed to those of the student himself) and to defend them in the face of opposition. This led in many cases to a gain in understanding of the problems of dealing with firmly held opposing views. It gives practice in handling interpersonal relationships; holding to one's views yet knowing when to compromise.

The simulations were evaluated in a number of ways:

Student questionnaires: These indicated that the time required for each part of both exercises was greater than had been allowed, the average for the exercises being four-and-a-half hours for LANGBRAE and about six hours for NEWHILL. The students considered the level of difficulty to be appropriate for them (they are all practising teachers and lecturers, many with considerable experience). The level of interest aroused and the relevance of the simulation to their own situations were both rated highly as was the degree of their own involvement. Many of the suggestions for improvements have been incorporated into the latest version of the simulations.

Observations of the teaching staff involved: These indicated that most students adopted their roles right from the start and did not step out of character, even after coffee breaks. It was interesting that the simulated committee meetings tended to cover the organisational aspects of the problem under discussion and ignore the key questions of the basic philosophy or rationale of what they were doing, unless under the chairmanship of a perceptive and forceful person. This initial failure to get to grips with the fundamentals of planning perhaps indicates that the simulation successfully recreated a typical situation, since many real-life meetings reveal similar inadequacies. The realisation of this common difficulty was a revelation to the students at the summing-up discussion, and a more effective way of highlighting the difficulty than any number of exhortations.

Observations of the course evaluator: These were taken during the course of the simulations and gleaned from course members in informal conversation afterwards. They revealed, among other things, that very few students had difficulty in adopting their roles initially, although one refused flatly to take part. However, once the session got under way, even the non-participant became involved, due to the chairman continually addressing remarks to her in her role name. Overall, the students agreed that the experience had been a worthwhile and extremely enjoyable one. They added that it had been very hard work, particularly for the chairmen. The effort of maintaining the concept of one's role and at the same time remembering all the factual detail relevant to the situation had been taxing.

Perhaps the main value of such simulations lies in their after-effects which are much more difficult to evaluate. As one student wrote on her evaluation form, 'I found the simulations interesting and thought-provoking, even more so in retrospect.'

The hidden curriculum in simulations: some implications of our applications

Nancy D Glandon, *University of Bradford*

This paper uses the concept of 'hidden curriculum' to examine some of the unintentional learning which occurs within simulation experiences. Because simulation games are partial reconstructions of some aspect(s) of particular social realities as apprehended by game designers, some 'hidden' learning is embedded in the structures of games; because simulation games are played 'live' by social actors, other unintentional learning emerges from the interactions within the simulations and debriefing sessions. The hidden curriculum in simulations includes the learning of Rules, Roles, and Reason. These categories, and some of their possible implications, are discussed in the paper.

Introduction

The majority of games players say they find simulations enjoyable; the majority of teacher-game directors say their pupils learn something from the experience (the same could be said of training or counselling); the majority of games researchers say simulations are no worse, and probably better in some aspects, than other learning tools (see Gibbs, 1974). This paper is an admittedly speculative (and occasionally polemic) inquiry into some of the learning that simulations may foster — learning that is not part of the aims and objectives of the game, but that may be inherent in the nature of gaming and simulation. This 'other' learning I have termed *the hidden curriculum*.

The hidden curriculum

Philip Jackson (1968) examined the 'facts of life' which exist in classrooms and which he suggested emerge from institutional demands, staff and societal expectations, and structural realities of the school. These social facts include ' . . . the crowds, the praise, and the power that combine to give a distinctive flavor to classroom life [which] collectively form *a hidden curriculum* which each student (and teacher) must master if he is to make his way satisfactorily through the school'. The learning which the hidden curriculum specifies includes learning to live in a situation fraught with delay, denial and interruption; the skills which the hidden curriculum demands include patience, apparent attentiveness, and overtly at least, unquestioning obedience to rules.

This hidden curriculum appears to be unintentionally embedded in institutional constraints and is made manifest to pupils through the ongoing interactions that characterise everyday life in the classroom. It may be said that the hidden curriculum provides the framework within which the official curriculum is taught and, hopefully, learned.

In much the same manner, simulations also contain a hidden curriculum — a set of facts and understandings which may be learned by simulation participants but which are not intended by either the game designer or director. Because simulation games are partial reconstructions of some aspect(s) of particular social realities as apprehended by game designers, some hidden learning is embedded in the structures of games; because simulation games are played 'live' by social actors, other unintentional learning emerges from the interactions within the games and debriefing sessions. The hidden curriculum in simulations includes the learning of rules, roles and reason; the skills which the hidden curriculum demands include acquiescence to the power of the Game Overall Director (GOD)[1], mastery of 'appropriate' sex-typed performances, and stress on technique, strategy, manipulation and rhetoric, rather than on meaning and ethical implications of behaviour. These learnings, and some of their possible implications, are discussed in subsequent sections of this paper.

RULES

Writers of simulation handbooks for teachers have stressed that simulations can alter the traditional authority structure of the classroom. The nature of simulations, they suggest, creates a situation where 'the teacher's role may be as interpreter of the simulation, and even as guide, but he does not have to pose as expert or as judge' (Taylor and Walford, 1972).

On the contrary, I would suggest that since the classroom game director is also the classroom teacher, he or she comes to the simulation situation with a recognised position of authority over the players, who remain pupils even while they play other roles in the game. In addition to this vested authority of the teacher, the simulation experience itself tends to add to the teacher's authority: he or she has advance knowledge of the game rules, scenario and aims[2] while the player-pupils bring to this new situation widely differing expectations and little knowledge of what is 'supposed' to happen. That 'what is "supposed" to happen' is important to game player-pupils is most visible in debriefing sessions — secondary school pupils and university students alike appear uniformly interested in comparing 'their' game-play results with that of other groups, as if to assure themselves that they have done it 'correctly', that is, as the teacher-director expected.

The possession of this 'secret knowledge' puts the teacher-game director in much the same position as the teacher of a reception class (Glandon, 1975): the player-pupils, newcomers in either setting, must look to the director-teacher to set the stage, establish the parameters within which they are expected to act, keep them and the game running to script, and lead the critical review after the play has run. It is because the teacher-director *is* in charge of introducing, keeping time and debriefing that I would suggest that the teacher remains an authority figure throughout the game. The functions of game-directing require that the teacher does pose as expert and as judge; the reality of playing games reinforces the authority of the adult-in-attendance to the player-pupils. Through the initial allocation of roles, the explanations and enforcement of rules, the calling to time, and through channelling the debriefing discussion the teacher asserts his or her authority just as in 'regular' classroom activities.

No matter how open the game form, no matter how non-authoritarian the facilitator, the unequal distribution of knowledge in a gaming situation places the game director in a potentially manipulative position. It is in the debriefing, where the learning should take place, that the manipulation is most subtle and most damaging, as the facilitator tries to draw the participants into an understanding of their experience that reflects his or her own interpretation of what happened. The most benign motives in the world do not change the fact of differential power (Cipinko, 1974).

From this perspective, simulations in classrooms, regardless of their overt curricular content, can be viewed as simulations of classroom life, which teach rules and obedience to those in authority, even where the rules of the game permit disobedience to those temporarily in authority within the game.

ROLES

Simulations are partial reconstructions of social reality. Because our particular social reality has necessitated a Sex Discrimination Act, it would follow that our simulations may also be in need of a similar exercise. Sex discrimination may be taught in simulations both in the game's basic structural components — or what could be called a 'simulation' of sex discrimination — and in the attitudes and behaviours of the director and/or participants during the playing and debriefing — or what can be called an 'acting' of sex discrimination within the simulation (Glandon, 1974).

While to my knowledge no one has yet carried out a comprehensive survey of the sex roles specified in games, a cursory look suggests that in simulations, as in reading schemes, traditional sex role understandings are taught (Lobban, 1974, 1975). Where sex roles are specified, those for women tend to be limited to housewives and mothers, with the odd corner-shopkeeper or working mother. It would appear that equal numbers of specified roles for males and females are rare, and roles of professional career women rarer still. All too frequently in decision-making games the 'swing' role — the person who doesn't have a definite position on the issue, but is open to pressure — is a housewife with two children, a veritable parody of the stereotyped woman who cannot make up her mind.

Sex discrimination may also emerge in the teacher-director's assignments of and directions for various roles: how many of us suggest that certain players should occupy specific high or low status positions based on our own perceptions of 'predictable' sex role responses? How often do we make suggestions for game role behaviour based on the sex of the player? How often in our simulations have we heard someone say, 'She can't be —; she's a girl', and laughed along with our class?

But perhaps it is in the debriefing where sex discrimination may be most effectively taught, for it is here where the teacher *as teacher* is once again in charge, and here where the two hidden curricula merge most closely with the need to suggest the overt learning that is supposed to come from the simulation experience. If the simulation also simulates sex discrimination, do we as teacher-directors discuss it, or take it for granted? Do we raise questions like these:

Were the roles and attitudes of the males and females different?
Did girls or boys have the power, or the authority?
Who were the unofficial leaders?

And most crucial of all:

Why is it this way?
Who is talking the most (during the debriefing)?
Who is really listened to? And why?

Some small group research has suggested that there is a significant difference between participants' perceptions of leadership and the objective criteria which define actual leaders; both male and female university students perceived females as leaders in less than 10 per cent of the cases, while they were actually leaders in 60 per cent of the cases (Coleman *et al*, 1973, Glandon, 1974). Are our own perceptions of simulation leaders and our pupils' perceptions similarly biased? Does our understanding of appropriate sex role behaviour limit our ability to be 'detached, objective' observers? Do we know who the decision-makers are in our games?

Boocock (1972) suggests that 'games may affect attitudes, in particular the individual's attitude toward his sense of control of environment'. If she is correct, and I believe she is, then it seems to me that we must deal with the attitudes of *all* our simulation participants — male and female — toward control of their environments. We must share with them our understandings of the sexual structures of our games, our perceptions of sexist acting in the game setting, and explore with them all the facets of the issues of life chances, leadership, decision-processes which our games reflect (Glandon, 1974).

Perhaps what is needed is a simulation of the Sex Discrimination Act, where an Equal Opportunities Commission hears cases of sex discrimination in our games!

REASON

There seems to be, to some extent, a shared consciousness [between the military and simulators] — one that exalts technique over meaning, innovation over insight, rhetoric over reality. There is a serious danger here — technical consciousness creates the world in its own image, replacing human values with machine values, so that it becomes difficult to tell *why* we are doing something as long as we continue doing it (Cipinko, 1974).

Virtually every commentator in the field has said that simulations are 'involving'; the most involving simulations would appear to be those which combine unequal distribution of resources with some need for semi-collective decision-making, giving rise to competitive clashes among individuals or groups of players (Shephard, 1971). This type of simulation frequently gives rise to the irrational in us; Taylor and Carter (1971) have suggested that exposure to the irrational is 'one facet of decision-making training which is often neglected', but which is certainly available in simulations.

Involving, competitive simulations which illustrate the irrational are, without doubt, reflective of 'real-life' situations, but at the same time tend to encourage particular forms of strategy and views of the world, which may be of only limited usefulness to the future generations we are educating. It *is* useful, I am sure, to develop skills of co-operation in order to pull off a *coup*, and skills of oratorical finesse (using only emotive hot air) in order to sway a local council. One does wonder at times, however, if our pupils enjoy learning the knife-in-the-back strategies so much that they lose sight of the social structural realities which foster such reactions.

My own five years' experience running SIMSOC with American university students in 'Introduction to Sociology' classes caused me a good deal of concern: some of my students had great difficulties getting past the 'fun' of the conspiracies to understand the social class differentials; a few students never did see further than the strategies. The fact that each year the students in the ghetto region wished to play it again, certain that they would use better strategies next time (such as kidnapping and arson — simulated, of course), makes me think that the game *as a game* was so involving, and being nasty and devious in a 'safe' situation so much fun, that learning about social structures was placed a poor second.

I am not suggesting that we eliminate such simulations from our repertoire, for they *are* models of real-world behaviour, but that we carefully temper their usages, encouraging post-game evaluation of the ethical realities revealed through the playing. For in our concern for overt curricular content, we may lose sight of the hidden learning in these games: that the way to 'win' is through strategy, technique, manipulation and rhetoric — and being better at these skills than the other players. This sort of covert learning needs to be made overt, and the simulated situations which encourage such skills need to be carefully discussed.

Conclusion

The aims and objectives of the game designer and the director are filtered through the constraints and understandings of the hidden curriculum of the simulation, so that the player-pupil learner may be getting different messages than we had intended.[3]

In none of these areas — *rules, roles,* and *reason* — is the content of the hidden curriculum in simulations markedly different from the school's general hidden curriculum. But because of the nature of simulation games — because they *are* fun, involving and motivating — the hidden curriculum in simulations is more insidious, and perhaps less likely to be seen, evaluated, challenged or rejected, unless we systematically help our pupil-players with that process. I wonder whether simulations as a classroom tool are as innovative and as liberating from the traditional order as we pretend they are?

Notes

1. This insightful title was used by Don Ifill in his presentation, 'Game Time', at the International Simulation and Gaming Association Conference, University of Birmingham, England, July 1977.

2. In most workshops for new simulation directors, advice|includes the caveat: 'don't let the players know you are unsure; when in doubt, make up a rule!'

3. The hidden curriculum may be one reason why attempts to evaluate content learning from simulations have proved so difficult.

References

Boocock, S S (1972) *An Introduction to the Sociology of Learning.* Houghton Mifflin.

Cipinko, S (1974) Paying the piper, or Pay us again Sam. In Moriarty, J E (ed) *Simulation and Gaming.* US Government Printing Office.

Coleman, M, McElroy, D and Whitehurst, C (1973) *Sex Differences in the Perception of Leadership in Small Groups.* Paper presented to the Pacific Sociological Association.

Gibbs, G I (1974) *Handbook of Games and Simulation Exercises.* E and F N Spon Ltd.

Glandon, N (1974) Simulating sexism: unintentional (?) replication of reality. In Moriarty, J E (ed) *Simulation and Gaming.* US Government Printing Office.

Glandon, N (1975) Socialization to Authority Structures: Kindergarten, a First Attempt. Unpublished PhD dissertation.

Jackson, P (1968) *Life in Classrooms.* Holt, Rinehart and Winston, New York.

Lobban, G M (1974) Presentation of sex-roles in British reading schemes. *Forums for the Discussion of New Trends in Education,* 16, 2.

Lobban, G M (1975) Sex-roles in reading schemes. *Educational Review,* 27.

Shephard, R W (1971) Notes on the uses of games and simulations for training and research. In Armstrong, R H R and Taylor, J L (eds) *Feedback on Instructional Simulation Systems.* Cambridge Institute of Education.

Taylor, J L and Carter, K R (1971) Some urban gaming-simulation assessments. In Armstrong R H R and Taylor, J L (eds) *Feedback on Instructional Simulation Systems.* Cambridge Institute of Education.

Taylor, J and Walford, R (1972) *Simulation in the Classroom.* Penguin, Harmondsworth.

Some aspects of the practical application of games and simulations activities to language training

Greta M Harvey and Martin S Wheeler, *Linguistics Systems Engineering, Isle of Skye*

This paper attempts to demonstrate the use and importance of games and simulations as *aids* to language teaching, and how they are gradually developing into a basic support and frame of reference for language training programmes at a sophisticated level. The paper also attempts to suggest the direction future developments with games could take. Consideration is given to: games and simulations exercises as *information carrying systems;* games and simulations exercises as *information processing systems*; practical *limitations* of games and simulations in language training; the *relevance* of games and simulations activities to language training in general; *developments* in games and simulations activities in English-language training (a) in remedial training for *native speakers* of English, (b) in training for the *immigrant learner* of English, and (c) in training for the *adult foreign learner* of|English; differences between the requirements of games and simulations activities for *military* and *management training* purposes, and the requirements for *language training* purposes.

Introduction

Language training is concerned with training learners in the efficient use of language as a tool for expression and communication. As with any other tool, this entails allowing the learner to practise using it with the minimum of interference and the maximum of opportunity to make mistakes. The problem with using a language, however, is that unlike most other tools it is extremely flexible and can be used for a variety of purposes. It is also unlike most other tools in that it is composed of a complex set of operations all taking place simultaneously, requiring great dexterity on the part of the user. Further, as languages function as a total system, use of *one* part implying knowledge of use of the *whole* system, it is very difficult to break up each operation into discrete units for practice. But practice there must be, and as there is very little learning required in mastering the basic principles of any language, the major effort is one of continued exercises with sets of patterns, or functions, until familiarisation with them becomes automatic. If the exercises in practising these set patters are too rigidly structured, or too repetitive, practice soon becomes boring, and interest is lost, and although the *principle* behind the set pattern may have been learned, the reflex action has not been acquired (there has been no transfer). In other words, the language learner is in the well-known situation of knowing all the rules, but somehow not quite being able to apply them. The requirement of the language trainer therefore is an exercise which ideally demands maximum involvement on the part of the learner, minimum interference by the trainer, and which can be adapted to provide the same exercise repeatedly without becoming boring, that is, it has a self-sustaining interest.

Games and simulations exercises are, by their very nature, practical activities which answer this need very well. Suitably devised, a good language training game should provide trainers with a support on which to build sets of apparently dissimilar exercises which will stimulate interest sufficiently long for the desired reflex being practised to become automatic. Games and simulations exercises also have the advantage that, being learner-oriented, they free the trainer to devote the greater part of his or her energy to the organisation and supervision of the activities. Let us examine then the possibilities offered by games and simulations exercises from the language trainer's point of view. There are a variety of areas for games and simulations. We will consider these one at a time.

Information carrying systems

The first requirement of any exercise in language training is that it should be capable of supplying or carrying information. Any game may be considered to be composed of a set of rules plus a set of game elements governed by those rules (and of course one or more operators or players to carry out the game). By interacting with the game, the operator or operators will cause it to assume a state or a series of states to which he or she must then react according to the rules of the game. In this way a single operator or player may be said to be carrying on a *monologue* with the game; more than one player may be said to be carrying out a dialogue through the game.

A game may therefore be considered as a simple communications interface carrying information about itself (about its own state) to the operators. Simple game rules will permit of simple, immediately foreseeable forms of dialogue, where more complex rules will permit of more complex, virtually unpredictable dialogue. Further, the more discrete states a game is capable of assuming, the more useful information it can carry (about its own state), and by extension, the more modulated information it may be expected to carry (in non-game terms). The number of states any game is capable of assuming is directly dependent on the rules of that game, and also on the number of discrete game elements it contains. An increase in either will result in an exponential increase in the information-carrying capability of the game. In communications terms, this corresponds to an increase in the *inherent bandwidth* of the system.

The question the practical language trainer has to consider is whether this information-carrying capability will also allow *modulation* of that information, thus allowing the game to be taken to the point where it provides a useful, practical communications tool, capable of reproducing some of those functions most commonly found in natural languages. This would seem to be possible if the correct degree of game complexity is achieved with the *minimum* complexity of rules to be learned by the operator, and the minimum of discrete game elements to be distinguished from one another.

A simple illustration of the reproducibility of natural language functions by the structure of games is that *all* games, from the very concept of rules contained within them, allow the positive and negative functions of permission to be expressed:

(this move) MAY be made

(that move) MAY NOT be made

Simple commands and various registers of request are also easily expressed:

DO (this)
DON'T DO (that)
PLEASE do (something else)

With a little ingenuity, interrogative functions may also be incorporated:

IS IT (now) POSSIBLE (to do this)?
WHAT (game element is to be used)?
WHERE (is this game element to be placed)?

also expressions of choice:

WHICH (game element is to be used now)?

By extension, more complex functions may gradually be built up — time relationships referred to past and future moves in the game, mutually inclusive or exclusive groups or sets (me, us, you, them). With modern technology at our disposal, a highly sophisticated degree of complexity need represent no real problem, as machines which work only according to certain rules may be constructed and programmed to recognise only certain elements, disregarding others entirely. This still means, however, that operators must be able to recognise (either by practice, or instinctively) the individual states of the game, or that the language trainer must be able to deduce by analogy what the information carried means in non-game terms. For the purposes of language training this need never become a major hindrance if the game can be devised so that it parallels the functions of natural language exactly. This is more easily done in practical terms than may be imagined from the above. For example, in a game which permits choice, the expression of natural language functions result:

IF (this element is moved in such a way THEN (such a state will result)

WHEREAS

IF (that were to be done)   THEN (another state would result)

This is quite easily simulated in game terms, and requires virtually no translation effort on the part of the operator from game terms into natural language terms in his or her native tongue.

The application of such techniques to the verbalisation of the same language functions in second or foreign language terms should be immediately apparent. This double demodulation technique is the one of most immediate interest to the language trainer, as with a little ingenuity it allows most natural language functions to be simulated and presented to the language learner in a highly stimulating form, with the possibility of providing (on the face of it, at least) infinitely different versions of the same game, thus allowing indefinite practice of the same language function. Bearing the above possibilities in mind, a further question the language trainer finds interesting to consider is whether games and simulations exercises may be adapted in similar ways to provide information *processing* tools, ie be used as information-processing systems to solve set problems.

Information processing systems

A useful enhancement to a language training exercise or game would be the capability not only of carrying or being modulated by information, but of being in some way able to process that information at the same time. This would increase its capability to reproduce some of the more complex functions of natural languages (working things out through argument or debate), and would result in a fairly powerful tool for practising simulated 'open-ended' dialogue under controlled conditions, where the response to a given stimulus could depend on a multitude of variables. In the ordinary way of things this is a fairly impractical exercise in the classroom, as a *semantic* context of ordinary conversation is infinite.

Any given stimulus can provoke almost any reply. If anything more than simple information processing or simple problem-solving is to be considered, then the complexity of the language simulating device required increases enormously. Imagine trying to devise a means of giving all the possible *types* of reply to the question: 'What's this?', and then all the possible types of response to that reply, and so on, *ad infinitum*!

With a game, however, any expression given in game terms is meaningful *only* within the limited semantic context of the game rules. Using games as natural language-simulating devices thus allows the trainer to define the semantic context much more sharply than would otherwise be the case. Given that a game has all the requirements for carrying information (either about itself, or by analogy, about a totally non-related subject which obeys the same rules) it should not be too difficult an exercise to write the rules in such a way that it is possible to use the game as a means of manipulating that information in order to produce hitherto (apparently) hidden information; in other words to solve problems. A problem may be considered as a game in reverse — where a game is a set of rules and game elements which adopt different states, a problem is a set of elements in a state or states to which the governing rules must be found. That is to say, the rules are implicit, but not immediately apparent to the player. The more states one has available for comparison the easier it is to deduce the rules governing them. A good example is the commonly found 'logic problem' of the type found in a lot of the work in *Language Training Pack 1: North Sea Challenge* produced by Linguistics Systems Engineering for BP Educational Services. In this particular case, the problem does no more than give statements of pre-processed information, and the operator himself (or herself) carries out the reorganisation of that information, using natural language as an aid (which, if verbalised, makes a very good language training exercise in itself). It is not too difficult, however, to introduce variables 'controlled' by the game itself, as in the case of other topographical problems; for example, jigsaw puzzles with a design or picture carried on separate differently shaped pieces, or fitting pentominoes into a set frame.

In other words, there is a built-in self-regulatory device as to the way in which the information contained is processed. It is interesting to speculate how complex this simple procedure may be made and yet remain within the practical bounds of exercises to be carried out in the normal training (classroom) environment; further, under what conditions exactly games may be used to solve the same *types* of problems natural language is used for solving. Whatever the conditions, it should by now be clear that it is theoretically possible to use simple games as automatic information processing systems and therefore as a tool for problem-solving. As even the most simple problem-solving tools can themselves be compared to relatively sophisticated communications systems, it should be possible to draw analogies between such types of games or simulations activities and natural language functions of a fairly complex nature. But what are the practical limits of such systems in the classroom?

Limitations

The basic limitation of games is in their nature; a game by definition (through its rules) has a beginning and an end. Once the end is reached, the game is over, and it must be started again. Similarly, simulation activities have a goal, or purpose, which, when achieved, indicates the end of the activity. As has been stated before, this is a useful device for the language trainer in that it presents a ready-made support whose limits are defined, making it suitable for repetitive practice exercises. The concept of an end-point, goal or result is also useful in that it contains a built-in element of satisfaction to players. *Aimless* repetitive moves are uninteresting and even boring, unless some sort of immediate result can be seen to have been achieved. This limitation is then an advantage rather than a disadvantage in language training. The exception is when a game always gives a fixed result — ie a jigsaw puzzle, or building-blocks which will only adopt one shape; as soon as this unique shape or result has been achieved, the game is no longer useful for immediate repetition. So games for language training should be capable of assuming (infinite) end-results, such as, for example, the variety of motor vehicles which can be assembled from a Meccano or similar construction set, and yet which nevertheless always concern the principle of a wheel revolving around an axle; or the endless variety of results in set card games, or chess. But to be of any use to the language trainer, the moves of the game must be capable of being verbalised *as an integral part of the game* in either spoken or written natural language.

Spoken chess is not a particularly suitable example (one of the unwritten rules of chess is that the game is played silently to aid concentration!) and even writing out each move is only suitable for certain limited spatial expressions; explaining the reasons for making each move is good language practice, but self-defeating in game-playing terms.

A more useful application of chess would be if players were composed of *teams* rather than individual players, each team having to discuss each move and arrive at a common decision, which would then be communicated to the competing team (in either verbalised natural language or game terms). Competitive simulations activities are very good exercises of this type. Perhaps by far the greatest practical limitation for the trainer unused to the application of games to language training, however, is in working out the correspondences between the natural language functions being taught and the game or exercise to be carried out, ie what game best simulates what language function.

It is not always easy to devise or even bring to mind a suitable game for practising a particular function or structure, particularly if one thinks in terms of set structures, such as 'to have to do something', rather than functions, such as 'expressing obligation'. For example, the basic function of comparison includes, among others, the structure 'used to' (a comparison in temporal terms between present and past habit). A game which demands rearrangement of a fixed number of elements in a totally new configuration, or enlargement of a previous configuration would be suitable here, and a trainer might eventually arrive at a hypothetical TOWN CENTRE game, in which players have to compete in rebuilding a fictional town shopping area on a limited budget, or to provide the maximum facilities in a limited area:

'Where the old Town Hall used to be there will be a bingo hall'
'We'll have green parks where we used to have factories' etc.

However, such games (which rapidly develop into simulation exercises) require careful forethought and demand a great deal of inventiveness.

In most cases, it is far more practical (and easier) for a trainer to *adapt* material which is already available (albeit for other purposes), such as games for pleasure, or management training, or to take a well-known game and go through it mentally, picking out the language functions it can be used to bring into play, for example MONOPOLY for the expression of relationships in time:

'Last time I landed on that property I didn't have enough money to buy it, but next time I will'
'That property has been bought since I last landed on it' etc.

With a little practice it will be found that even very simple games, requiring little vocabulary proper to themselves and therefore a minimum of extras to burden the actual playing of the game, can provide a suitable support for practising an astonishing number of language functions. It should be noticed that, pedagogically, the competitive element contained in all games is not of much practical use to the language trainer apart from its purpose of stimulating play, or in providing a suitable means of dividing a large class into smaller competing groups.

A further difficulty in deciding which game or exercise to use for giving training in given language functions is that of being able to foresee easily what other language functions are going to be brought into use during play. This is particularly relevant in the case of complex simulations exercises. A game which generates the need in its players for a form of expression which they are unable to verbalise in natural language terms can lead to frustration and, if left unattended, to abandonment of the game, or worse, to continuation of the game in another tongue. This natural breakdown point in the usefulness of the game may also be reached if interest in playing the game overrides the desire or agreement to play in a given language. For foreign language learners this is a disadvantage, whereas for mother-tongue learners the need to express oneself can be usefully harnessed to developing dexterity in the use of the language for self-expression or communicative purposes. From a purely physical point of view, any game should be easy to transport into and from the classroom (the normal language-training environment). If composed of many separate elements, they should be relatively easy to keep neat and tidy, with very easy access to each of these elements for the players. Furthermore, the game should ideally be cheap to produce (trainers have always had notoriously limited budgets) — ideally there would also be the possibility of the language trainer producing the game himself or herself, or at least being able to add to, or replace, the elements from which it is composed.

Briefly, then, to be suitable for language training purposes, games should:

parallel the functions of natural language as closely as possible,
contain many repetitive moves of the same nature,
be suitable for verbalising each move (games should contain a certain amount
of choice at each move which may be challenged by other players),
give as high a degree of social exchange as possible, that is, lead to discussion,
or group participation, team decision, etc,
be unpredictable from the start-point (unlike jigsaw puzzles),
be capable of adopting an infinite variety of end-points, like card games or
board games, or give an infinite variety of routes towards a fixed end-state.

Further, in common with games used in other training areas, they should:

involve class-sized numbers of players,
be simple and easy to transport into and from the classroom or training
environment,
be sufficiently interesting to both trainer *and* learners to create the desire to
play,
be composed of elements which do not depend on complex manoeuvring or
assembly skills, such as film-making, model-making, or direct use of a
machine such as a typewriter keyboard input for moves.
not take too long to complete, that is, give the satisfaction of achieving the
end-result within the usual period allotted to classroom activities,
be cheaply and easily reproducible,
be extensible by the trainer or players.

There is the further consideration that although the principles underlying
'man-devised' games are usually (and by definition) very easy to understand and
assimilate, paradoxically the principles underlying 'man-devised' languages are as
yet only very imperfectly understood. Hence any game used for language
training purposes should state very clearly in the instructions on its use what
particular language functions it relates to and is intended for practising, giving as
many examples as possible. This has been a major defect in games applied to
language training so far. From the above, then, it will be seen that the practical
limitations to the use of games and simulations activities in language training are
relatively small in number and extent, and that the possibilities such activities
offer in this field are therefore quite large.

Relevance

From what has been said, the general suitability of the application of games and
simulations activities to language training will be obvious. It should also be
obvious that games and natural language activities are very similar and, the
competitive element apart, that the two activities are very closely related.

Like gaming activity, language activity is basically composed of a set of
objects to manipulate (vocabulary); and a set of rules for their manipulation
(grammar); and of course, operators to use the language. This relationship has
been realised for some time, but not sufficiently thoroughly investigated as yet,
nor has any fully worked-out methodology of application been put forward. In
actual fact, language trainers have been using games, role-playing exercises and
simulations activities for many years now as teaching or training aids, but so far
in a largely unco-ordinated way, with only very few attempts made at relating

the language functions under consideration to the type of game or exercise being carried out. A more thorough investigation and description than has yet been published would be welcomed in the language training field (indeed, a workshop on the subject of 'Language Games in the EFL Classroom' had been organised in October 1977 in London, under the auspices of IATEFL). Nevertheless, it must be borne in mind that there are many factors acting *against* the use of games and simulations activities in language training, sometimes directly, sometimes indirectly. These include resistance on the part of both trainer and learner to 'playing', instead of practising by well-known methods considered to be more 'serious'. Playing at learning will not become acceptable to this type of person until a valid rationale can be clearly perceived behind the activity — which means that in language training, a direct relationship to the language functions under study must be clearly and carefully spelled out beforehand. There is also the fact that a trainer, because of a better grasp of the language and language techniques being taught, may simply not perceive, or may overestimate, students' capabilities of carrying out a given game (which may demand unexpected skills), and become more enthusiastic about carrying it out than the activity itself warrants. Coupled to this is the fact that, outside the private sector, many language students are following a set syllabus towards a set goal (examination or certificate) and the terms of this syllabus may not permit of much change from traditional teaching methods, even if both learner and trainer would prefer this.

Games, role-playing and simulations are notoriously time-consuming activities and, in the absence of any quantitative method of assessing relative efficiency, a point is reached where known and well used methods are preferred to the unknown in the interests of pure efficiency. In the commercial and industrial sectors of language training, where competence in a language very often has to be expressed in terms of hours of training to achieve a certain level, this is not conducive to the use of games as a training aid. In other words, games and simulations activities are not yet considered as being *essential* aids to language training. Despite this, however, their practical usefulness is such that they are rapidly becoming recognised forms of teaching in those areas where freedom to experiment with teaching methods and materials exists, and where a need is felt (such as in intensive training courses) for a suitable means of breaking otherwise intolerably intensive training rhythms.

It is doubtful if games *per se* could ever form the single basis or method for a language training course (and indeed this is highly undesirable, as is any single inflexible teaching method), but their degree of importance and the role they can play is beginning to attract the attention of publishers. Although their use in state-controlled teaching institutes has received very little official approval, the most sophisticated programmes to reach the market in recent years (*English for Business* [Bellcrest] , *State Your Case*, and the *Crisis* series [both from OUP] ; and the *Decisions Language Training Packs* [BP]) have all, in some way or other, been dependent on role-playing, and, in the case of the *Decisions* materials, simulation activities.

Apart from the above programmes, simple games and simple role-playing exercises are widely used at the present in language teaching, but do not go beyond the type of simple counting games such as BINGO, or anything more complex than re-enacting previously presented *set* situations allowing very little development or unexpected use of self-generated *unfamiliar* language structures or functions. The teaching of language through drama activities is a highly specialised application which it is not possible to deal with thoroughly within the scope of this paper. Games at the level of the *word* are also very common, and widely used (SCRABBLE, LEXICON, crossword puzzles); games at the level of *sentence* construction (JABBERWOCKY, FIND A STORY) are slightly less common, and at the level of language *functions* or connected discourse are virtually non-existent in widely distributed form.

Complex simulations of the type of the Robert Gordon's/Aberdeen *Press and Journal* BRUCE OIL MANAGEMENT GAME are only being attempted in experimental forms as yet. Although popular and well-known parlour games such as MONOPOLY are sometimes used in business and commercial language training, this is usually only to give a background context vaguely associated with a particular theme of 'English for specific purposes', and such games are most commonly used as a vehicle on which to hang practice in 'free' expression in a loosely defined context, rather than being closely related to defined functions or structures. Management training exercises have also been used, but again, usually only for the intrinsic interest value of the game or exercise, or as an exercise in group and interpersonal relationships (hopefully) generating the related expression of those relationships.

In fact, most of the so-called language teaching games on the market may be better classified as group animation activities than as true games of competition and skill (eg *English Language Teaching Games for Adult Students*, Books 1 and 2, Evans). In 1973-1974, the *English for Business* series (Bellcrest) was released by Oxford University Press in collaboration with the BBC, and represented the first serious published attempt at relating role-playing to language functions. As a complete multi-media package including filmed or videotaped story-line material it has proved rather unwieldy in the classroom in terms of time scale of application, as well as being beyond the reach of the average budget in its complete version. Nevertheless, most other materials appearing since have followed the role-playing lead set by Bellcrest (with a very wide semantic context), and the pure games aspect (with a very narrow semantic context) has been neglected.

Developments

First, developments will come in remedial training for native speakers of English. Native speakers of English fall into two broad categories where language training is concerned: the school-age learner, and the adult, working learner. For both categories the stigma of being assigned to remedial work is a strongly emotive force countering any motivation that may exist, and any games or exercises designed to be used in this context should attempt to diminish the effects of this. A good example of this is the BBC TV programme *On the Move*. The programmes, however, deal specifically with the problems of *literacy* as opposed to those of general performance in all language skills. The accompanying handbook for tutors, *BBC Adult Literacy Handbook*, contains a useful list of games for use in development techniques of literacy. With the school-age learner, games and simulations which deal with the *techniques* and *skills* of language use would be appropriate, as these should prove helpful in handling information in other areas of learning. Also appropriate are games which promote an increase in vocabulary, parallel forms of expression, basic sentence construction, and those which permit batteries of grammar or structure drills to be presented, or which give practice in difficult areas of reading, writing and spelling. A card game might be devised where language constructs are coded symbolically onto each card, and players have to communicate correctly (as defined in the rules of the game) in the artificial coded language.

For the working adult, those games dealing with the art of communication would be more appropriate, directly linked if possible to job improvement. They could also be linked to interpersonal and intergroup relations within the working environment (channels of communication with colleagues, subordinates and superiors) and could also encompass techniques of accessing and processing information (how to find out *where* to get hold of information likely to lead to job improvement, and, once obtained, how to organise it and use it efficiently — creation of a databank, report and résumé writing, etc). As an example here, a game might be devised where data is accumulated in the form of cards, a databank compiled, and then the information contained in that databank used to solve set problems, also distributed in card form. The solution to the problem could then be set out, or communicated, to other players according to the type of language exercise under consideration (writing or speaking skills). There are great opportunities here for the adaptation of already existing material, such as the ILEA's set of nine graded simulations exercises, or role-playing exercises as exemplified by IT'S YOUR CHOICE (Edward Arnold). Virtually any game or exercise intended for native speakers which involves them in creative language expression can be adapted and developed if the correct linguistic approach is used. There is also a large opening here for games of the self-instructional type. Perhaps the new forms of televisual or telephonic data transmission could be called upon to provide the necessary support hardware (Teletext, CEEFAX, Oracle, Viewdata and Telesoftware).

Second, there will be developments for the *immigrant learner* of English. The problems encountered here are basically the same as those above, with the extra complication of cross-cultural differences. Appropriate games to be developed would therefore be culture bound, and would give knowledge about, or emphasise, the principal culture differences expected, such as women driving cars, owning property and enjoying equal education opportunities, as well as giving practice in the use of the related ways of expressing these differences. Useful areas of application would be in dealing with the bureaucratic machine, filling in forms (most native speakers require training in form-*reading*, even after university education), and the skills associated with map and plan reading, decipherment of public transport timetables, using the public telephone system, etc. A possible game might involve the compilation of a cartoon strip using all the fixed expressions of visual art in British comics (burglar = black mask, striped sweater and swag bag), the recognition of red post boxes (not yellow, or blue), with the appropriate verbal associations which are part of the native speaker's automatic cultural heritage. How do you express 'Ouch!', 'Bang!', or 'Wuff!' in French or German? 'Jumbo' is obviously (?) an elephant, but what sort of affectionate name do we use in English for a house-snake, or the family ox? Here, not only does the correct linguistic approach require to be used, but also needed is a comprehension of the problems that some of the very fundamentals of game-playing we take for granted may present to the immigrant learner. The very concepts of playing games for pleasure, and of developing great skill in playing techniques, are probably culturally loaded in our favour.

Third, there will be developments in language training for the adult *foreign learner* of English. The total range of development possibilities here is truly vast. As well as combining some of the points mentioned above, games could range from the simplest vocabulary practice for adult beginners, to the most sophisticated computerised job simulation exercise for students wishing to gain experience of carrying out their own professional speciality in English, in competition even with native speakers (BRUCE OIL MANAGEMENT GAME type of activity). Games and exercises would also reflect a cross-section of adult occupations rather than an adaptation of children's games (as is the case at present). It would also be appropriate to develop games and exercises here designed to offset the teaching difficulties of persuading foreign learners to communicate with each other voluntarily in what is basically an artifical medium of expression.

Context-specific games would be useful, if designed so that basic vocabulary and information required to play the game or carry out the exercise were presented as an integral part of the game and in English only. This would thus tend to circumvent any tendency to translate back into the mother tongue and deal with the game in mother-tongue terms.

A set of materials based on the principles outlined in this paper has been prepared by the authors, from which it is possible to take examples to highlight the points above. Based on the successful *Decisions* materials developed by Bath University School of Education and published by BP Educational Service, *Language Training Pack 1: North Sea Challenge* presents three related role-playing and simulated social activities exercises and gives comprehensive training in all the language functions generated by the decision-making process. The background context of the pack is the North Sea oil industry; in presenting *new* information essential to the working of the exercises to the foreign learner *in English*, it minimises the risk of mother-tongue interference during the working out of the exercises; and in providing a comprehensive set of language drills related *specifically* to those language functions used during the working out of the exercises it provides the English language trainer with a powerful training aid.

It can be seen that games which are capable of being played on a cassette tape recorder for practice in the spoken word might represent a future development possibility. There is at the moment a definite lack of games dependent on the *acoustic* (as opposed to visual) recognition skills. Perhaps it may even be possible to envisage an adaptation of sound games for the blind for this purpose. With the application of games to specific language training areas perhaps the traditional visual or graphic printed support for games will be able to be replaced by the imprinted magnetic tape support, and associated forms of aural and visual display.

MILITARY AND MANAGEMENT

Games and simulations which have so far been applied to language training have rarely been specifically designed for that purpose, and have usually been those originally developed for either *military* or *management training* purposes. As such, they have tended to emphasise, and were usually developed to provide training in, those qualities most commonly considered useful to management and the military — the personal qualities of leadership, group dominance, aggressiveness, ability to make rapid decisions under conditions of stress, and so forth. Very few have been specifically concerned with the exploration of channels of communication, increased comprehension of alien concepts and cultures, the techniques of self-betterment in a broad range of mental skills, or the development of skills of self-expression for self-improvement. A few notable exceptions have been training courses for reception personnel, but these are not widely available. The saturation language courses and materials provided by the armed forces during the Second World War gave training in *reacting* to an alien situation in an alien language, but made very little attempt to teach an *understanding* of that situation in any other terms than those of the mother culture. This monocultural pattern has been adhered to ever since. It is hardly surprising that the reception of the games and exercises developed from these techniques when applied to language training has been mixed, and that discussion generated by a game (for the purpose of free expression) can turn to a discussion of the *ethics* of the game being played, rather than a discussion related to actual play. Further, it is not surprising that the purpose of the game can be totally misunderstood, and a language student refuse to play because he or she feels there is an ulterior motive due to previous exposure to military or management games of exactly the same nature.

It should be pointed out here that a great deal of language training activity is dependent on brainwashing techniques, and is therefore more susceptible to being used for the 'wrong' purposes than even military or business training techniques. Take, for example, the language courses and materials for immigrants to Soviet bloc countries which, to Western minds, are no better than advanced and highly efficient propaganda implantation exercises; then take a look at our own business training games from an Eastern point of view, and imagine the horror they must generate. It would be interesting to try playing MONOPOLY with all property under communal ownership. The topics and subjects chosen for language training games and exercises for the *foreign* learner must therefore be very carefully evaluated. On the one hand they are basically required to give a clear representation of cultural values and interests, and on the other they also have to do this without giving offence or being incomprehensible to other cultures. The non-cultural approach may be used to good effect for training the native speaker, and sometimes for the immigrant; but for the foreign learner a cultural approach should be attempted.

Games designers should bear these points in mind when devising and preparing games aimed at the general language training market. Perhaps what is eventually needed is a game or exercise which, rather than representing a pure communications interface between natural language A and natural language B, using game language as a common denominator, is a game designed with a variable logic system such that, starting in perfectly comprehensible terms in natural language A, it gradually evolves to terms in natural language B. Whether such a hypothetical game is feasible in practical terms or not remains to be seen.

Conclusion

There is now sufficient interest and demand to warrant a full and proper investigation of the development of games and simulations exercises specifically as language training aids in their own right, not as training tools to condition *how* one thinks and expresses oneself, but as training tools to allow one to develop *freedom* and *flexibility* in the way one thinks and communicates. That is to say, their development should be seen as that of *communications* tools, rather than that of *conditioning* tools.

In this way, language training games and simulations may eventually give something back to the original training areas that gave birth to them, and perhaps even influence the further development of games and simulations in those areas. The language trainer's most pressing need at the moment, in practical terms, is a comprehensive directory or list of *all* academic gaming and simulations exercises involving creative self-expression, classified in three ways: first, in the order of complexity of operation, from simple to sophisticated; second, by principal language *functions* used in carrying out the game; third, by degree of mastery of expression of natural language required to carry out the game efficiently. Chess, for example, requires no use of the expression of natural language, whereas a simulated public debate requires a great deal of fluency and art in the use of language as a tool of persuasion or aggression which not even the native speaker finds easy to acquire.

HYDROPOWER 77

Eric Addinall and Henry I Ellington, *Robert Gordon's Institute of Technology, Aberdeen*

HYDROPOWER 77 is a competitive multi-disciplinary design project based on the assumption that a decision has been reached to construct a 1,000 MW pumped-storage scheme in a hypothetical area. The project package was devised and developed by the authors and was subsequently presented by the North of Scotland Hydro-Electric Board as a competition for senior pupils in secondary schools in the north of Scotland. This paper describes the development of the project package, and its educational aims and objectives. It then discusses the organisation, the response, the judging and the final outcome of a competition based on the game.

Introduction

It has been argued (Ellington and Percival, 1977) that science education should do more than deal with purely scientific content, and should contribute to the development of other general skills required in later life, and that suitable science-based multi-disciplinary simulation-games constitute a method whereby such wider educational objectives can be achieved. The authors have been associated with the development of several simulation-games of this type in recent years, and one such venture, in which the authors collaborated with the North of Scotland Hydro-Electric Board (NSHEB) to produce a competitive design project, is described in this paper. During the early summer of 1976, the authors were approached by the NSHEB to consider developing a suitable design project which could be used as a competition for senior pupils in secondary schools throughout the NSHEB area in the north of Scotland. It was decided that the design of a hydroelectric pumped-storage scheme would provide a suitable vehicle for the competition. The subject area was extensively researched with the co-operation of the NSHEB and a suitable scenario on which to base the competition was developed. The competition was launched in September 1976, and the final judging took place in Aberdeen in June 1977.

General description of the project

The central feature of HYDROPOWER 77 is a realistic, thoroughly researched scenario. This scenario was developed only after the authors had spent three full days visiting conventional hydroelectric and pumped-storage schemes throughout Scotland in order to obtain the necessary background knowledge, and had made a number of visits to the Hydro Board's Edinburgh office in order to discuss details of the project with one of their leading technical experts on pumped-storage. Development of a realistic scenario for the competition would have been practically impossible without this co-operation.

(a) THE SCENARIO

Players are told:

> A decision has been reached to construct a pumped-storage scheme in the (hypothetical) Loch Haddon area in the West of Scotland. The proposed scheme is to have a generating capacity of 1,000 MW, maintainable over a period of up to eight hours, and is to be used to supply roughly 1,200 million units of electricity per annum to the national grid. Six possible sites for the scheme have been identified in the Loch Haddon area. [In a hydroelectric pumped-storage scheme, surplus electricity is removed from the grid system at times when supply exceeds demand and used to pump water from a low-level reservoir to a reservoir at a higher level; this water is then used to generate electricity at times of peak demand.]

(b) THE OBJECTIVE OF THE PROJECT

The objective of the project was to decide which of the six possible sites was the most suitable and to present a case for its development. Specifically, the participants were required:

(i) to assess the potential of each site from both a technical and an economic point of view,
(ii) to make a decision as to which site to develop, taking account of all relevant technical, economic, geographical, amenity and enviromental factors, and to justify this decision in a written report,
(iii) to prepare a multi-media presentation of the selected scheme.

The multi-disciplinary nature of HYDROPOWER 77 is demonstrated by the following educational objectives:

(a) to make the participating pupils *aware* of the principles and applications of hydroelectric pumped-storage and of the various factors involved in choosing a site for and designing a pumped-storage scheme,
(b) to provide *experience* of participating in a complex planning exercise involving a wide variety of technical, economic, geographical and environmental factors and thus requiring a high degree of co-operation between pupils with different disciplinary backgrounds,
(c) to provide pupils with an opportunity to *use their initiative* and develop their creative ability.

Contents of the project package

All schools participating in the competition were provided with a project pack containing:

(a) a short introductory leaflet describing the scenario for HYDROPOWER 77, explaining the object of the project and listing the contents of the project package;
(b) a background information leaflet introducing the participants to the

concept of pumped-storage, discussing the various economic and technical reasons why it is becoming increasingly widely used, describing the development of pumped-storage in Britain, and reviewing the main features of pumped-storage schemes;

(c) a leaflet providing all the technical and economic data needed for the project;

(d) two of the Hydro Board's own technical leaflets (describing the Cruachan and Foyers pumped-storage schemes), so that pupils could make direct reference to the design parameters, diagrams and photographs of existing schemes;

(e) three maps of the hypothetical Loch Haddon area on which the project is based dealing respectively with general topography and communications, existing hydroelectric developments and land utilisation. The maps are all drawn to a scale of 1cm = 2.5km;

(f) maps of each of the six individual sites identified as being suitable for the construction of a pumped-storage scheme. Each map describes the basic topography of the site and is drawn to a scale of 6cm = 1km;

(g) a leaflet giving background geographical information on the Loch Haddon area and detailed geographical and environmental information relating to each of the six sites;

(h) a general guidance leaflet designed to help participants organise their work on the project.

The HYDROPOWER 77 Competition

The competition was organised from the Hydro Board's Edinburgh head office by its press and public relations officer, who was closely involved with the project from its inception. In September, at the beginning of the school year, each senior secondary school in the NSHEB area in the north of Scotland was sent a complete project package, together with a letter inviting the school to enter the competition. An article publicising the competition was published in the September *Bulletin of the Scottish Centre for Mathematics, Science and Technical Education* (Ellington and Addinall, 1976).

Since the object of the exercise was to provide a multi-disciplinary teaching aid which could be usefully integrated into the school curriculum, the NSHEB made the project package available to all the secondary schools in their area, irrespective of whether or not they actually entered the competition. Schools receive many invitations to enter competitions each year, and the initial entry of twenty-six schools (from the north of Scotland area) reflected the considerable interest shown in the competition. In addition, several teachers have since indicated that, although they did not enter the competition, the project package will be put to good use as a complement to the normal teaching programme in future years. Schools which entered the competition were then given a timetable so that the teams could organise the work on the project. The preliminary judging of written reports took place in April 1977, and six 'semi-finalists' were subsequently chosen. These had their multi-media presentations assessed in May and, as a result, three teams were chosen to take part in the live final, which was held in Aberdeen Grammar School on Wednesday 15 June 1977.

The competition was deliberately structured so as to eliminate progressively all but the most able and enthusiastic teams by a process of 'natural drop-out'.

Towards this end, the project was designed to be extremely demanding both in terms of the intrinsic difficulty and the time needed to complete it successfully. As a result of this policy, only six of the twenty-six schools which originally entered the competition lasted through to the final stages. They had their entries assessed according to a detailed marking scheme, and the authors feel that the standard achieved by all six teams in both their written reports and their multi-media presentations was very high indeed. The three finalists, Aberdeen Grammar School, Hazelhead Academy (Aberdeen) and Lawside Academy (Dundee), produced reports and presentations of exceptional quality, showing that the demands made within the competition were fully justified. At the final, the multi-media presentations of the three leading teams (all of which had been encouraged to make any improvements or revisions they wished) were assessed by four judges.

The three teams then took part in a question-and-answer session in front of an invited audience. Their overall placing was based on a mark carried forward from the original assessment to which was added a mark based on the opinions formed by the judges at the actual final. At the end of the day, Hazelhead Academy (Aberdeen) was first, followed by Aberdeen Grammar School and Lawside Academy. The third place achieved by Lawside Academy (Dundee) deserves special mention. It was only during the judging of the multi-media presentation in Dundee that the authors discovered that the team was composed entirely of fourth-year pupils. Their performance was, therefore, all the more remarkable since nearly all the other teams were composed of fifth and sixth formers.

Conclusions

In the opinion of both the organisers and the participants, HYDROPOWER 77 has proved to be an extremely worthwhile and useful exercise. Firstly, it has helped to stimulate genuine interest in and appreciation of the process by which the Hydro Board tackles a major development project such as the building of a pumped-storage scheme. During the winter months, many schools visited the Board's existing pumped-storage schemes at Cruachan on Loch Awe and at Foyers on Loch Ness. This interest was undoubtedly aroused through the schools receiving the project package prior to the competition.

Secondly, it has provided schools with a self-contained package of multi-disciplinary material which can be used by teachers in a number of different departments (physics, geography, economics, etc) to demonstrate the interaction and interdependence of the various factors associated with a major technological project. In order to increase the effectiveness of the package in the general teaching situation, the authors sent specimen solutions of the various stages of the project to all the schools who entered the competition. Some idea of the participants' views can be had from comments made by two of the teachers involved in the competition:

> As well as integrating the physics and geography departments it proved that, when solving a practical problem, it is always worth listening to views from other departments . . . The project was good training for the boys in presenting their materials in an exciting and imaginative way. I feel that the boys gained as much from tackling this problem as they gained from sixth-year studies in physics (Aberdeen Grammar School).

As a project it is very well thought out and presented. It is also very well balanced . . . [The] pupils have learned many new skills, techniques and attitudes as a result of working through the project. They have learned how to: (i) tackle a problem, (ii) organise themselves and work as a team, (iii) work independently and use reference material (ie without staff help), (iv) write a lengthy, highly technical report, which should stand them in good stead for CSYS [Certificate of Sixth-Year Studies]. It is interesting to note that one or two members of staff, including myself, are becoming aware of the part which models and model-making can play across the curriculum. The project also provided an opportunity for some interdepartment co-operation within the school — a facet of school life which is often missing . . . In general, the project has béen an unqualified success (Hazelhead Academy).

Postscript

While developing the scenario for HYDROPOWER 77, the authors realised that it would make an ideal source of in-depth case studies and design exercises at a variety of levels and in a variety of disciplines. Following discussions with the Institution of Electrical Engineers (who had collaborated with RGIT in the publication of THE POWER STATION GAME, Ellington *et al*, 1977), a new type of educational package embodying this idea, 'The pumped-storage multi-project pack', was developed (Ellington and Addinall, 1977a); this was subsequently published by the IEE under the name HYDROPOWER. The general philosophy of packages of this type is described in detail in a separate paper by the authors (Ellington and Addinall, 1977b).

'The pumped-storage multi-project pack' (HYDROPOWER) can be obtained from the following address: IEE, Station House, Nightingale Road, Hitchen, Herts SG5 1RJ, England, at a price of £12.

References

Ellington, H I and Addinall, E (1976) HYDROPOWER 77. *Bulletin of the Scottish Centre for Maths, Science and Technical Education*, 9, 9-10.

Ellington, H I and Addinall, E (1977a) The pumped-storage multi-project pack — a new type of simulation exercise. *Proceedings of 1977 ISAGA Conference*. University of Birmingham.

Ellington, H I and Addinall, E (1977b) The multi-disciplinary multi-project pack — a new concept in simulation/gaming. *Programmed Learning & Educational Technology*, 14, 3, 213-222.

Ellington, H I, Langton, N H and Smythe, M E (1977) The use of simulation games in schools — a case study. *Aspects of Educational Technology XI*. Kogan Page, London.

Ellington, H I and Percival, F (1977) Educating 'through' science using multi-disciplinary simulation-games. *Programmed Learning & Educational Technology*, 14, 2, 117-126.

Games and simulations for secondary school chemistry teaching: the periodic table

Uri Zoller *Haifa University*
and Y Timor, *Israel Institute of Technology, Haifa*

This paper reports a project that was intended to develop an educational simulation game to be used as a teaching device in theoretical and applied chemistry for high school students with various backgrounds. The game was designed to develop higher levels of thinking through learning and discovery-by-playing. The general idea was applied to the teaching of the periodic table by simulating the process that real scientists went through. The student is presented with the challenge of constructing the periodic table, applying its laws and derived rules for solving unknown problems within the framework of selected simulated case studies. Thus, the first part of the game consists of the construction of the periodic table according to the data of the elements and the understanding of the principle of periodicity, followed by the understanding of the laws involved and the electronic structure of the elements. Each group of players consists of two pairs who compete for about 75 minutes using the various components of the game.

Introduction

The value of learning through pleasure and interest, both of which facilitate motivation, appears to be agreed upon. Nevertheless, in spite of the rapid growth in the creation and use of educational instructional games and simulations for school courses in general, their availability in the area of natural sciences is rather limited, particularly as far as chemistry is concerned. Furthermore, while many agree that the most important function of a game is probably the reinforcement of previously learned skills, the claim that many games and simulations attain predetermined instructional objectives with regard to *previously unlearned skills* has been recently challenged (Reid, 1977).

Rationale and objectives

In an attempt to meet the above challenge, we have developed an educational simulation game, THE YOUNG CHEMIST, within the framework of our ongoing research and chemistry curriculum development programme. The game is designed to be used as a teaching device for theoretical and applied chemistry for various target populations (ie science- and non-science oriented, disadvantaged and gifted students) in the secondary school. Specifically, the developed game is designed to teach students the concept of the periodic table by simulating the process that real scientists (Mendeliev for one) presumably went through. The student is presented with the challenge of constructing the periodic table and applying its laws and derived rules to solving unknown problems within the framework of selected simulated case studies. Most important, the developed game is designed to develop *higher* levels of thinking through learning and discovery-by-playing.

The idea of the game was not necessarily a consequence of the realisation that games would be an effective means of filling an existing gap in the chemistry curriculum (Ellington, 1977), but rather a logical result of our conviction that both games and simulations are *not* sufficiently being used as instructional and learning tools. Consequently, our main objective was the development of an educational aid for theoretical chemistry instruction which combines a high level of learning with enjoyment of the study process.

If one considers all the well-established characteristics and parameters of games and simulations (Berne, 1964; Raser, 1969; Tansey, 1971), then their use within our project, in the form of a simulation-game for achieving our objectives, appears to be straightforward. Moreover, the active involvement of the participating students within the learning process can be effected both cognitively and affectively.

The game

The developed game, THE YOUNG CHEMIST (Timor, 1977), consists of three parts each of which is designed to be played by two pairs of players who compete for about 75 minutes using the various elements of the game. The first part consists of the construction of the periodic table according to the *physical* data of the elements and the understanding of the principle of periodicity. This is followed by the understanding of the laws involved. This stage concludes with the development of the participants' skills in predicting the characteristics of unknown elements by drawing on these laws. Methodologically, this is the so-called historical approach for science teaching which was strongly advocated by *Harvard Project Physics* (Holton, 1976).

Part two of the game develops the concept of periodicity based on the *electronic* structure of the elements and concentrates on the combination of elements to form chemical compounds in accordance with evolved rules. Part three develops the student's capability for applying the governing laws on which the periodic table is based for solving previously unknown problems within the framework of selected applied chemistry case studies.

The educational and methodological analysis of the game, from the chemistry instruction point of view, as well as the discussion of the teaching problems involved are beyond the scope of this paper, and have been dealt with elsewhere (Timor, 1977).

The game consists of the following items: game story; game instructions; question cards, answer cards; information cards (about the learned subject matter); game boards; 32 numbered element cards (cards of the first 18 elements of the periodic table); four graph cards (to be constructed and completed by the participants); miscellaneous aids, such as arrows to point towards the direction of change in characteristics and other aids. Some detail of these items would be helpful.

Game story provides the participants with the background of the game as well as their expected role. It follows the inquiry and discovery process which real chemists *allegedly* went through when the periodic table was first constructed. The essence of the simulation is thus presented to the players.

Question cards present the questions with which the participant students have to cope. In case of difficulty one can use available clues (the 'price' being the loss of some game points).

Answer cards contain the right answer which is an essential form of feedback to the participants as far as the learning process is concerned. They also serve as an aid to scoring the ongoing competition.

Information cards provide the essential information including definitions of new concepts which are not being grasped independently by the participants.

Element cards contain the basic data of each element on both sides (including the symbol of the element, its name, the atomic number, atomic weight, density, etc).

As stated before, at the end of stage one, the construction of the periodic table (in which only the first 18 elements are included) has to be completed by each pair of the competing participants. The desired result is shown in Table 1.

Group\Period	1	2	3	4	5	6	7	8
One	H							He
Two	Li	Be	B	C	N	O	F	Ne
Three	Na	Mg	Al	Si	P	S	Cl	Ar

Table 1. *Completed periodic table at the end of stage 1*

In principle, the two competing pairs have to pick simultaneously the question cards in numbered order, discuss (within each pair) the presented question in an attempt to reach the right solution against the clock. The answer agreed upon is then written down on the appropriate sheet, and after the opposite team has finished its discussion, the two answers are compared and checked against the corresponding answer card. Finally, the scoring on each item is summed up by taking into account whether or not clues were used. The winning pair is the one who has scored more points over the entire game. The role of the teacher is basically passive during the game period unless he has to serve as a referee in case of partial or incomplete answers. In this respect, it is worth mentioning that individual competition is appreciably reduced and co-operation is *increased* by designing the game for two competing *pairs* rather than for individuals.

As indicated above, a special effort has been made to demand a high level of thinking by constructing questions of as high a level as possible throughout the game. For example:

> There are 32 cards in front of you. On each card you will find an ordinary number and a Roman number in different colours. Arrange the given cards in such a manner that they will best illustrate and demonstrate the laws you have discovered through dealing with them.

An analysis of the level of questions has been made according to Bloom's taxonomy. This is summarised in Table 2.

No of Question \ Level	Knowledge	Comprehension	Application	Analysis
1		+		
2				+
3		+		
4		+		
5		+		
5a				+
6		+		
7		+		
7a			+	
7b				+
7c		+		
8				+
8a		+		
8b			+	

+ a question of this type present

Table 2. *Analysis of question level*

Research and pilot field test

Understandably, the development of an educational simulation-game which is interdisciplinary as far as its different components are concerned, involves many aspects, each of which deserves formative and summative evaluation in accordance with its unique framework of self-contained rules, instruments and frames of reference. Both the cognitive and the affective domains should be taken into account. Needless to say, a full-scale evaluation is beyond the capabilities of a small team within a limited period of time. Nevertheless, some results of selected areas of research, follow-up and evaluation concerning the newly-developed game have been undertaken. The results are worth noting. Stage one of the game has been fully developed and has been field-tested by small groups of 14- to 15-year-old students. Cognitive tests and attitude questionnaires were administered (Timor, 1977) to this sample of the target population. The feedback from this formative evaluation has been used for further modifications and improvements. The final version of the first part of the game has been redesigned accordingly. The other two parts, although developed, have not yet been field-tested and therefore the *final* modified version is not yet available.

A special cognitive post-test for stage one of the game has been developed and administered to the students after they have completed the game (Timor, 1977). The game was field-tested only with students whose entry behaviour can be described as *'never having learned'* the periodic table in their chemistry courses prior to their playing the present game. Thus the results of the post-test reflect their cognitive gain via the game. Seventy-five per cent of the sample students scored >60 per cent on a specially devised objective test (a test which *we* consider to be satisfactory). The sample for field-testing of the first stage of the game consisted of 170 students from eight different classes. Since several modifications of the game did take place during the development stage, the attitude questionnaires of only 64 students remained for final analysis in the preliminary field test.

A summary of results concerning the participants' attitudes with respect to enjoyment (in playing the game) and learning and comprehension (of chemistry principles and laws through the game) and the structure of the game, is given in Table 3. It should be pointed out that the *total* in the figure refers to the total number of questions in the questionnaire and not only the four categories listed.

Subscale	Number of items in subscale	Mean score	Standard deviation
Enjoyment	6	2.81	0.45
Learning	3	2.74	0.79
Comprehension	4	3.21	0.52
Game structure	6	3.24	0.55
Total score	34	2.94	0.29

$N = 64$
Scale: strongly agree: 4 / strongly disagree: 1

Table 3. *Scores on attitude questionnaire (preliminary field test)*

Conclusion

In conclusion, the emphasis of the present project was not on inventing a better instructional educational device for *every* learning situation, but rather on the development of an additional instrument which increases the variety of instruction options in the field of chemistry and consequently helps achieve specific, predetermined objectives in both the cognitive and affective domains.

It is hoped the specific interaction between students with different characteristics and the newly developed game, in different learning situations under a variety of conditions, will simultaneously maximise meaningful understanding of the periodic table on the one hand and the enjoyment of methodological thinking on the other. The contribution of our game towards the achievement of the above goals seems to be clear. Summative evaluation of the newly developed game, as well as its educational instructional value concerning both the cognitive and affective domains involved, will constitute the final phase of the project.

References

Berne, E (1964) *Games People Play*. Grove Press, New York.

Ellington, H I (1977) Systems approach to the development of education. *SAGSET Journal,* 7, 1, 14.

Holton, G (1976) The Project Physics Course-Notes on its educational philosophy, *Physics Education,* 330-335.

Raser, J R (1969) *Simulation and Society — an Explanation of Scientific Gaming.* Allyn and Bacon, New York.

Reid, N (1977) Games and simulations for 'O' grade chemistry. *SAGSET Journal,* 7, 2, 48.

Tansey, P J (1971) *Educational Aspects of Simulation.* McGraw-Hill, London.

Timor, Y (1977) *MSc thesis.* Technion, Haifa, Israel.

SPACE QUEST: a mathematical game

Thomas Doherty, *Cranhill Secondary School, Glasgow*

To solve some of the problems of teaching mathematics to RSLA pupils, the author has devised a science fiction-based board game. The game capitalises on the pupils' interest in science fiction and is intended to teach co-ordinates and vectors. The aim of the game is for players to 'travel' from the Earth to Mars and back to the Earth. Various problems have to be solved *en route*. Using a board made up of squares (co-ordinates) the players learn to move their pieces using co-ordinate geometry and become aware of the nature of vectors. The game can be played by a class (in groups) and completed in a double period.

Introduction

The raising-of-the-school-leaving-age (RSLA) revolution still has not had much effect on classroom practice. Courses for pupils of lower ability have rarely been adopted due to the policy of topping-up 'O' grade classes rather than putting lower ability children through a more appropriate course for their needs. Nowhere is this policy more prevalent (and more misguided) than in mathematics where the attitude usually adopted is 'If they're not very bright they can drop maths and go for "O" grade arithmetic only'. Unfortunately this mentality persists and leaves the classroom teacher in a situation where he would like to teach these children by the variety of methods which are necessary to ensure their continued interest but finds himself stuck with 'chalk and talk' which alone is not sufficient. To make matters worse, he has not the time to develop an adequate amount of material on his own, and so he must continue trying to make something out of nothing. This last area of frustration is made worse by the fact that such courses as *are* available for the RSLA pupil have been designed so as to ensure the minimum of teacher involvement, as a result of which the teacher often finds that the material needs extensive modification before he can use it in his classroom. In an attempt to alleviate this problem to some extent, I felt the need to develop two types of back-up material which can be used with all my classes, and which I hope can be modified and used by other teachers (see Bloomer, 1975). My main efforts so far have been to design a board game called SPACE QUEST. In attempting this I took into account six basic procedural rules suggested by Watts (1975) in a paper first presented at the SAGSET conference in 1974:

1. A game should possess *simplicity* of its rules and procedure.
2. The *language* in which it is written must be simple. (In the case of SPACE

QUEST it was very tempting to use scientific and mathematical jargon.)
3. The game must be *short* (less than an hour).
4. The *whole group* must be involved in the play of the game.
5. The *teacher must be involved.* The point made earlier about problems in material design is backed up by Stenhouse (1975) who has pointed out that the teacher plays such a vital part in the learning process that 'teacher proofing' cannot work. This is partly because teachers will not condone moves towards their own obsolescence, but largely because the teacher's natural value as a *formative evaluator* of the ongoing classroom processes makes it essential that he be included.
6. The game should be *part of a planned course.* In no way should it be seen as a replacement for more traditional methods but should be used in conjunction with them.

The next section of this paper describes the game, which has been designed to incorporate Watts' criteria.

SPACE QUEST

SPACE QUEST, as the name suggests, is a game which has space as its theme. This was considered to be an area of interest and stimulation to children in view of the current success of TV programmes such as *Space 1999* and *Star Trek.* SPACE QUEST is a race where rival space crews leave Earth, travel to Mars and return to Earth, where the game ends. During the journey crews will encounter various problems, such as damage to the spacecraft, loss of power, etc. These difficulties are overcome by means of solving mathematical problems. The winning crew is that which completes the journey to Mars and back again in the least time. ('Time' here refers to the game's scoring system, which is measured in terms of 'Earth Days', where Earth Days are added to the mission time in relation to mistakes made. So the first craft to land back on Earth is not necessarily the winner.)

Duration: The game is designed to last between 40 minutes and one hour. This allows the game to be completed within the time normally allotted to a double period. Ideally, if the game could be trimmed to perhaps 30 minutes this would allow adequate time for a debriefing session.

Players/teams: All members of the class play the game. Although it would be more suitable from a management point of view if the numbers were smaller, in a typical classroom it will rarely be possible to operate on a small scale when one considers that first- and second-year classes in secondary school normally comprise 30 or more pupils. The game is played by two to six crews, each crew consisting of three to five members. Each player has a title, eg Commander, Navigator. All titles, with the exception of the Commander, are meaningless as far as their tasks in the game are concerned. Tasks will, however, take the form of specific instructions for each crew member. An example of the type of instructions given to crew members is given below. Each turn of the game begins with all the Commanders going to the front of the classroom where each throws the dice to determine the movement of the craft. He may then consult his crew with respect to the optimum alternative, but it remains his decision as to which alternative to choose. After each turn, that is, when everyone in the crew has completed his calculation, the Commander picks up a Translation Card from the pack if no mistakes have been made in the calculations. This responsibility which the Commander possesses is in no way intended to suggest that the Commander has to be the most capable of the crew in academic terms. In fact this role could be played by the poorest pupil. The restriction which does obtain is that all Commanders should be of approximately the same ability. Similarly, all Navigators should be equals, whether of high or low ability. The reason for this limitation is to ensure, for testing purposes, that each team is approximately the same as every other, which minimises pupil difference effects on the game. In a homogeneous group, such as a fourth-year Certificate class, less emphasis could be placed on this kind of division and some measure of co-operative effort, as suggested by Leith (1967), might be appropriate.

Seating: There should be no need of any special seating arrangement in the non-cooperative version of SPACE QUEST to be played by primary and early secondary children. The arrangement of one crew/one row seems satisfactory here. In a co-operative situation as mentioned above seats should be placed in such a way as to enable all members of a crew to be close enough to each other to consult each other easily; perhaps a circular arrangement of seats. The seating arrangement should not place too much stress upon the standard classroom set-up, which can easily accommodate six such groupings.

The object of the game: The spacecraft which has taken the fewest Earth Days to complete its journey to Mars and back again is the winner. Alternatively, the round trip can be split into two separate missions and the winner decided by aggregation of the two.

The scoring system: Each move consists of a dice throw, the manoeuvre of the craft (see (c) in section on play), response to the 'Alert' Call (see (d) and (e) in section on play) and the picking up of a Translation Card (see (c) in section on play). Once all calculations have been completed and answers checked the turn is finished. At this stage, each crew adds one Earth Day to its total plus one Earth Day per incorrect answer. No Translation Card is awarded to any team which has made any errors. It is important that corrections are postponed until the game has been concluded, although the Controller may be consulted by any player in extreme difficulties. Any player who feels the need to consult the Controller does so at the expense of one-half of an Earth Day, which is added to the total for his team. The reason for penalising such consultation is to discourage those children who usually ask the teacher for help without properly thinking the problem through — a not uncommon phenomenon. At the same time, for the one or two pupils who really do need the teacher's help at any given time, the loss of a half-day can be an investment if it prevents costlier and more frequent penalties.

In addition to the penalties to be incurred, a bonus system also applies. Any player who finishes his task quickly continues working through the remaining stock of Alert Cards. No penalties will be incurred for mistakes on these, unless they subsequently become involved in the game in the usual way. The bonus score, which is subtracted from the crew's total, is one-quarter of an Earth Day per correct solution. It should be noted that although this bonus system is a reward for speed to some extent, the weighting of the penalties and rewards is undoubtedly in favour of accuracy rather than speed. If pupils can combine both then so much the better. If these fractions prove too difficult for a particular group of children, it is easy to adjust the scoring to a whole number base.

The board: The board consists of a peg-board twenty units square, which is divided into four equal regions by means of a horizontal line and a vertical line which bisect each other. The board has eight Red Alert areas (shaded areas). The board is illustrated in Figure 1.

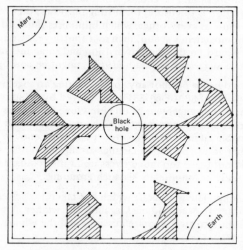

Figure 1. *The SPACE QUEST board*

All holes on the peg-board which are on, or contained within, any boundary lines are considered to be part of that region of space, so that, for example, the points on the surrounds of the Red Alert areas are also considered to be red.

All points on the periphery of the board are considered to be in play and craft may land on them. The circular area in the centre of the board designated 'Black Hole' is impassable. The reason for employing such an obstacle is to prevent craft travelling directly from Earth's sector to Mars's sector via the horizontal axis, thus gaining excessive advantage over the others. With this obstacle in existence, only very rarely can craft move in this way, and then only with high dice totals. As an optional feature, each person playing the game could be issued with squared or graph paper upon which to chart the progress of the craft, or to try out and plan possible translations which might suit. This aspect might be useful, for example, for groups working on co-ordinate geometry or vectors.

The units: The spacecraft are represented by pegs of different colours. They are positioned on the launch pad on Earth on one of the 15 holes within Earth's limits.

THE PLAY OF SPACE QUEST

(a) *'Briefing' (optional section):* This takes place immediately prior to take-off. Briefing consists of giving each pupil a programme containing the learning component of the game. The players complete the programme, taking a

post-test to ascertain their acquisitions. This done, the play of the game may begin. There are severe practical difficulties involved in this section:
- (i) preparation of a programme is a lengthy process and hence difficult for a classroom teacher to find time to attempt;
- (ii) some programmed materials exist, but few will do without extensive modification, which brings us back to point (i) above;
- (iii) given the time restrictions on the game it is difficult to provide a small programme which can teach a significant amount in such a short time.

It seems that unless the game is extended to last more than an hour, little use can be made of programmes in conjunction with it.

(b) *Take-off/landing:* The Controller informs each crew member to consult their take-off instructions. These consist of some fairly straightforward problems of the type which the players will encounter as the game progresses. The reason for offering the players an easy beginning is so as to make them comfortable in the novel situation, to provide some positive reinforcement early on and to motivate them favourably towards the game. Once everyone has completed their take-off exercise and checked their answers the craft are ready to move into space. The Commanders then go to the front of the class, ready to throw the dice which will determine where the craft go. Landing the craft follows a similar pattern. In this case, when a dice throw brings a craft on to the target planet the crew may then, on their next turn, consult their landing instructions. Neither taking-off nor landing is counted as penalty time unless errors are made, which incur the usual penalties. The procedure for in-flight problem-solving is different from this.

(c) *The dice and movement round the board:*
- (i) At the front of the room, in the possession of the Controller, is a pair of ordinary dice, one black and one white. The black die determines horizontal movement, the white one is for vertical movement. When the dice are thrown the Commander has a choice of four possible moves. An example will best illustrate this. Suppose that the Commander throws a black 4 and a white 3. This means that the choices (in translation number pair form) are:

$$\begin{pmatrix} 4 \\ 3 \end{pmatrix} \qquad \begin{pmatrix} 4 \\ -3 \end{pmatrix} \qquad \begin{pmatrix} -4 \\ 3 \end{pmatrix} \qquad \begin{pmatrix} -4 \\ -3 \end{pmatrix}$$

  It might sometimes occur that one or more of these translations is impossible, but the dimensions of the board ensure that at least one of them *can* be accomplished.
- (ii) Movement from Earth to Mars and back again takes the form of a clockwise journey round the board. (Speaking in terms of Cartesian quadrants, this means that spacecraft must go from the 4th to the 3rd, 2nd and 1st *in that order* before re-entering the 4th quadrant [where Earth is] in order to complete the mission.) Further, once a craft has left a particular sector it cannot go back into it.
- (iii) After each turn a crew which has made no errors in its calculations may collect a Translation Card. These cards are kept until needed. They can be used instead of a dice throw. Each card contains a number, and any two in conjunction can replace a dice throw. The advantage in having

these cards is twofold. Firstly, by awarding a card only for error-free solutions, it provides a source of constant reinforcement, and, secondly, its long-term effects within the game are to lessen the luck factor of the dice and, once again, encourage crews to take extra care in order to obtain this strategic advantage. The object is to collect at least two of these cards until the holder wishes to use any two in place of a dice throw. These can be combined in any way the holder wishes in order to give a suitable translation. Figure 2 illustrates a possible situation where Translation Cards may be used to advantage.

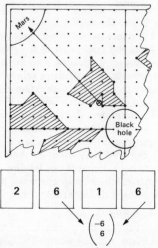

Figure 2. *The cross in this figure represents a craft heading for Mars. Below the board are the Translation Cards held by its crew. In this situation, only a dice throw of double six would take the craft safely to Mars. Now, this has odds of 35-1 against, whereas, by using two of the cards held, as indicated, the landing can be made.*

(d) *The Yellow Alert:* During the mission each crew is always on Yellow Alert. This situation involves each member of a team in solving a mathematical problem. Each player has, on his desk, a file containing a stock of Yellow Alert Cards and a stock of Red Alert Cards. Each of these cards is given a reference number, such as Y/6, R/23, etc. During the Commander's participation in the throwing of the dice he collects an Instruction Card which corresponds in terms of colour to the type of alert. For example in a Yellow Alert situation, that is, one in which the craft has avoided landing on a red area, the Commander might pick up a yellow card which reads: 'Your craft has suffered minor damage by asteroids. All members of your crew should take Yellow Alert Card Y/12.' When the Commander relays this information to his crew each takes the appropriate card and tackles the problem on it. The benefit of this type of arrangement is that game and academic content are separate as advocated by Cowan (1974); so that the stock of Instruction Cards for the game can be used every time, whatever the content.

(e) *The Red Alert:* This operates in the same way as the Yellow Alert except that the problems posed here are more difficult. A craft is called to Red Alert when a dice throw takes it into a point in one of the eight red areas in space or when a collision occurs (see below).

(f) *Collision course:* If two or more craft land on the same point they are deemed to have collided and each Commander picks up a Red Alert card. Where a choice of movement is available no craft can choose to follow a collison course.

LUCK

As is obvious, luck plays a part in SPACE QUEST, although this is intended to be less than is usual in games which involve dice. The fact that every dice throw allows a crew a measure of choice involves a certain amount of judgement. In addition, the use of the Translation Cards goes further towards eliminating the randomness of the dice. The luck factor of the dice is not eliminated, however. The advantage in retaining some degree of uncertainty is to ensure the novelty which a dice throw provides, as well as maintaining motivation, where the players can put defeat down to bad luck and try again.

THE CONTROLLER

Apart from the obvious role for the teacher to play in organising and generally supervising the class, he may also help pupils who are having difficulties with their calculations.

DEBRIEFING

As soon after each session of the game as possible teacher and pupils should discuss the game, its successes and failures. After all, what is the point of bothering to use a game without taking account of its affective outcomes?

Comment

The game SPACE QUEST is still in the early stages of development, and so it is perhaps presumptuous to speak of extending the game. However, if the game can be seen to be successful in backing up some standard mathematical material it is not beyond the bounds of reason to anticipate its use with a variety of subject matters. The sciences and modern languages spring readily to mind as possible subject areas to 'plug in' to the game superstructure.

References

Bloomer, J (1975) Reply to question in open forum of SAGSET Conference 1974. In Gibbs, G I and Howe, A (eds), *Academic Gaming and Simulation in Education and Training.* Kogan Page, London.

Cowan, J (1974) Identification of standard game forms with definable objectives. *Programmed Learning & Educational Technology*, 11, 4, 192-196.

Leith, G O M (1967) Developments in programmed learning. In Robinson, J and Barnes, N (eds), *New Media and Methods in Industrial Training*. BBC.

Stenhouse, L (1975) *An Introduction to Curriculum Research and Development*. London.

Watts, D (1975) Simulations and games with less able pupils. *SAGSET Journal*, 5, 1.

Evaluation procedures for simulation/gaming exercises

F Percival, *Robert Gordon's Institute of Technology, Aberdeen*

Despite the many impressive claims which are often made concerning the educational outcomes of gaming and simulation methods, many of which are non-cognitive, there is a paucity of sound experimental evidence to indicate if these benefits are actually achieved. The art of evaluation in this area is still in its infancy. Too often a simulation or game is judged to be successful merely on the grounds that it 'works', although this tells us nothing about the extent (if any) to which the aims of the exercise were achieved. This paper attempts to summarise what has emerged from evaluation research to date and will offer some reasons for the apparent slow rate of progress. Following this general survey, a selection of evaluation *tools* are explained and discussed with particular reference to their individual strengths and weaknesses including validity, ease of application and statistical treatment. Examples from the author's own experience of simulation evaluation are used to illustrate some of the difficulties which can arise. This paper highlights some of the problems, but does not claim to have all the answers.

Introduction

Claims concerning the advantages and effectiveness of using gaming and simulation techniques in education are manifold. Less common, however, is the presence of hard evidence to support these claims. If gaming and simulation exercises are to play an increasing role in education, the effectiveness of such methods must be more critically studied than has so far been the case. It is apparent that research in this area is still in its infancy, possibly due to a combination of the diversity of thought on the direction of evaluation, the poor quality of much of the previous evaluation work, and lastly the difficulty of devising valid and workable assessment tools where attitude and broader skill changes are involved.

The direction of evaluation

One current area of debate in education evaluation (not only in the field of games and simulations) is concerned with the respective merits of two distinctly polarised approaches. On one side there is the so-called agricultural/botanical approach and on the other the social/anthropological approach. These contrasting evaluation models have been discussed in some detail at a previous SAGSET conference (Bloomer, 1974). Briefly the agricultural/botanical paradigm is the *scientific* approach and originates from experiments set up to assess the effects of certain variables (soil, fertiliser, etc) on the growth of crops. The experiments have tight controls and the resulting outcomes can be relatively easily measured. This approach in educational experiments has led to systematic, objective-orientated evaluation procedures. The social/anthropological approach is more concerned with studying the ongoing process and uses far more subjective methods — the argument being that the variables in educational experiments cannot be readily controlled and the inputs and outputs are not easily measurable.

Within the narrower confines of the evaluaton of gaming and simulation situations a similar polarisation exists. Several experimenters have adopted the traditional scientific approach based on the intended objectives of the exercise in question. Some of these have used this approach to compare gaming methods with more traditional instruction — an exercise which is itself fraught with difficulties. Some workers have, however, argued that the worth of games and simulations cannot be expressed by formal evaluations and statistics (Tansey, 1973).

This was echoed by Bloomer (1975) when she stated that formal measurement of *input* and *output* in simulations is often invalid as the so-called *input* and *output* is varied, complex and often cannot be specified with certainty let alone accuracy. In addition, she argued that simulations involve complex human interactions which input/output evaluation methods ignore. Walford (1975) has also attacked the application of traditional objective-orientated evaluation methods to simulations, citing the following major objections:

(a) simulations usually involve complex mixtures of cognitive and affective intention and these are not easily specified,
(b) simulations are essentially open-ended, and therefore unpredictable in outcome.

On the validity of evaluation methods, Shubick (1972) has criticised the small amount of attention paid to sorting out different simulation uses and the corresponding slow development of a *range* of assessment and evaluation criteria relevant to particular uses. This degree of discrimination could lead to the construction of more evaluation procedures which could then be applied to the particular objectives under consideration in individual simulations.

It is obvious that many workers are unhappy with the purely traditional *scientific* approach to evaluation and many of their reasons are valid. On the other hand, however, a simulation or game is too often judged to be a success purely because a teacher has considered the package to have 'worked' with his pupils, which tells us very little about what the pupils actually gained from doing the package. The usual grounds for this conclusion are that the mechanics of the exercise worked and that the pupils 'appeared to enjoy the experience'. A further criticism of this type of subjective assessment is that the teacher's impression may well be coloured by novelty or Hawthorne effects, ie the success of the package may be due more to the enthusiasm of the teacher than the materials themselves.

Clearly there must be some middle ground between what purports to be a purely objective approach and a purely subjective one. It is, however, impossible to generalise where this middle ground should lie — this is surely a function of what the simulation or game is trying to achieve.

Previous evaluation work

Many attempted evaluations of simulations and games have been published, by far the majority of work being American. However, despite the quantity of work it is apparent that very few well-planned and unambiguous research attempts have been reported. Fletcher (1971) and Wentworth and Lewis (1973) have published useful and critical reviews of research on the evaluation of games and simulations in education. Fletcher criticised the approach of many researchers who investigated particular simulations or games, each study employing its own battery of tests to measure different sets of variables. Such approaches made attempts to replicate findings virtually impossible. Among the reasons cited by Fletcher for the low quality of available research were:

(a) standardised, workable games and simulations were lacking,
(b) simulations varied enormously in objectives, structure and level of sophistication,
(c) most simulations studied were not adequate models of reality.

Fletcher, however, made little mention of the lack of adequate evaluation methods which would appear to be a major contributing factor to the level of research quality. Point (b) above does not appear to be valid criticism as one of the major attractions of simulation techniques is the very fact that they are so versatile as to be able to vary enormously in objectives and sophistication.

Wentworth and Lewis were also very critical of much of the research they reviewed mainly because of 'inadequate testing procedures and research design, use of unsophisticated statistics, and inability to determine important variables'. Despite their reservations about the standard of much of the work, Wentworth and Lewis concluded from the research which had been done that:

(a) simulations do not appear to have any advantage over other methods in teaching content, ie the lower cognitive aspects of learning. If content learning is the major instructional goal, then it appears that other less demanding techniques, such as lectures, reading or programmed learning, may be at least as effective. On the purely cognitive side it seems that the most important function of a game or simulation is that it can be used to *reinforce* previously learned skills;
(b) simulations appear to have a positive influence on student attitudes. However, this may be due to the novelty and quality of such exercises rather than any other factors;
(c) simulations appear to be influential in encouraging students to become actively involved in the learning process. This appears to be one universally observed advantage, ie students become motivated and appear to enjoy the activity and in this, the less able appear to be marginally better off than the others.

However, Wentworth and Lewis appreciated that more research of a better quality is required if these tentative conclusions are to be confirmed and if solutions to many more unanswered questions are to be provided. They suggested a fruitful line of enquiry might be to use observation instruments to measure identifiable learning behaviours, arguing that paper-and-pencil assessment methods have limited measurement capabilities when applied to simulations and games. One further tentative finding of research to date is that transfer of learning *may* be taking place. If this were to be confirmed the status of games and simulations as educational tools would rise considerably as transfer of learning appears difficult to achieve.

Problems in measuring attitude and broader skill changes

From what has been said previously, it would appear that the value of using gaming and simulation methods in education lies in the *affective* domain and in the development of broad skills such as communication skills, problem-solving skills, decision-making skills, and interpersonal skills. It is often attempted to achieve such changes via cognitive content, so that the cognitive, affective and broad skill areas are closely interwoven. The measuring of changes in these areas is no simple task. There is no one right way and it would seem prudent to adopt several approaches, mainly of a paper-and-pencil kind, although observational and interview techniques also have a place. Written tests lead to all sorts of linguistic problems and such tests also have problems of validity — students may give the answer they feel the examiner wants. An associated problem is how to analyse the information once it has been obtained — much attitude research can be criticised on this score. However, some attempts have been made, despite all the difficulties, to adapt and develop evaluation tools which, although not perfect, may provide some insight into the effectiveness of gaming and simulation techniques; some of these are discussed below.

Some evaluation procedures

The assessment procedures commonly used in education are concerned almost entirely with measuring the attainment of *cognitive* objectives, eg knowledge gained. Such procedures include essay-type questions, objective items and unique-answer questions. In terms of reliability, validity, ease of application and statistical treatment the last two question types appear well suited to measuring purely cognitive attainment from a game or simulation. The actual experimental design adopted is dependent on several factors including numbers available, availability of suitable control groups, etc. The main problem arises when one attempts to measure the development of attitudes and skills which are not purely cognitive as traditional assessment methods are often inappropriate. The suitability of assessment techniques is further restricted by the necessity of having procedures which are simple in application, acceptable to students, as valid and reliable as possible and which can be meaningfully analysed.

Such conditions limit the choice to methods which could be broadly classified under two headings: observational techniques and self-reporting techniques.

OBSERVATIONAL TECHNIQUES

When certain attitudinal objectives are involved, or when development of communication or interpersonal skills is a major aim of a simulation or game, direct observation of individual or group behaviour can be of use in monitoring achievement. Closed-circuit television or a simple audiotape recording of the activities in a group session can act as a permanent record of the exercise so that subsequent analysis of the session can be attempted. The analysis can take the form of simply cataloguing the numbers and patterns of communications within a group or may reach the complexity of an interaction process analysis (Bales, 1950) which may provide an insight into the social psychology of groups and the personalities of group members.

SELF-REPORTING TECHNIQUES

Several such techniques have been devised. *Likert scales* are commonly used in attitude measurement and appear deceptively easy to devise and administer. There is, however, a lot of skill required to produce good Likert items which are valid and which provide good discrimination. Essentially, a Likert rating scale consists of a list of statements, and the person answering has to make a judgement on every statement, often selecting one response from a number of degrees of agreement and disagreement. The number of points on the scale depends on the requirements of the setter, although the provision of an even number of possibilities makes it impossible for students to take refuge in a completely neutral category. Although common practice, it is statistically unwise to add together scores for separate statements on a Likert scale to obtain an overall attitude score. This may only be done if the statements are measuring the same dimension and if the frequency of responses from agree to disagree form a ratio scale. It should, however, be possible to use Likert-type scales to recognise variations in attitudes and opinions by comparing students' responses to individual statements in a test administered before and after a teaching unit designed to modify such opinions, or by comparison with a matched control group.

The *semantic differential technique*, first developed by Osgood *et al* (1957), has been used as a tool for various types of assessment to measure connotations of any given concept for an individual. Word pairs of antonyms, such as 'valuable/worthless' and 'interesting/boring', are joined by a scale from, for example, +3 to −3 including zero. The method assumes that the word pairs are opposites. This assumption may not always be valid as different words may have different meanings to individual students. A major advantage of the method is that it is very rapid to construct and complete. Hadden (1975) has pointed out that rating scales such as +3 to −3 or 1 to 5, not only in semantic differential techniques but also in other assessment techniques, are often statistically groundless, and if used, are a basic fault of such techniques. This is because the scores are on ordinal and not interval scales, eg a person who 'strongly agrees' with a given statement and is given a score of 3, does not necessarily agree three times more strongly than a person who 'slightly agrees' with the statement and is given a score of 1. Such scores provide only an *indication* of the relative strength of opinions or attitudes between different people. A further criticism has been that adverbs such as 'extremely', 'very', 'fairly', 'slightly', etc do not mean the same to all people, and hence the interval between, say, 'slightly interesting' and 'fairly interesting' on a rating scale may not be the same as the interval between 'fairly interesting' and 'very interesting' to some students.

Rating objectives by means of a grid in which the objectives of an exercise are listed and the student asked to indicate whether each objective has been 'well achieved' through to 'not achieved at all' has been reported by Vesper and Adams (1969) in addition to other workers. The rating is usually done on a five-point scale, but variations are possible. Most of the statistical criticisms levelled at other rating scales discussed also apply to this method if responses are scored on an ordinal scale. However, this method may prove useful in some cases where no other suitable technique exists for assessing the achievement of certain objectives, or as a check on other measures.

Situational techniques were first described by Handy and Johnstone (1973), and have recently been used by Hadden (1975) and N Reid (personal communication, 1977). Such techniques have so far been used to assess the modes of thought and scientific attitudes of students, as compared to their attitudes *to* science. Students are involved in tackling a problem or situation which in itself need not be of a scientific nature, but which requires students to think scientifically to solve it, for example by controlling variables. Such situations involve students using the 'broader skills' of a science education such as problem-solving and decision-making skills and rely little on previous lower cognitive skills.

Although little work has so far been done on the use of this technique, it would intuitively appear that it should have a reasonably high validity compared to the rather artificial assessment procedures discussed above. One problem may be that the method is cumbersome, and questions may be difficult and time-consuming to construct and apply.

Interviews with students have sometimes been used to assess the effectiveness of simulations or games. A well-constructed interview procedure is, however, not easy to achieve and administer fairly, and even more difficult to analyse effectively. However, it would appear that the validity of this method of evaluation would be high.

The above list is by no means exhaustive, but gives examples of techniques which the author has found useful when attempting to evaluate simulations. They vary quite markedly in ease of construction and validity — an inverse relationship being apparent, with interviews being most difficult to construct yet most valid and rating objectives easiest to construct but least valid.

Each technique has certain drawbacks and no single technique is the best in all situations. It is probably most profitable to use a battery of evaluation procedures, using alternative methods to reduce the limitations of validity and reliability of any one technique, and to note whether a pattern of responses emerges — always allowing for the fact that a score on one scale cannot be directly compared to a score on another.

Analysis

Much educational research where rating scales are involved can be criticised in terms of invalid statistics. For example, some researchers have added up scores from items on an attitude scale and arrive at a number expressing the student's attitude to the subject in question. This is unreasonable, simply because there is no assurance that individual items test the same attitude dimension. It seems obvious, therefore, that items must be analysed individually, and several methods have been used including simple statistical analysis (eg chi-square), graphical methods or even presentation of raw data. Also, while it is important that overall trends should be identified, it is equally important that individual measurements against the general trend are identified and explained.

References

Bales, R F (1950) *Interaction Process Analysis.* Addison Wesley, New York.

Bloomer, J (1974) Future developments in evaluation. Paper presented at 1974 SAGSET conference.

Bloomer, J (1975) Paradigms of evaluation. *SAGSET Journal,* 5, 36-37.

Fletcher, J L (1971) The effectiveness of simulation games as learning environments: a proposed programme of research. *Simulations and Games,* 2, 473-488.

Hadden, R A (1975) *A study of affective objectives in the teaching of chemistry.* MSc thesis, University of Glasgow.

Handy, J and Johnstone A H (1973) Science education — what is left? In *The Discipline of Chemistry — Its Place in Education.* The Chemical Society, Education Division, London.

Likert, R (1932) A technique for the measurement of attitudes. *Archives of Psychology,* 140, 55-70.

Osgood, C E, Suci, G J and Tannenbaum, P H (1957) *The Measurement of Meaning.* University of Illinois Press.

Shubik, M (1972) *On the Scope of Gaming.* Rand Corporation.

Tansey, P J (1973) Evaluation, statistics both slammed. *Simulation/Gaming News,* 1, 4-12.

Vesper, K H and Adams, J L (1969) Evaluating learning from the case method. *Engineering Education,* October, 104-106.

Walford, R (1975) Evaluation. *SAGSET Journal,* 5, 20-22.

LANGUAGE ASSISTANT GAME

Ray McAleese, *University of Aberdeen*
and Geoff Hare, *University of Bradford*

Each year some 1,500 language students go abroad from this country to European cities and towns where they work in schools as language assistants. Until now little or no training has been provided locally (in their own college or university). This paper describes a game that is part of a larger training programme developed in the University of Aberdeen. LAG is a game that simulates explaining; it is currently in two forms, TRAINING and CONTEST. It has been used for two years with assistants both in Aberdeen and abroad.

Background

A unique feature of courses in universities, polytechnics and colleges of education leading to a language degree or teaching qualification is that students spend part of their time abroad. Since 1930 an annual total of some 1,500 students go to Europe under the language assistant scheme. In return more than 4,000 language assistants from Europe, Africa and America come to this country. The majority of students go abroad under the foreign language assistant scheme, run by the Central Bureau for Educational Visits and Exchanges. Others, in order to fulfil residence requirements from their colleges, perhaps attend a foreign university or go in conjunction with firms (Willis, 1977). One of the main purposes of the assistant scheme is to give students additional experience in learning a foreign language by enabling them to live in the foreign country.

English language assistants normally spend an eight-month period in a school, acting in the capacity of an assistant to English language teachers. They take conversation classes and act as 'representatives' of the UK. For this they are paid a reasonable salary by the host government. In return they *experience* living, talking, working, being in a foreign country. For some time there has been doubt about the quantity and quality of preparation these students receive before they take up their jobs. The common view was that 'if they are able to get by without getting into serious trouble, then it's a good scheme'. Not all teachers in this country took this view . . . fortunately.

For some time the departments of French and education in the University of Aberdeen have been collaborating on providing initial training for English language assistants going to France. At a national level, there is a short course run by the Scottish section of the Central Bureau in the June before the students go to France (in September). In late September a further three-day course is organised by the British Institute in Paris, in conjunction with the Office National des Universités et Écoles Françaises. Although these courses have their uses, they tend to be large, anonymous and formal gatherings. In Aberdeen we have been attempting to provide a more personalised approach (Hare and McAleese, 1976a). One particular emphasis has been a concentration on *teaching skills*. After all, the students will spend a full academic year acting as teachers, if not being teachers. It seems a curious situation that untrained students should be unleashed upon unsuspecting French pupils without a hint of some *professional* training. (Few other examples of this behaviour exist, apart from teachers in universities and polytechnics!)

In order to provide some training materials, the authors undertook an action research project partly funded by the Nuffield Foundation (Hare and McAleese, 1976b). As part of this work they visited France, talking to and observing assistants in their day-to-day work in schools. One of the more interesting training materials developed is an explaining game, LAG.

Development of the game

The LANGUAGE ASSISTANT GAME (LAG) is an academic game (Tansey, 1971); its aim is to give language assistants practice in the teaching skill *clarity of explanation*. Explaining has been defined in various ways:

> To explain is to relate an object, event or state of affairs to some other object, event or state of affairs; or to show the relationship between an event or state of affairs and a principle of generalisation (Bellack *et al*, 1968).

Or

> An explanation deals with the way something works or fits together, causes something, leads to something, is attained, has purposes, functions or goals (Smith and Meux, 1962).

In the language assistant context it simply means 'the general type of activity that assistants use to help pupils understand or comprehend textual passages, reading, etc'. Explaining is an integral part of teaching or speaking a language, and a very important part of the *comprehension* phase of language learning.

We realised, from our discussions with French teachers, that in general they were dissatisfied with the way assistants were able to explain passages in conversation classes. The idea of a game to help our assistants came after a particularly useful conversation with an English teacher in Bourg-en-Bresse. We reproduce here a transcript of the salient points from the interview.

Q: You would discourage absolutely the use of French by the assistant in the classroom?
T: Yes, that's the most important problem, and we have trouble every time with that, because they find it so much easier to speak French to the pupils than English.
Q: What techniques do they need to know to be able to do without the use of translation?
T: When a pupil says he doesn't understand a word, the assistants don't know how to explain it, so they just translate it. What I try to do when I have an assistant in my class is I show her how to give examples to illustrate words and idioms.
Q: So to explain in English another English word you must give examples . . . for example, 'pulling one's leg' . . . is a key point in your teaching method?
T: And with a word like 'Cheers', you'd have to demonstrate it, mime it . . . This is very important. It is a skill that the assistant must know. This is the main problem.
Q: You're not asking them to explain something in the sense that explaining something is rather complicated in English. You're asking them to give relevant and related examples so that the pupils make a link and say 'the penny's dropped'.

T: So after the explanation, the pupil associates a phrase in English with a situation. They don't need the translation, because it comes to them like that, in the situation. That's what they want to say and so you give it to them when they need it. But you've got to check to see if the pupils have understood or not, by asking them to give their own examples.

Q: What would the assistant do to help you with this role? How does the assistant fit in to this teaching strategy?

T: Well, the assistant should do the same. The problem is they can't usually. They don't know how to do it. When the pupil says, 'I don't understand such and such a word', they give a synonym, which is no good because it's sometimes more complicated than the word itself and it doesn't say anything. There are no true, absolute synonyms. So one word is no good. What we need is a sentence — we need the word in its situation. That is very difficult. You've got to be trained to do it.

Q: I don't think any of the students we saw could do that successfully.

T: No, that's the problem. That's why we take them with us in our classes, because we can help them. When somebody stops them and says, 'I don't understand such and such a word', and the assistant can't explain what it means or show them what it means, I do it. If the assistant is clever she gradually becomes able to do it herself. One of our assistants is quite good at it now. But she didn't understand it at all at the beginning.

The problem was quite clear. We had to devise methods of training assistants in using various methods of explaining meanings. As will be seen, the solution to the explaining problem came about because, as well as looking at the content in training our assistants, we were trying to introduce *self-instructional* methods, in order that the assistants, after some initial training, could work on skills on their own or in small groups outside the university. It also became clear that we would have to 'simulate a French classroom' in order to provide prior practice for our students. This idea gave the first part of the solution: a *simulation* or game that enabled the assistants to practise explaining. By making the exercise a *game* we were also introducing an element of enjoyment into the situation as well as an incentive element (Tansey, 1971).

Our solution to the problem of explaining was to devise a game that assistants could play in pairs, or groups, that simulated the explaining situation in a class where a number of words, etc, had to be explained to French pupils.

The first attempt was to simulate the real situation with role play where in certain instances, eg in an oral or written test for comprehension work, the words and phrases used by the assistants can be 'nonsense' to the French pupils. That is, they are unknown and as a result the assistant has to explain. We thought of associating *nonsense words*, eg a *blut*, a *splod*, to *prive*, etc, with real words, and requiring the assistants to work in pairs, as first one used a nonsense word in a sentence and the other tried to guess the real word, and so on. For example:

nonsense word	to *splod*
real word	to break

One student would have to explain 'to break' without using the word but using the nonsense word, 'to *splod*': if I jumped out of the window I would *splod* my arm.

Other students would have to guess the meaning of *splod* or rather, in practice, supply the verb, to break. The basic assumption behind this simulation is that the nonsense word in the simulation corresponds to the unknown word in the real classroom situation. If, in the simulation, the explanation is precise enough to generate the original word in the guesser's mind, then the same explanation of the word encountered in the real classroom situation would (the game assumes) suggest the meaning of this new word in the foreign language learner's mind. This hypothesis underlies the game as a whole in all its versions, but in the original version, as described above, the nonsense element of the game became intrusive in practice. A modified solution was needed. The solution we adopted was to use the initial letters of the title of what we were doing — a Language Assistant Game — to represent the unknown word we were using, and to use a *lag*, to *lag*, *laggish* and *lagging* in all possible situations. This was the only major change.

Explaining so far has been assumed to be a homogeneous skill. Clearly this is not so. There are many types of explaining: we identified six types commonly usable in the conversation class (there are certainly others, but these six cover the most frequent usage in conversation classes):

1. giving an example
2. giving a description or definition
3. using the unknown word in context
4. giving a synonym
5. demonstrating
6. giving the French translation.

We now had a game where assistants had to explain to a partner a word or phrase, without using that word, but *using one of six different types of explanation*. For example, explaining 'the penny's dropped' by using it *in context*, or 'closing time' by *giving a definition*. At this stage we were able to have some trial sessions with assistants to see if we could devise a suitable set of rules to enable the game to be useful. From some French school textbooks we identified a list of words from passages on 'the British way of life'. Some 20 Aberdeen assistants volunteered to be guinea-pigs! The rules for these sessions were:

The game was played in groups of four or five. The assistants took it in turn to be *explainer* or Teacher with the others acting as a guessing panel or class. (In this sense the game is not unlike CHARADES.)

We constructed two packs of cards that were to contain instructions and words to be explained. Before each turn two packs of cards were shuffled — *a Technique pack*, containing cards with the type of explanation, ie in *context*, *translation* etc, and a pack with the words to be explained; *a Word pack*.

The Teacher then selected the top card of each pile, first a Technique card and then a Word card.

Using the technique indicated above, the Teacher attempted to explain the word on the Word card without actually using it. Where it was necessary (for reasons of syntax) to use some replacement he/she substituted *lag*, to *lag*, etc. For example, the *word* 'policeman', and the *technique* 'context' gives: 'This morning as I was coming to school, a *lag* put up his hand and stopped the car, he said; "Hello, Hello, Hello."'

The class, after consulting, attempted to guess the word; only three guesses were allowed. Two rules governed the scoring:

1. *If the word was guessed* by a member of the class, the Teacher scored a mark related to the difficulty of the explaining technique. The following scores applied:

give translation	*1 point*
demonstrate	*2 points*
give an example	*3 points*
give a description	*4 points*
use a synonym	*5 points*
use the word in context	*5 points.*

The hierarchy was based loosely on an idea of the relative usefulness of each method in foreign language teaching. This was an arbitrary and subjective decision, but there seemed to be some agreement among players as to the order, if not the magnitude, of the marks. The member of the class guessing scored one point in all cases.

2. *If the class did not guess*, the Teacher was allowed two additional tries. If the explanation did not elicit the correct answer, then the Teacher scored no points and the turn passed on. If a Technique card was turned over that was impossible (*demonstrate: bacon and eggs*), then the next card was turned over. Only one pass was allowed.

The rules proved adequate, although there was some explaining required to begin with! These rules gave the game a fairly competitive spirit. There was a chance element, but the dominant feature was that the better at explaining the Teacher was, the more points he scored.

During these trial sessions the game was played in a variety of ways:

(a) randomly selecting the technique,
(b) the Teacher or explainer selecting the most appropriate technique — in practice this meant that one where the Teacher could be sure of scoring points!
(c) in teams: the group were divided into two teams. Each team drew up a series of words on a topic they selected. Among those selected were 'my home town' and 'school life in the UK'. When the word lists were complete they were exchanged, with members of team A taking it in turn to explain team B's list to other members of their group and *vice versa*,
(d) in pairs: an explainer and a guesser,
(e) in threes: an explainer, a guesser and a referee.

The participants generally agreed that the game was fun to play, and that they found explaining more difficult than expected. There was some reservation about whether the game actually 'taught anything' but it was agreed that in a further modified form it would be usable as a language teaching game in French classrooms, particularly with the top three classes (by age).

After the initial trials we felt that it might be possible to organise a contest for our assistants to find 'the *lag* of the year'! The idea was to keep up interest in explaining by having a public contest where contestants would try to explain to a distinguished panel a list of words, phrases etc. The panel would try to guess the 'mystery' word and the contestant would score one point for a correct guess. The following set of rules was devised:

1. Each contestant will be given two minutes to explain 15 words or phrases.
2. The words must be taken in the sequence given. A contestant may pass if unable to explain.
3. Any technique of explanation is allowed except using the French translation (for reasons related to the methodology of language teaching [direct method]).
4. None of the words appearing on the cards may be used. Instead the words *lag, to lag, laggish* and *lagging* may be used.
5. The panel will be allowed three guesses at an explanation, if the contestant wishes.
6. The winner will be the contestant scoring most points. In the event of a tie, an elimination round will be held.
7. The referee will be the final arbiter in the event of a dispute.

The rules were a development of the original idea. The modifications, eg the time limit, taking the words in a sequence, etc, were introduced to increase the gaming element and to introduce an element of strategy into the rules. In its final form the contest was not unlike the BBC television series MASTERMIND.

Eight future assistants took part in the contest, with a number of others including university staff in the audience. The panel was made up of members of the university, the local college of education and the Director of the Scottish section of the Central Bureau for Educational Visits and Exchanges. A winner was found at the end of one round; he scored 13 out of a possible 15 points. The university French Club provided a small prize and it was presented by the headmaster of the local *Total* French school. The lists of words were arranged so that each one contained an equal sample of phrases, single words, nouns, adjectives, idiomatic expressions, etc.

A post-mortem after the contest identified one or two problems both with the rules and with the 'spirit of the game'. Contestants, panel and audience enjoyed the afternoon, and the atmosphere was relaxed and informal. The specific points needing attention were related to the gaming side of the contest. One or two of the contestants used a fairly liberal interpretation of the rules to explain words — to explain the word 'how' a contestant held up her hand in a Red Indian-type salute! We felt afterwards that this type of explanation, while it did not spoil the contest, and if anything improved it, was not sufficiently in keeping with the educational aim of the game. It depended too much on a shared cultural experience of contestants and panel — something that is not relevant in the English assistant/French pupil contact in France. The very fact, however, of discussing this problem with the assistants helped to make them more aware of which types of explanation were useful in the teaching situation and which were not.

As a result of our experience with LAG we have been able to devise two sets of rules for the game. One is intended as a proper training simulation, the other suitable for a class game in France or as a contest in this country. We have called these games LAG (TRAINING) and LAG (CONTEST). (For details of LAG (CONTEST), see Hare and McAleese, 1976b, and McAleese and Hare, 1977.)

LAG (TRAINING)

LAG (TRAINING) is intended to give trainee assistants practice in the general teaching skill of explaining. Explaining is defined as the skill of helping pupils understand or comprehend, of relating or saying how objects, events or affairs fit together, function or come about. Explaining has a number of subsets;

sometimes they are mutually exclusive, sometimes they overlap.

giving an example	Harrow, Eton and Gordonstoun are examples of *public schools*
giving a description or definition	a large vehicle that can carry up to 50 fare-paying passengers on the roads is a *bus* *to stump someone* is to say something that the other person does not understand
using a context	before I go to bed I take my clothes off, I get *'undressed'* (implied)
giving a synonym	policeman and *bobby*
demonstrating	*cheers!* . . . the player holds one hand as if holding a glass and then raises it to his mouth and says 'Cheers!' *(Lag)*
giving a translation	*uniform* means *uniforme* or to be *homesick* is *avoir le mal du pays*

RULES

1. The game is played in threes. Players take it in turns, during a playing session, to be explainer, guesser or referee (see below).
2. A concept is agreed upon, for example 'British characteristics', 'my home town', etc — one that would arise in classroom teaching (see suggested words in the Appendix to this paper for three concepts).
3. All three players write down 15 words or expressions related to the concept. Five minutes is the maximum time permitted. You can write the words as a list on a sheet of paper, or on the blank cards provided.
4. Players are called referee, explainer and guesser. The referee gives his list of words to the explainer (the person on his right) who attempts to explain the words to the guesser on *his* right.
5. On completion of a turn, the explainer becomes the referee, the guesser becomes the explainer, and the referee is the guesser. Play rotates anti-clockwise. On each occasion, the explainer uses words devised by the player on his left.
6. You are provided with a pack of cards relating to the technique of explaining to be used. Shuffle the cards and turn them face down (the words 'Technique card' showing on top). Word cards are placed adjacent (make sure the guesser cannot see the words).
7. The explainer selects a Technique card from the top of the pile and places it face up on the table, so that all three players can read it. He then selects the first word on his list or the top card on his Word pile and makes a discreet note on his score card of the technique and the word. The explainer attempts to explain the word to his partner (see example below). Where the explainer must use the word being explained in order to make syntactical or grammatical sense, he substitutes the words *lag, lagging,* or *laggish*. The word being explained must *not*, of course, be used. It is likely that it may

sometimes be impossible to explain a particular word using the specific technique, for example, 'demonstrate' a 'public school'. If this is the case the next Technique card is turned over. The explainer is not penalised. (Avoid using this let-out wherever the combination is only difficult rather than impossible.)

Example
The explainer turns over the Technique card *context* and the Word card *butterfingers*. He explains '. . . when a player in a ball game like rugby or cricket drops the ball, when it has been thrown or hit towards him in such a way that he could catch it easily, the crowd may call him . . . *lag!*'

8. The guesser is allowed one attempt and if a word is guessed correctly the explainer gets the score related to the technique used. The following scores apply:

example	*6 points*
context	*6 points*
description/definition	*5 points*
demonstrate	*3 points*
synonym	*3 points*
translation	*1 point*

If the guesser cannot guess the word, there is no score.

9. If the guesser challenges the technique, ie thinks that the technique used by the explainer is not that selected, and the referee agrees, then no score is given for that attempt.
10. Normally there is no time limit for the explainer to complete his list, but a maximum of five minutes may be agreed in advance.
11. When there is a dispute, the referee is the sole arbiter.
12. The game should emphasise practice at *explaining* not at guessing. The guesser is playing a collaborative role, judging whether in the real situation a pupil would have been able to understand, *not* acting as a member of a panel. He should be helpful. However, the competitive element does add further interest to the game.
13. The winner is the player with most points.
14. Players should keep a record of the techniques used. Practice is then possible in seldom used categories.

A slightly modified version of the game is available from the authors (McAleese and Hare, 1977); it consists of a game manual with examples and pre-printed packs of technique and word cards. Sample word lists appear in the Appendix to this paper.

Conclusions

The evaluation of this game has been formative and not summative. However, we have some evidence that is rather more quantitative than the evaluations so far referred to. During the 1976 training programme for assistants, we asked all the participants to complete a questionnaire which measured how *useful* the students found individual parts of the training, and how *enjoyable* individual parts were. On both dimensions LAG came top: 5.34 (enjoyment) and 5.52

(usefulness), on a range 1.00 poor, 6.00 excellent. The mean scores for all training were 4.65 (enjoyment) and 5.21 (usefulness). Clearly such figures *prove* little, but they *indicate* worth of the game and the general approach.

The potential of such an approach has yet to be fully identified. We recognise that our attempts are initial and at best tentative, but we can indicate some features that may show the strength of the approach. Educational games are in accord with modern attempts to innovate in teaching and training. They are (as is LAG) *dynamic, problem-based* and *participatory* (see Teather, 1978): LAG deals with a constantly changing and infinitely variable situation — the language assistant in the classroom (dynamic). LAG was a response to a specific problem. It is however multidisciplinary and transferable to other languages and other training situations (problem-based). Lastly, there is active participation in the ongoing processes of their own training by the assistants (participatory).

Boocock and Schild (1968) writing in the last chapter of their book say: 'Games design is not only *not* a science, it is hardly a craft, but rather an art in the sense that we have no explicit rules to transmit.'

We would have to agree wholeheartedly with their sentiment. The ten years since they wrote their book has hardly changed the situation; however, we put forward LAG as a paradigm for a particular class of simulation game, a paradigm that will no doubt be bettered.

Acknowledgements

We are grateful to the following for their help and encouragement: The Nuffield Foundation, Total Oil Marine, M Hervier and the pupils of the Lycée Total in Aberdeen and, of course, our students without whom none of this would have been possible.

References

Bellack, A *et al* (1968) *The Language of the Classroom*. Teachers College Press, Columbia University, New York.

Boocock, S S and Schild, E O (1968) *Simulation Games in Learning*. Sage Publications, USA.

Hare, G and McAleese, R (1976a) Training the modern language assistant — a personalised approach. *Modern Languages in Scotland*, 9, 104-109.

Hare, G and McAleese, R (1976b) *Language assistant training — a report of work supported by the Nuffield Foundation*. University of Aberdeen (available from ERIC, ED 134 005).

McAleese, R and Hare, G (1977) *Language Assistant Game — Playing Manual*. University of Aberdeen.

Smith, B O and Meux, M O (1962) *A Study of the Logic of Teaching*. University of Illinois, Urbana, USA.

Tansey, P (1971) *Educational Aspects of Simulation*. McGraw-Hill, London.

Teather, D C B (1978) Simulations. In Unwin, D and McAleese, R *Encyclopaedia of Educational Media Communications and Technology.* Macmillan, London (in press).

Willis, F *et al* (1977) *Residence Abroad and the Student of Modern Languages: A Preliminary Survey.* Modern Languages Centre and Postgraduate School of Studies in Research in Education, University of Bradford.

Appendix

Words which can be used in LAG (TRAINING)

British characteristics (average difficulty)	General expressions (very difficult)	School (difficult)
town planning	to fall in with	assembly
dour	to stump someone	uniform
out of date	to undress	comprehensive school
to care about	to come again	public school
pub	to be afraid	a double period
darts	to be afraid of	bicycle shed
policemen	over and over again	prefect
cheers!	the morning after the	school council
fish and chips	night before	homework
helmet	near at hand	take 100 lines!
kilt		class exam
time gentlemen please!		boarding school
bacon and eggs		form master
public school		

Computer-based games and simulations in geography: a problem in innovation and diffusion

D R F Walker, *Loughborough University of Technology*

Games and simulations are of growing importance in the teaching of geography, reflecting important changes in the content and methodology of the subject. Many of the games and simulations that have been developed involve tedious calculations, and this is often a limiting factor in the design of potentially valuable new developments. The use of the computer can resolve this problem as will be shown by widely used examples. As with many aspects of educational technology the problem is in institutionalising this new development, which involves providing easily used materials and information. Supported by a research grant from the National Development Programme in Computer Assisted Learning, the Geographical Association has established a service to geography teachers to remove barriers to the adoption of computer use and to diffuse information. This service may provide a model for further work by subject associations in the adoption of subject related educational technology. The activities and findings of the research project are described.

Introduction

Towards the end of a two-year period of research into the use of the computer for the teaching of geography, much of it concerned with computer-based games and simulations, it is possible to give some preliminary thoughts and findings that may be of interest not only to geographers but to all those concerned with the development of teaching strategies and with games and simulations in particular. Early use of the computer in geographical education occurred in the very early 1970s, and by 1973 the Geographical Association undertook a survey to find out who was involved and to discover what type of use was being made of the computer as a resource. The survey showed that there was considerable potential for the use of the computer and it seemed likely that the limited number of teachers with access to computing would increase. The problem was that the computer is a very difficult resource to use without some form of external assistance, preferably from educationists who understand the teachers' objectives. In 1975 the National Development Programme in Computer Assisted Learning offered a research grant to the Geographical Association to discover what sort of assistance teachers needed and the extent to which a subject association could provide it.

Both games and simulations and the use of the computer are new developments in geography teaching although both are firmly rooted in the development of the subject itself. It has been argued that new curricula innovations should not be introduced until they have been carefully evaluated, but in the case of both these innovations evaluation is patently inappropriate or even misleading, largely because the innovations are not new ways of achieving old objectives, but are strategies for achieving new objectives, objectives which are to a certain extent suggested by the strategy.

The problem with evaluation of innovations is that it can only be applied to situations in which two strategies are used to achieve the same ends. Some research into games in geography teaching in 1974 (Walker, 1974) showed that for the imparting of factual information games were certainly no worse than traditional methods and need take no longer, but of course it was not possible to compare the important understandings that were imparted by the game to those that are imparted by traditional methods or to evaluate any supposed advantages that traditional teaching had over games and simulations. Similarly, the use of the computer has been evaluated only for those tasks where it replicates or replaces a traditional method in seeking objectives that are already well established. It may not necessarily do well in such comparisons. In the USA the major use of the computer has been in the field of programmed learning where the machine in effect replicates the teaching machine, and is known as Computer Aided Instruction (CAI). Fielding (1974) prepared a course text in geography relying heavily on CAI units, but had to admit that

> they are not presented as computer listings for two reasons. First, CAI is still uneconomic. User costs have not fallen as was anticipated when the first units were prepared in the latter 1960s. Second, the wide range of languages and the even wider range of equipment used for CAI make computer listings difficult to use (Fielding, 1974).

Where the computer has been used there have been reservations about the effectiveness of that use. The Carnegie Commission on Higher Education in its 1975 report concludes that

> the primary target opportunity for the computer in higher education is in enrichment activities. For almost all kinds of material problem-solving, games and simulations can provide the learner with better ways of integrating and testing the knowledge that he has acquired.

Evaluation tends to compare two strategies for reaching the same objective. For a number of reasons it seems quite inappropriate to use this approach to computers and games and simulations; both of them reflect a revolution in the nature of academic geography and this revolution is now having a major impact on the teaching of the subject. New 'O' and 'H' grades in Scotland and new 'A' level examinations in England and Wales reflect these changes. The academic revolution took place largely in the 1950s, and Burton (1963) describes the nature of the changes and the fact that all the substantial argument is over. It took some time to cross the Atlantic, and even longer to penetrate to the schools. The revolution consisted of a shift from a qualitative, classificatory and descriptive mode, without theorising and generalisations; as Hartshorne stated, 'No universals need be evolved, other than the general law of geography that all its areas are unique' (Hartshorne, 1939); its main aim was to provide an 'accurate, orderly and rational interpretation of the variable character of the earth's surface' (Hartshorne, 1959). The new mode described by Burton and amplified in greater detail by Harvey (1969) is that of geography as a social science, attempting to explain by the formation of theories.

The search for explanation is of a slightly different nature in the social sciences, such as geography, compared to the natural sciences. In the natural sciences the basic unit is the molecule or atom, in the social sciences the basic unit is the person, and the person is much more variable than the atom or molecule. So attempts to explain by means of predictive theory must be supplemented either by the use of stochastic models in which the variations introduced by humans are simulated by the introduction of random numbers, or human behaviour must be simulated by games and simulations as understood in the context of this society. Games and simulations can involve a considerable amount of data processing and computation, and these have become much more accessible with the introduction of the computer. Indeed, as Unwin has argued, 'although the quantitative revolution in geography had its origin significantly before computers became widely available there can be little doubt that computer use has greatly accelerated its course and acceptance' (Unwin and Dawson, 1976). New developments in the subject at research level clearly present a challenge to the teachers of the subject both at secondary and higher educational levels and the new geography that is now coming into the educational system would seem to have a new set of objectives. These are, very broadly, that pupils should understand the processes which operate to produce the landscape and learn to evaluate the importance of different processes, and that they should learn the use of the scientific method in their understanding of these processes.

The survey which the Geographical Association carried out in 1973 indicated that uses of the computer were developing which could be of considerable assistance to the attainment of these objectives, and it soon became clear that the research tool that had made much of the new geography possible would be of direct relevance in the teaching of the subject. But some major initiative was necessary to make this happen; teachers could not be expected to make use of a computer as easily as even a slide projector. It was appreciated from the outset that teachers could not use the computer unless they had access to packages, a computer program and associated documentation, hence the name 'package' in the title of the project. The main scope for the assistance to teachers has therefore been seen as the provision of packages to teachers, combined with demonstrations and explanations indicating how these could be used in geography teaching.

Developments

The first stage was to inform geography teachers about the existence of the service and this was achieved by articles in the relevant journals, by seminars and workshop sessions at the Geographical Association annual conference and by visits to a large number of teachers' groups in different parts of the country. For demonstration purposes 12 packages were collected and edited. These were then catalogued so that interested teachers could order those that they felt would work on their machines and which would fit in with their teaching. As a result of the initial publicity over 300 teachers have requested the catalogue and 270 packages have been ordered and despatched, largely since January 1977. Some 60 of the teachers who have received the packages have now written to the organisers describing the use that they have made of them. Clearly in this respect the project has been successful, and it is now planned to continue a package exchange service financed by a small charge per package.

Three hundred interested teachers is a small proportion of all geography teachers, and if it only represents the ones who are enthusiastic about computing rather than new developments in geography teaching then the future is rather limited. Since it is not possible to convince teachers by the use of the results of evaluation the main method must be by description of some of the implications of the use of computer-assisted games and simulations, and this can best be done by an analysis of some sample material.

Consider, first, two simulations, one deterministic and one stochastic. The deterministic simulation relates to the problem of the location of industry. It is known that very many factors are responsible for the location of industries, and that not many fruitful generalisations can be made, but one generalisation is that industry locates so as to minimise its total transport costs. This is the theory developed by Weber (1909) in his *Theory of the Location of Industries.* The computer package WEBER allows the user to set up a simple simulated network of places and links, to locate the raw materials and to specify the size and location of markets, the amounts of each raw material used and the transport costs, and the program will then produce a detailed analysis of all the costs involved including the least cost location for the industry. The calculations for one set of data would take rather more than an hour, yet the computer takes only a few minutes used interactively, and has the further advantage that any alteration can be made to the data and a new analysis performed, so it is possible to simulate the progressive reduction in the amount of one raw material needed and to see the effects that this will have on the location or to progressively change any of the other variables.

Use of this simulation with students raises one most interesting reaction, which I think tells us a great deal about the nature of the learning process. The role of the computer is to remove from the teaching exercise the boring and repetitive calculations that are involved; it is a saving of non-educational labour, yet many students clearly miss this and feel at a loss when they go straight from the formulation of their problem to being presented with the results of the calculations. Is it possible that teachers and pupils are still wedded to the puritan work ethic to the extent that they are not prepared to let the computer take over those tedious and boring human activities which it is good at and deprive the human being of the masochistic pleasure to be derived from repeated addition and multiplication? In fact, the computer does not make life simpler, it does the opposite. It takes away the time-consuming but mentally undemanding activities so that the pupil is faced with the much more demanding tasks of drawing conclusions about results with a much higher frequency. This is good educationally, but it can destroy some cosy educational customs.

The next simulation is one which would never be tackled at all if the computer were not available. It is one of the class of simulations that are known as stochastic simulations, since not all the variables can be operationalised and a deterministic model would fail to predict reality; to represent the unaccounted-for variables random numbers are introduced. If this ever is done by hand it is extremely tedious. Even more tedious would be repeating the operation several times to see if the range of predictions made included some or all of the real-life cases studied. With the computer providing the random numbers as well as carrying out the calculations, several runs can be carried out and the results compared. When students realise the extent of the labour that would have been involved they are inclined to make less protest about the machine taking over from them. The simulation that has been used by GAPE has been the simulation of the growth of an offshore spit.

Two different types of games have been included in the first issue of these packages; one is a well-known computer game modified for a specifically geographical application. HURKLE uses the random number generator in the computer to locate a mythical beast in a grid reference system which can use two, four or six figure grid references; after entering a location for the beast, the user is told in which direction to go to find it. Even those experienced in the use of grid references have to think quite hard to relate directions and grid references, and it has been quite widely used with children of 11 to 13 as a supplement to conventional map teaching techniques. The other type of game is perhaps closer to the manual games used in geography teaching. It is basically a farming game in which the student has to make strategy decisions in conditions of uncertainty about future weather, the typical problem faced by farmers, but also a feature of all decision-making. The context of this computer simulation is the Chagga farmers of East Africa and the computer is used to simulate the vagaries of the climate and to control the progress of the student through the game, as well as leaving him with a clear record of his choices and the results of the reaction of his choices with the subsequent weather.

Conclusions

These four examples give some indication of the type of package available at present. The computer-based game and simulation clearly opens up considerable possibilities and at the same time forces on both student and teacher the need to rethink where the major effort should be in the teaching process. All the tedious tasks so often set to keep the class quiet for the last 20 minutes of a session, all the laborious sorting of materials, all the time spent in doing the calculations involved in a game, can be taken over by the computer and immediately one is faced with analysing results, drawing conclusions, thinking harder and probably going a lot further. The Geographical Association is well aware that these are very early stages in the use of the computer, but widespread availability of cheap computing power and a growing list of packages for the use of geography teachers could make a considerable impact over the next five or so years. The computer-based game and simulation is going to have a big impact and to be rather more important than the teaching machine or the slide projector.

References

Burton, I (1963) The quantitative revolution and theoretical geography. *Canadian Geographer*, 7, 151-162.

Fielding, G J (1974) *Geography as a Social Science*. Harper and Row, New York.

Hartshorne, R (1939) *The Nature of Geography: A Critical Survey of Current Thought in the Light of the Past*. Lancaster.

Hartshorne, R (1959) *Perspective on the Nature of Geography*. London.

Harvey, D W (1969) *Explanation in Geography*. Edward Arnold, London.

Unwin, D and Dawson, J A (1976) *Computing for Geographers*. David and Charles, Newton Abbott.

Walker, D R F (1974) An evaluation of the use of games in the teaching of geography. *Profile*, June, 124-128.

Weber, K (1909) *Theory of the Location of Industries*.

Chapter 5

Retrospect and prospect

Jacquetta Megarry, *Jordanhill College of Education, Glasgow*

Taking the last decade as its unit for analysis, the first part of this paper is a retrospective selection of issues from the published literature of simulation and gaming. The preoccupation with the 'comparative experiment' is noted and criticised as fruitless. The influence of 'new wave' evaluation is charted, together with its emancipation from the blinkers of behavioural objectives, the greater concern with instruments to measure process rather than product and an interest in unanticipated outcomes. The common assumption that the use of games and simulations is somehow 'democratic' is challenged and indicators of authoritarianism detected. The role of debriefing is discussed and four distinguishable tasks for debriefing identified. To conclude the discussion on retrospect, the last section is concerned with issues of realism and reality. Specifically, consideration is given to the problems of how much realism is optimal in a simulation and the difficulty of assessing transfer to the 'real world'. The idea that reality may be socially constructed is linked to the notion of games of 'multiple reality'.

The last section of the paper attempts a look into the future. Firstly, technological impacts are considered, especially of cheaper and smaller electronic data processing and of systems like CEEFAX. Secondly, the need for closer links is stressed, with the human relations movement, with mathematical theory of games and among simulation gamers of different nationalities and disciplines.

Genesis

The idea that play and games have value in education and training has a long and distinguished intellectual pedigree. It can be traced back through the writings of eminent theorists like Jerome Bruner, Jean Piaget, George Herbert Mead, J L Moreno, John Dewey and Jean-Jacques Rousseau all the way to Plato (Boocock, 1968; Bloomer, 1972). Indeed Plato sounds uncannily modern on the subject; in the *Laws* he says 'the future builder must play at building, and the husbandman at digging . . . all the thoughts and pleasures of children should bear on their after profession' (Jowett, 1953:24) and in *The Republic* ' . . . enforced learning will not stay in the mind. So avoid compulsion, and let your children's lessons take the form of play' (Cornford, 1941:252).

In these circumstances, it is curious that most *published* work on educational simulation and gaming dates from the 1960s. Pioneering examples were the JEFFERSON TOWNSHIP SCHOOL DISTRICT simulation (Hemphill *et al*, 1962) and the publication in 1961 of the WFF 'N PROOF non-simulation games in mathematical logic (Allen, 1971:67). Moreover, the techniques do not appear to have been developed as a belated application of the theoretical writers mentioned

187

above. Nor did they seem to have grown from a natural extension of the widespread use of 'make-believe' role play and structured games in many primary schools, which might have been expected to spread up the age range to secondary and tertiary education and outside the classroom walls into training applications and adult education. Instead, curiously, the techniques seem to have derived from business and management training; the first well-known business simulation game was developed in 1956 by a research group of the American Management Association (Ricciardi *et al*, 1957). That they, in turn, owed a great debt to the ancient tradition of military gaming was made clear by their prior visit to the US Naval War College (Taylor, 1971:25). Again, the Rand Corporation pioneered political gaming as 'a natural extension of their extensive involvement with sophisticated military games' (Taylor, 1971:26). Thus instead of education supplying the training methods for business and military activities, 'this process has been reversed, and education has taken from business a method which business in its turn had borrowed from military training' (Tansey and Unwin, 1969b:1).

Exactly why the educational potential of simulation and gaming should have been 'discovered' in the sixties is not clear. Perhaps the prevailing climate of educational ideas was right; like kidney transplants, educational innovations are likely to be rejected without careful tissue-typing (Bloomer, 1973). To change the simile, if adoption of simulation and gaming (like educational technology — McAleese, 1977) is similar to the transmission of an infectious disease, perhaps the resistance was low at the time. In any event, the early sixties marked the birth of a new field in American publications; British work followed on from the late sixties. Selecting any particular year as a starting point is always somewhat arbitrary, but the year 1968 is a natural choice. A seminal paper was presented to the 1968 conference of the Association for Programmed Learning and Educational Technology (APLET) in Glasgow (Tansey and Unwin, 1969a). Entitled 'Simulation and academic gaming: highly motivational teaching techniques', it attracted great interest among delegates. Out of this arose the group who gathered at Bulmershe College of Education in 1969; they formed the nucleus for the first annual conference of SAGSET in August 1970 at Reading. Another conference paper on simulation and gaming attracted great interest in 1968; this was at the University of London Institute of Education's conference on innovation in university teaching. In turn it led to a symposium on 'Instructional simulation systems in higher education' in Birmingham in 1969 whose proceedings were published the following year (Armstrong and Taylor, 1970). 1968 also marked the publication in the US of *Simulation Games in Learning* (Boocock and Schild, 1968) which provided a useful benchmark of progress in American simulation and gaming (and contains a striking amount of material which has not yet been superseded or followed up).

So the decade 1968-1977 forms a convenient unit of analysis for this paper. It can be considered the first decade of life for simulation and gaming in the UK and not quite the second of its US counterpart. In addition, the bulk of published work on both sides of the Atlantic falls into this period. Major periodical sources became available — *Simulation and Games* (since 1970), *SAGSET Journal* (since 1971), *Simulation/Gaming* (started as *Simulation/ Gaming/News* in 1972) — supplemented by conference proceedings of the National Gaming Council (now the North American Simulation and Gaming Association: NASAGA), the International Simulation and Gaming Association

(ISAGA), and SAGSET (from its sixth annual conference onward). The continuing interest of APLET has been documented by three dedicated issues of their journal *Programmed Learning & Educational Technology* (July of 1973, 1974 and 1976) and papers given at their educational technology international conferences and published in their Proceedings, the series publication *Aspects of Educational Technology* (numbers 2, 3, 5, 6, 7, 10 and 11). There is now a wealth of published information on both sides of the Atlantic. This is in sharp contrast to the state ten years ago when Tansey and Unwin dismissed published British work in 12 lines (Tansey and Unwin, 1969a:175).

Before turning to the two main tasks of this paper — a retrospective glance at the last decade and a prospective attempt to anticipate the future — a couple of caveats are necessary. Evidently this account is highly personal, possibly idiosyncratic in its preoccupations; it makes no attempt to summarise or classify the now voluminous literature but deliberately seizes only on those ideas and developments that seemed significant or illuminating. Moreover, it is largely dependent on the sources mentioned above for a picture of work in progress. The difficulty is that *published* work forms the uncertain tip of an unknown iceberg, which may be unrelated to the whole both in shape and (unlike the real iceberg) in volume. With these two reservations in mind, then, the retrospect and prospect may be attempted.

Retrospect

A large proportion of the published research in the US (and a growing proportion in the UK) has related directly or indirectly to the problem of evaluation. The major concern of this part of the paper is to look at the trends and problems in this work. A number of subsidiary problems will also be highlighted.

THE COMPARATIVE EXPERIMENT

A striking and depressing feature of the last decade is that a high proportion of evaluation effort has been directed toward empirical comparisons of learning from simulation games compared with traditional teaching techniques. Apparently, when confronted with a new technique, educational researchers feel an overwhelming compulsion to investigate the comparative question. Thus Boocock and Schild (1968:20) state,

> Ideally the research design for a comparison study would be a version of the classical experimental design in which the control group or groups would be taught the same subject matter covered in the game by one or more alternative methods

and complain that the studies presented in the book all 'depart in some respects from the ideal model'. Again, House (1973:457) regrets that 'few [studies] prove *scientifically* that games either teach better or teach something that cannot (or is not) taught by other means' (emphasis added). The comparative preoccupation is now less forgivable. A decade of inconclusive experimentation with programmed learning ought to have encouraged researchers to ask themselves what, if anything, their null hypothesis meant, and whether it was fruitful to try to test it (ie whether it could ever *convincingly* be falsified). The hoary chestnut has not yet been discarded: Keys (1974) quotes four recent review articles, presenting results from 17, 56, 43 and 16 studies respectively. On the learning of factual material, these are more or less evenly distributed among those that find games more effective, less effective and 'no significant difference'. More recently, Pierfy (1977) reviewed 22 studies and found that games were 'no more effective in fostering student learning [than traditional methods]'.

There have been various responses to these apparently disappointing results. One is to point out the many and various methodological weaknesses of the studies, especially those which do not support the researcher's expectation. In most cases, the studies present fairly easy game. Thus Pierfy (1977) notes that in some or all of the studies reviewed the following faults were present:

1. researcher was also game designer or adapter,
2. testing instruments not validated, reliability questionable,
3. no account taken of pre-test interaction effects,
4. intact classes used: teachers not comparable,
5. test/re-test design: effects of boredom, practice, specific answer memory,
6. Hawthorne[1] effect (researchers' presence and interaction affects results),
7. novelty[1] effect (positive results merely because technique new),
8. inconsistency over whether debriefing integral or separate,
9. poor information about supposedly comparable 'traditional technique'.

It would be easy to add to this list (eg see the Stanley [1971] criticism of Allen, Allen and Ross' claimed gain in non-language IQ of 20.9 points in high-school students after playing WFF 'N PROOF). Keys goes further and denies that the most tightly designed traditional study imaginable, comparing game learning with that of lectures, cases or other media, could ever measure potential for learning in games. He believes that their potential is more likely to be realised in combination with other media, that traditional learning objectives are inappropriate and that traditional tests are unlikely to tap the potential (Keys, 1974). The latter point has been made emphatically by Shirts when criticising the use of conventional tests of facts and ideas in comparative experiments:

> Books and lectures present carefully processed ideas and facts to the students in grade-A, enriched, homogenized form. The students, in turn, have been trained by many years of conditioning to accept this rich diet and to return it to the lecturer on demand. In simulations, on the other hand, facts are frequently hidden in scenarios, messages from other participants, decision-making forms, statements by people in hot debate, and announcements from the directors or the simulated mass media. Other facts are specific to the game being played and have to be translated before they have any meaning in the real world (Shirts, 1970).

It is undoubtedly true that test instruments have been inadequate in the past, and the efficient presentation of factual information is in any case not foremost among the claims made for simulation and gaming (Greenblat, 1973:66). But Pierfy is surely diagnosing the symptoms rather than the disease when he concludes 'the major weaknesses which qualify the conclusions stated in this paper concern inadequate instrumentation' (Pierfy, 1977:266). However much the instrumentation is refined, no research report in this comparative mould will be immune to criticism from both supporters *and* critics of simulation and gaming (or perhaps not even from either). The search for a conclusive answer to this question is like the quest for the elixir of youth. It has exacerbated the repetitive and non-cumulative nature of much of the 'little' research by 'isolated academic entrepreneurs' to date (Follettie, 1973). Although it is probably now too late to attract funding for the kind of 'big' research which Follettie advocates, an agreed set of assumptions and categories for data collection would help to improve the *possibility* of research which 'added up' to something. A start was made on this by Fletcher (1971b) but with little success; few subsequent papers have even referred to his proposals, either to reject his categories or to implement them (though Pierfy [1977] is an exception).

The persistence of the quest for the answer to the comparative question (simulation/game versus 'traditional technique', whatever that may be) is illuminating for what it reveals about the assumptions implicitly made by the researchers. To expect to be able to hold constant *all* the other input variables so as to be able to attribute any change in output variable to the difference in treatment suggests either colossal faith or a degree of naivety about what variables are important. For example, Pierfy comments regretfully that 'Since most of the research on simulation has been conducted in school settings, many researchers have had no choice but to experiment with intact classroom groups' (Pierfy, 1977:262). But what possible interest would attach to data gathered from specially constituted classes, brought together only for purposes of the experiment, disbanded immediately after? The excitement, disruption and social regrouping caused in any school in which a team of researchers moved in and rigged up special classes would all themselves be likely candidates to explain any experimental results; by contrast, the teaching technique used might be a relatively marginal detail. Relevant here is Inbar's finding that 'the group effect is the major determinant of the differential impact of the game over players' and that the 'capability of the person in charge of the session' was also unexpectedly important (Inbar, 1968:185). This was echoed in another context (using programmed texts in Nigeria) by the recognition that the effectiveness of programmed materials is 'largely a function of the reception conditions. Achievement depended more on the stability of the school and the teacher's confidence than on the quality of the materials themselves' (Roebuck, 1970).

These findings should be a salutary reminder that the differences between teaching techniques may be far greater as perceived by the teacher or researcher than from where the student sits. From his viewpoint, the fact that school attendance is compulsory and unrewarding, or that attendance at the training course is imposed by the employer and generally believed to be a waste of time, may take precedence. In the general context of educational research, it has been suggested that

> all our findings of 'no significant difference' are in effect telling us that, do what we will with the factors we can control, they will . . . always be of marginal importance compared with the factors we cannot control — the elements that go to make up a total human being, with all its heritable and environmental influences and prejudices (Hubbard, 1972:225).

Nor is this defeatism; Hubbard believes in evaluation which provides information that is *used* in decision-making. He is pointing out that the results of a 'controlled experiment' are unlikely to assist in a choice of method.

> It is seldom really controlled, in the sense even that experiments with mice are controlled, and of course one of the most obviously uncontrolled factors is the teacher in the classroom. Given such major uncontrolled variables, the better the coverage of the experiment, the larger the sample, the more the results of our particular controlled

perturbations are submerged beneath greater disturbances (ibid).

In these circumstances it is surely wiser to leave the *comparison* and to concentrate on improving and refining the learning system in question (Hubbard, 1972:225). If he is right, it follows that the call for 'replication' of comparative research (eg Pierfy, 1977) is misconceived; instead of converging on a reliable conclusion, results may 'hunt' wildly because of uncontrolled and uncontrollable inputs. Small-scale classroom-based research may be of greater utility to the practising teacher than the large-scale 'macro' approach (Teather and Whittle, 1971).

INSIDE THE BLACK BOX?

The results of a decade of research which has been cast in the traditional 'scientific' framework of varying the inputs and trying to measure consequent changes in output have been relatively modest. Even when not chasing the comparative hare, in relation to the effort and money invested, researchers are not greatly the wiser. It is perhaps time to stop blaming the researchers, their experimental design, their test instruments or their subjects and ask instead whether the input/output model of research is appropriate to evaluating simulation and gaming, if indeed it is appropriate to educational research at all.

Over the last decade there have been increasing self-awareness and explicit statements by curriculum evaluators about their models or 'paradigms' of evaluation. (A 'paradigm' is used here to indicate a concept prescribing problem areas, research methods and acceptable standards of explanation.) The traditional (classical, scientific, input/output, agricultural/botany) paradigm

> takes its origins from studies of the effects of different soil and fertiliser conditions on the growth of seedlings; the inputs are well-defined and easy to measure, and the seedlings (presumably) do not interact, socially or otherwise, with each other or the experimenter (Bloomer, 1975:36).

This paradigm has been under increasing criticism over the last decade (eg see Stake's 'Introduction' in Tyler, 1967). Its limitations as applied to evaluating classroom simulation and games are obvious: not only are the inputs multiple, complex and only partly known, but the outputs are disputed, difficult to isolate, detect or measure and the interaction among participants is considerable. Interaction forms, in some views, a major part of what simulation and gaming is about; it is *not* merely a source of 'noise' or experimental error. Classroom events are too complex to shut in a black box and turn a blind eye toward — we require better techniques for understanding what goes on *inside* the black box.

Moreover, the traditional type of evaluation effort, whether comparative or not, has been linked to the belief that the objectives of any curriculum materials should be specified in advance, preferably in behavioural terms, and that evaluation should be with reference to these objectives. This notion has also come under fire not only from curriculum developers (Stenhouse, 1975:70-83) but also from educational technologists, who originally developed and institutionalised the cult of the behavioural objective (Macdonald-Ross, 1972, 1973; Mitchell, 1972). Clearly the open-endedness which is the very essence of many simulation games presents a special problem for an objectives-oriented evaluation, since goals may be tentative, fuzzy and probabilistic (Bloomer,

1974). It is to be hoped that recent criticism of the 'objectives' school may reduce the simulation gamer's sense of sin and general defensiveness at this state of affairs. Clearly, if Stenhouse is right, it is no wonder that the attempt to state behavioural objectives for simulation games has not always been possible or fruitful: 'Education as induction into knowledge is successful to the extent that it makes the behavioural outcomes of the student unpredictable' (Stenhouse, 1975:82). Many would share his greater concern with *process* than with product.

However, while there is widespread agreement about the criticisms of the 'agricultural/botany' paradigm, there is no consensus on which of the ever-multiplying alternative paradigms should replace it. There is no shortage of candidates: Stenhouse discusses four — the holistic approach (MacDonald), illuminative evaluation (Parlett and Hamilton), portrayal and responsive evaluation (Stake) and transactional evaluation (Rippey *et al*). Popham (1975) summarises evaluation models under four different headings and a further quartet are presented in 'Four evaluation examples: anthropological, economic, narrative and portrayal' (Kraft *et al*, 1974). One problem, then, is not the absence of an alternative approach to evaluation, but an embarrassment of riches. Widespread dissatisfaction with the science-derived model has left no consensus on which discipline to substitute. Social anthropology, psychiatry, sociology, history, detective work/electronics troubleshooting, economics, literary criticism, journalism and legal theory and practice have all been advanced as candidates (Butts and Megarry, 1977).

A further problem relates to criteria, safeguards and quality control in these 'new wave' styles of evaluation.

> The whole anthropological approach relies on an explicit stance and on a willingness to take scrupulous precautions on questions of partiality, bias and confidentiality. In essence it is an entirely open system of reporting which is often candid and disarmingly straightforward (Taylor, 1975).

Unfortunately, the 'scrupulous precautions' are never spelled out and 'disarmingly' may conceal 'deceptively' straightforward: Stenhouse warns that:

> [new wave evaluators] aspire to 'tell it as it is', and often write as if that is possible if they allow for some distortion due to their own values. But there is no telling it as it is. There is only a creation of meaning through the use of criteria and conceptual frameworks. The task of briefing decision-makers in language they readily understand can too easily lead to the casual importation of unexamined assumptions and criteria . . . it is too easy for the evaluation which aspires to the condition of the novel to degenerate into the novelette (Stenhouse, 1975:116-7).

Take just one example from the field of published evaluations of simulations and games; Goroff's (1973) account of 'simulated incarceration experiences' is colourful, informative and readable. In style it is not unlike Brauner's 'narrative evaluation' in Kraft *et al* (1974). Neither account pays explicit attention to the problems of corroboration, alternative viewpoints or how comments were selected or elicited.

It is essential that if we import concepts and models of evaluation from other disciplines, we should also import and develop safeguards and rigour. The illuminative evaluators, for example, have been justly criticised by Parsons for failure to acknowledge and implement standards of sociological case study work (eg as codified by Becker and Cicourel) and on other grounds; 'we should [not] be trying to re-invent the wheel, and there are very real dangers in importing the spokes alone' (Parsons, 1976).

However, while evaluators are trying to achieve some degree of consensus on their assumptions, develop new procedures and refine their safeguards, life in educational and training establishments goes on. The danger is that impatience will breed a reaction which has recourse to teachers' intuitions as a substitute for serious evaluative effort. This seems to be the position taken in an article entitled 'Evaluation, statistics both slammed' in which the possibility of showing that a simulation had 'made its point' is denied as follows:

> But statistics will not prove it, never while proof by induction is an accepted part of mathematical theory. For proof by induction depends on the phrase 'therefore, intuitively', which is the phrase that we, as experienced teachers depend on at the moment whether we use simulation or not in our teaching (Tansey, 1973).

Leaving aside the confusion this shows over the nature of mathematical induction (a rigorous procedure which proves a theorem in two stages and owes nothing to intuition), it would be useful to know the cause of the remarkable reversal this shows since the same author's proposal three years earlier:

> What is now urgently required is research . . . concerned with finding evaluative systems . . . Too often, we hear of 'hunches' and 'intuitions' (Tansey, 1970:300).

Evaluative research is easy neither in theory nor in practice, but it at least attempts to resolve the fruitless deadlock of arguments between teachers with equally passionately held but mutually incompatible intuitions. Education may not necessarily wish to derive its evaluation techniques from agricultural/botany, but without any publicly observable data its activities are no more susceptible to scrutiny than those of psychiatrists, astrologers or priests. Ironically, the stalemate created by incompatible subjective data was one of the major problems inherent in nineteenth-century introspectionist psychology and partly explains why Skinner's black box behaviourist psychology was adopted with such enthusiasm in the twentieth century.

However, several papers have described promising leads for the development of 'anthropological' type techniques like survey and interview data, observer rating schedules and tape recordings, and a start has been made on more rigorous techniques of analysis — for example, Dukes and Kidder (1974), Boocock (1972), and also Steffens (1977). There is a significant paper which treats the topic at length (Keys, 1974). He stresses the need to 'give more serious attention to the learning "processes" in games by systematic observation, systematic recording and intensive analysis of these observations' (Keys, 1974:16). He goes on to describe six types of measures which are capable of corroboration and correlation with less subjective measures: (a) his own use of narrative reports (and the incident process applied to game behaviour); (b) Whitlock's (1973) use of checklists gathered from students' recollections of outstanding positive and negative learning experiences. This capitalises on students' demonstrated ability to recognise productive and preventive learning experiences; (c) a strategy by Vora, based on Herzberg's motivation-hygiene approach, for identifying major game stimuli; (d) McKenney's (1967) faculty diary; (e) the Player Diary and Personal Application Assignment. The latter encourages players to relate ideas and concepts learned in games to other areas of their lives (Kolb *et al*, 1971); (f) the instructional interview described by Jerome Bruner as follows:

It is instruction, carried out with an individual pupil or small group, that has as its object not simply to teach but also to provide information about how children are learning particular materials and skills and how we can help them. The instructional interview is a tutorial in which materials and pedagogy are tested by an interviewer-teacher conversant not only with the substantive materials but also with the cognitive processes of children. The same children are interviewed repeatedly over varying numbers of sessions, to them it is a form of instruction (Bruner, 1966:167-168).

This last technique has been quoted at length because it is seldom referred to in the literature despite the stature of the author, and although it is low cost and high yield. It also has high student/trainee acceptability since 'to them it is a form of instruction'; it does not exhaust their limited 'evaluation patience'. Like other techniques cited by Keys, it is small scale, detailed and close to the process itself rather than the product. As Bruner comments earlier, 'the closer evaluation is to the end of the process, the more it becomes a "test" of a completed product, with all that implies in defensive vanity all round' (Bruner, 1966:165).

It is exactly this defensive vanity that has been so sterile an influence on the evaluation tradition. There has been a tendency to assume that the kind of techniques described above may be a necessary part of *formative* evaluation (which is reported on seldom and scantily), but have no place in a report of completed *summative* evaluation. The implied dichotomy (between formative and summative evaluation) has had unhelpful effects; quantities of useful data must have been thrown away by people who are reluctant to document their false starts, second and third thoughts and changes of direction. Defensive vanity has also contributed to the myth of the immaculate conception; we could profit by exchanging more information about the process of developing a simulation game and more ideas about its unintended, unanticipated and even undesirable outcomes. Reports of the latter are rare (but see Rosenfeld 1974:10) and the question has attracted surprisingly little interest. Perhaps an immediate benefit of questioning the dogma about evaluation having to be tied to pre-stated objectives is that it may help to reduce the massive blinkers which tend to prevent us from detecting unexpected effects of our learning materials.

The issue of evaluation is so massive and problematic that it overshadows the other issues and unbalances this paper. It demands serious attention because it is vital that evaluation studies of the next decade should not repeat the mistakes and blind alleys of the last. Let us turn now to some other issues, all of which could and should be illumined by the evaluation studies of the 1980s.

AUTHORITARIANISM AND SIMULATION GAMING

It is frequently asserted, and perhaps implicitly assumed even oftener, that the introduction of simulation and games into a classroom or training situation automatically makes it somehow more 'democratic'. Thus Boocock and Schild explain:

> Because the rules are in the game itself, rather than being imposed by the teacher's authority, and because the outcome of the game, not the teacher, decides the winner, control of the class shifts from the teacher to the learning materials themselves — and in a sense ultimately to the students (Boocock and Schild, 1968:262).

My argument is that this (quite common) belief is an illusion — at best it is misleading, at worst it is quite dangerous. In the first place, most activities in education and training classrooms are imposed by the authority of the teacher, backed up by the weight of the institution. It is on this basis that the game and rules are accepted and operated by the students. Furthermore, no one who has survived as a classroom teacher for long is under any illusion about where control of the class lies. He may or may not choose to exercise it but if he has lost control, it will not be to the learning materials. Again, leaving aside the more blatant ways in which teachers are sometimes obliged to 'stack the decks' in running games, it is doubtful whether student success in games is any less influenced by the teacher than in 'conventional' techniques. The self-validating effects of the teacher's expectations, the geometry of social relationships established in the classroom and the pattern of positive and negative reinforcements distributed (often unwittingly) by the teacher — all these are still powerful. In fact, simulation and gaming offer extremely powerful and sometimes subtle vehicles for authoritarian teachers to manipulate their students and project their ideas and personalities. In many ways, contrary to popular belief, it is a far more interventionist technique than the humble lecture.

Dorothy Heathcote exemplified this unexpectedly humble aspect of the lecture in a talk on 'Drama as education': 'the best use of me is, the first time I say anything that rings any bells, to cut off and go your own route of your own thinking . . .' This door is not open to a participant in a simulation game, and is only slightly ajar for an observer. 'During game play participants are forced to accept the game designer's viewpoint regarding the phenomena being modeled' (Goodman quoted in Dukes and Seidner, 1973:172). It is all very well to say, as many designers do, that the issue of value judgements built into the game is a non-problem because it can be thrashed out in the debriefing afterwards. This underestimates the imposition on a student who is first obliged to be involved in an exercise whose premises he wishes to question; he will probably have to wait far longer than the traditional 50-minute lecture period for his opportunity to disagree.

The insensitivity with which neophyte gamers ride roughshod over their participants' wishes will be familiar to many. It was brought home to me forcibly once on arrival at a simulation gaming conference feeling tranquil, detached and in need of space to reflect and cogitate. Straight from the train, much travelled, unwashed and unfed, I had two role cards thrust upon me by a well-meaning enthusiast who had not time or tolerance for non-participants. A streak of authoritarianism pervades the literature; the language is usually of persuasion and control, not of sharing or co-operation. One has the impression that the designers have, or think that they have, all the answers and the game is used as a means of transmitting received wisdom. Somewhere the potential for open-ended exploration appears to have been lost to view.

Writing of the need for the teacher to clarify his objectives at the outset, Elder emphasises that

> the post-game review should be structured around these objectives, which may be discussed in the light of the simulation experience. Without the discipline imposed by such specific learning objectives, the results of the exercise are likely to be nebulous and disquieting no matter how well it is structured and administered (Elder, 1973:349).

Disquieting for whom, one wonders? Presumably the answer is that it would be disquieting for the instructor, if any of the students were to divert the discussion into unexpected avenues.

Also writing of debriefing, Fennessey states flatly: 'It is best to organise the questions so that they focus first on the experiences the players had in the game, next on the players' evaluation of the realism of the game model, and finally on the principles the game is designed to teach' (Fennessey, 1973:216). That sounds rational, if slightly dogmatic; but often human emotional needs should take priority. Writing of 'game literacy', Zelmer unconsciously betrays a disregard of this; she comments on a trial run of a simulation with 'an inexperienced test group' which was 'in all other respects a good group . . . well motivated and highly (print) literate'. She explains that 'after the designers played through three rounds of the game they indicated that they wanted to omit a debriefing . . . and proceed immediately to a discussion of the mechanics of the game'. She complains that 'the participants seemed to have a great deal of difficulty in separating their own internal feelings from a discussion of more general game principles — a problem which I would attribute in good measure to their lack of game literacy' (Zelmer, 1974:125).

Unless the game was extraordinarily uninteresting, the participants' desire to discuss feelings and ideas recently aroused by the game seems entirely understandable and encouraging. In fact, if the implication is that a more game-literate group would have dropped the bone obediently and scampered on to discuss the game mechanics as instructed, then game literacy seems to be a highly undesirable and (fortunately) rare quality. Curiously, Rowntree quotes a rather similar description by Bates of a conflict of intentions between tutor and student. Bates' description is in terms of student distraction by irrelevancies; Rowntree reminds us that 'distraction' and 'relevance' are not solely for the teacher to decide (Rowntree, 1975:284).

It would be wrong to neglect the clues given by the language used in the 'literature' of gaming; there was, for example, an illuminating exchange between Goodman and Duke in an NGC symposium session on the future of gaming simulation (Duke, 1971:173-4) in which the connotations of Duke's phrase about 'running people through his games' was explored. Again, Boocock and Schild reveal a belief in the absolute correctness of the designer's method of using a game irrespective of the context of use: 'It would be naive to assume that because a handful of researchers have had some gratifying successes with the technique . . . that it will automatically be adopted by school systems and *correctly used* by classroom teacher' (emphasis added) (Boocock and Schild, 1968:261). The words emphasised suggest a wistful desire for a teacher-proof simulation game.

A refreshing contrast is afforded by the 'frame game attitude' which 'involves setting people to work developing their own game within a framework supplied by the original designer' (Goodman, 1974). His rationale explicitly includes the idea that 'in many areas of gaming there is more to be learned from designing games than there is from playing them', as well as the seditious idea that teachers, too, can engage in learning, and that they should respect the ability and interests of students (Goodman, 1974:303). Extending this to the notion of respecting also their values and linking it with the problem mentioned above there is scope for experimentation with student-constructed scoring systems slotted into a frame game supplied by the teacher. It avoids imposing the teacher's (or designer's) set of values although problems remain when (as frequently happens) there is no consensus among the students. More radically, there would seem to be scope for encouraging students to design games entirely by themselves, and play them a number of times under different design conditions to discover relationships among variables. In social studies, simulation gaming can provide the opportunity for practical activity analogous with the laboratory for physical science. But just as in science education, it is relatively rare for students to design experiments entirely from scratch, similarly with simulation gaming, having students innovate *within* a framework offers a time-saving compromise.

DEBRIEFING

It is not clear why this word has come to mean the discussion after a simulation game. Originally it was a military term, used, for example, in the Second World War to describe the pilot 'telling all' about the events of the flight; presumably it was coined because the process was in some ways the converse of the briefing which preceded the flight — in which he was on the receiving end of the 'telling'. This debriefing was clearly a very different process from the discussion which follows many games; the pilot had been alone, did most of the talking and his audience was eager to hear the vital information he brought. Participants in a simulation game, by contrast, often have to compete for air-space, frequently have shared the same experiences, and often they are expected to listen to the director as well as each other. The latter is sometimes over-anxious not only to tell them what they thought, saw or learned but also to tell them what *should* have happened in the game and why.

The term 'debriefing' is unfortunate; there are up to four distinguishable tasks for the post-game discussion, and the use of a single term with a military connotation of one-way communication is misleading. In the first place, there is often a need perceived at least by the participants to talk about the events of the game itself, though it is not always perceived by the director (see above). Second, if the game was also a simulation, the director will want participants to relate the in-game events to the outside world, to question the fidelity of the model and to examine their position in relation to the value judgements embedded in the design. Third, it may be appropriate to open up a free-ranging discussion of emergent principles and wider issues raised by the game. Lastly, there may also be a stage in which the director collects evaluative reactions to the game, asks for comments, criticisms, suggestions for improvements and variations. These four components may not occur in sequence and, indeed, may not happen at all (eg after a routine play of a well-validated non-simulation game). We know far too little about whether and when debriefing is necessary, how, if at all, it should be structured, and whether game-learning and debriefing-learning are independent or interactive; nor do we know whether the answers to these questions may not differ for different individuals.

Some clues exist in the literature but remain to be followed up. For example, there is the suggestion (Boocock and Schild, 1968:257-8) that game learning may be intrinsically limited in its effect. In Bruner's terms, games may assist 'enactive' and 'iconic' learning but may not lead unassisted to 'symbolic' representation. If that is correct, debriefing (especially the second and third components just identified) may have a special role in helping this transformation. This idea is akin to Whitehead's celebrated notion of the 'rhythm of education' (Whitehead, 1962); playing the game corresponds to the stage of romance, debriefing (first component) to the stage of precision, and debriefing (second, third and fourth components) to the stage of generalisation. Another important lead is the use of videotapes, observation checklists and peer-evaluation questionnaires as 'reflexive devices' (Kennedy, 1973:337). These can assist the ruminative, inward-looking reflection which is a necessary stage before turning the scope of the discussion outward and may thus be helpful, especially in the first stage identified. In the context of evaluating caribou-hunting games, Fletcher demonstrated a significant 'increase in learning brought about by reflection on the game experiences' (Fletcher, 1971a). This is not unexpected from a game where strategy learning requires repeated plays and subsequent analysis; but the development of efficient and unobtrusive recording systems — for use both in game play and debriefing — requires further work. Although some progress has been made toward identifying the multiple functions of debriefing and proposing techniques (eg EIAG: Stadsklev, 1974:52-65), major questions remain unanswered.

REALISM AND REALITY

Another set of key issues for simulation surround realism and reality. The cardinal sin committed by designers of early simulations was to build models of overpowering complexity, with a multiplicity of variables; this was probably caused by an understandable desire to make the simulation as realistic as possible. However, while this 'hi-fi' approach may be appropriate to simulations for research purposes, it is often unsuitable for simulations with pedagogic intentions. For the latter, the optimum degree of realism is an empirical, not an armchair, question.

The question is reminiscent of studies to discover what degree of realism is optimal in visual illustrations. Dwyer (1972) summarises a considerable body of research and quotes earlier theorists who thought that visual illustrations should be as realistic as possible. More recent work casts doubt on this, particularly his own research using illustrations in teaching anatomy and physiology of the heart to medical students. In those instructional situations where visuals made a difference, illustrations containing relatively small amounts of realistic detail were most effective. Dwyer offers the explanation that even though the more realistic illustrations contained more information, it was excessive and distracting and interfered with learning. Plausible and simple though this sounds, interpretation is more complex; Dwyer's studies raise again the thorny question of how learning is to be measured. His conclusion must be placed firmly in the context of the nature of his test items (yet it is often quoted in isolation). He used four types of test; in general it was only on the drawing and identification test that illustrations were demonstrated to be effective. The terminology test consisted of completion items and the comprehension test of multiple-choice questions; it is unsurprising that verbal teaching was adequate to produce verbal learning. Moreover, since both drawing and identification tests involved drawing, labelling or identifying parts of a line diagram, it is hardly surprising that the abstract line visual was the best preparation. The question Dwyer's work leaves unanswered is which type of visual illustration is most effective for training doctors in the anatomy of a human heart *in vivo*.

It is *this* question which is parallel to the question of how much realism is desirable in a simulation which seeks to teach students about the real world.

Ideally it should be tackled by evaluation of how far learning from the simulation *transferred* to the real situation it purported to simulate. In common with the idea of letting untrained doctors loose on open-heart surgery, it is not necessarily practicable. Nevertheless we should not confuse learning as displayed on tests of simulation learning with learning displayed 'on the real thing'. Only the latter can validate the former.

Meanwhile, the case can still be argued that 'distortion, simplification and exaggeration can be legitimate and effective, when used appropriately' (despite the 'Case of the Serbian King' — Shirts, 1976:38). If the reality to be grappled with eventually is appallingly complex and difficult, it does not follow that an appallingly complex and difficult simulation should be developed. The learner's attempts are much more likely to succeed on a 'shallow end' approach which starts from a crudely simple model and gradually elaborates and refines it toward greater fidelity.

Implicit in the preceding discussion is the notion of a reality 'out there' which the simulation can and should recreate. This resembles pre-impressionist views of the relationship between painting and the 'real world'. It is challenged by Shirts who asserts that 'in reference to educational simulations and games, there is not one reality but many, depending upon how an idea, process, or fact is approached' (Shirts, 1971:379). The phenomenological approach denies that reality is a fixed entity 'out there', waiting to be discovered; it is socially created (Berger and Luckmann, 1966). We perceive the world with our brains, not our eyes; we ascribe meaning to people and things by defining situations and constructing realities from memories and experience (Greenblat, 1974).

Interestingly, she goes on to explore the implications of this idea for game design. 'Players should be given different and conflicting information, corresponding to the different and conflicting perceptions held by their real-world counterparts' (Greenblat, 1974:7). This notion is worked out in an example in which different groups of players have equal access to resources but perceive their shares unequally. (This is the converse of Shirts' game STARPOWER in which different groups of players have unequal access to resources but are supposed to perceive their shares equally.) The idea is highly ingenious but the practical disadvantages which Greenblat lists are formidable: the need for secrecy and contrivance, greater expense and complex packaging, the fact that it is inherently 'one-off', possible loss of trust in or hostility toward the game director, and perhaps a growing general expectation among participants of 'trickiness' in game design (cf STARPOWER).

Prospect

The only way to stand a good chance of success in predicting the future is to be vague, like the astrologers. It seems preferable to risk being wrong and even to risk confounding predictions with prayers. The greater difficulties of writing about the future than the past are responsible for the imbalance of length between this section and the previous one. Although these speculations may be off target, at least they will not be in the air for long.

LESSONS OF THE PAST

The first group of expectations derives directly from the observations offered in the retrospective section, and they are expressions of hope as well as of belief. The first is that the comparative experiment will very soon be laid to rest; its 'results' have not justified the effort. Moreover, more inventive and diverse process measures will be developed, along the lines suggested above. But in addition to devising methods for collecting 'anthropological' data, there will have to be serious spadework on the problem of corroboration, with rigorous procedures for limiting and exposing sources of bias. More effort will be expended on investigating unexpected and undesirable results — for example, the effects of half-hearted or stereotyped role play.

The issue of authoritarianism in simulation gaming will come out in the open with the realisation that authoritarianism is more a product of the individual teacher's personality, experience and professional security, than of the teaching method used. Nevertheless, there will be more exploratory, open-ended uses of games and simulation by some; students will gradually be emancipated from the fixed roles of participator/observer and experiment with adapting, designing and running through multiple plays with variations.

A lot of attention will be paid to the functions and problems of debriefing outlined above. The use of observation media as an adjunct to debriefing will grow, and the nature of the interaction between learning during and after the game will be illumined. With any luck, growing awareness of the distinct components implied by the word itself might even lead to its timely superannuation.

There will be further investigation into the effects of different types of realism and a greater divergence between simulations for research and for education. More simulation games should be explicated at a variety of levels of realism and complexity so that participants can move up (and down) a hierarchy and explore this dimension. It seems unlikely that many 'multiple reality' games will be developed but there will be greater awareness of the subjective theory of reality and its implications for social simulation games.

It seems unlikely that there will be many additions to the current repertoire of a dozen or so simulation game structures. Simple and timeless ideas have already demonstrated astonishing versatility and longevity (Megarry, 1975) and different subject matter will continue to be injected. What is more likely (and highly desirable) is that a greater variety of people will become involved in design, with greater freshness of approach. Cozette Shirts has remarked that 'white middle-class men trained in western universities had developed 95 per cent of the games in existence today, and that many contained stereotyped or non-existent roles for women' (reported in Shirts, 1976:38). Whether the percentage is correct or not hardly matters; and the comment about stereotyped roles could as easily have been made about blacks, or workers, or non-Europeans.

TECHNOLOGICAL IMPACTS

Two hardware developments are likely to have their impact on simulation-gaming if we develop the software to exploit the opportunities. The first is the tumbling price and increasing miniaturisation of electronic data processing. Already, games with pocket calculators have become a growth area (Thiagarajan and Stolovitch, 1976). More important, the spread of cheap mini-computers will offer the benefits of on-line interactive simulation in the classroom without the inflexible administrative constraints which inhibit computer-based simulation at present. However, this will only be true if development in the technology of terminals starts to catch up with that of central processing units. At present, the visual display unit with light pen, graphics capability and hardcopy facility is the most promising combination for interactive simulation and gaming. But there will have to be a dramatic fall in price, rise in flexibility and reduction in size before this catches on. Potentially, miniaturisation could do for computers what videocassettes are doing for the use of television in education.

The second development is the CEEFAX system which will exploit the fact that nearly all British homes have a television and an increasing majority will also have telephones. Link the former via the latter to a large central computer with massive databanks and a library of good simulation/gaming programs and the possibilities are wide open. Lifelong education in the full range of subjects could be available in the home on an individualised basis; games could be picked up and put down at will, difficulty levels and strategy manipulated. The computer could link players in their own homes around the world or offer 'beat the program' or solitaire educational games as required. Access to the data files could help people with personal decision-making as well (including careers guidance, or simulating the effect of another child on the family finances?). The possibilities are legion . . .

CLOSER LINKS

The final set of predictions centres around links between simulation/gaming and other fields of work. At present the field is rather isolated and self-contained, with specialist societies, journals and the rest. This is understandable in the early stages of an innovation, but the time must come soon for integration.

There are a number of barriers to be breached soon. Perhaps the most immediate candidate is that between simulation gaming and the human relations movement. Interestingly, the vocabulary of transactional analysis has just begun to be exchanged at APLET's conferences as well as at SAGSET's. Apart from informal links between SAGSET and the Group Relations Training Association, there has been surprisingly little cross-fertilisation. The March 1977 (vol 8 no 1) issue of *Simulation and Games* was therefore an especially welcome sign as it is devoted to the human growth games and attends to the 'transpersonal' movement in psychology and education. It ranges widely over the role of fantasy, improvisation, altered states of consciousness, meditation and sport, and the self-nouns: self-knowledge, self-direction, self-actualisation, self-integration. Lest this sound unduly mystical and 'far-out', it should be noted that there are hard-headed applications. For example, the role of fantasy and addressing the 'right brain' (cerebral hemisphere) is illustrated in the high-school teaching of electromagnetic induction, and a whole article is devoted to rigorous and validated measurements of self-knowledge development and levels of consciousness (Alschuler *et al*, 1977).

Another interesting possibility is that mathematical theory of games and educational gaming might draw a little closer. It is disappointing that a branch of mathematics developed to analyse goals and player strategies should thus far have remained incarcerated in prison on the horns of a dilemma. Again, until recently there has been a near-total separation between the literature on and marketing of domestic ('leisure') and educational ('serious') games and simulations. There are signs that this division is being eroded — the monthly

Games and Puzzles has started to give space to overtly 'educational' games in recent years. The Games Centre in Hanway Street, London, now carries materials and books of both types, as well as accessories like blank card and dice, hex sheets and the like, to assist designers.

However, first we need to set our own house in order. Barriers still divide simulation gamers. Workers with similar interests in simulation gaming are failing to learn from each other or even to acknowledge each other's existence. The columns of the three periodicals mentioned above contain references mainly to work in the same country as the author. There is little knowledge of research interests in other countries and still less genuine exchange of ideas. Nor have annual international conferences solved this problem. We need to devise more helpful forms of academically respectable communication than have been perpetrated in the past.

CODICIL

Paradoxically, the best hope for the future is extinction. While simulation and gaming is still a tender plant it may need its special societies and publications for protection and interest. However, if it is to survive in the cold hard world it must be planted out and take its chance with the rest. To change the metaphor, if the seventies marked the infancy of simulation and gaming in Great Britain, the eighties will represent the formative years of adolescence. Before the turn of the century it will need to marry and settle down. Only when we have lost our *separate* identity as simulation gamers and become accepted as educationists interested primarily in fostering learning by *whatever* technique is most appropriate — only then will this most fascinating and frustrating set of techniques come out of its present incubator, and take its rightful place as part of the standard range of media to which every good teacher on occasion will turn.

Note

1. Pierfy confuses these two (as do Boocock and Schild, 1968:20 and Greenblat, 1973:75); reference to the original studies (of the relationship between illumination and productivity at the Western Electric Company, Hawthorne) shows complex effects (eg productivity increased in the control room — illumination constant — as *well* as in the experimental room — illumination decreased); these were probably caused by teamwork among the workers and co-operative attitudes to the project resulting from the researchers' interview technique (Mayo, 1949:60-76).

References

Allen, L (1971) Some examples of programmed non-simulation games: WFF 'N PROOF, ON SETS and EQUATIONS, pp 63-90, in Tansey (1971).

Alschuler, A *et al* (1977) Education for what? Measuring self-knowledge and levels of consciousness. *Simulation and Games*, 8, 29-47.

Armstrong, R H R and Taylor, J L (eds) (1970) *Instructional Simulation Systems in Higher Education.* Cambridge Institute of Education.

Austwick, K and Harris, N D C (eds) (1972) *Aspects of Educational Technology 6*. Pitman, Bath.

Baggaley, J *et al* (eds) (1975) *Aspects of Educational Technology 8*. Pitman, Bath.

Bajpai, A C and Leedham, J F (eds) (1970) *Aspects of Educational Technology 4*. Pitman, Bath.

Belkin, J and Hazi, H (1974) *Proceedings of the 13th Annual Symposium of the National Gaming Council*. University of Pittsburgh.

Berger, P L and Luckmann, T (1966) *The social construction of reality*. Doubleday, New York.

Bloomer, J (1972) Evaluating an educational game. Unpublished MEd thesis submitted to Glasgow University Department of Education.

Bloomer, J (1973) Games and simulation. *Times Educational Supplement (Scotland)*, 23.11.73.

Bloomer, J (1974) Outsider: pitfalls and payoffs of simulation gaming, pp 32-37, in Gibbs and Howe (1974).

Bloomer, J (1975) Paradigms of evaluation. *SAGSET Journal*, 5, 1, 36-37.

Boocock, S S (1968) From luxury item to learning tool, pp 53-64, in Boocock and Schild (1968).

Boocock, S S (1972) Validity-testing of an intergenerational relations game. *Simulations and Games*, 3, 1, 29-40.

Boocock, S S and Schild, E O (1968) *Simulation games in learning*. Sage Publications, Beverly Hills, California.

Bruner, J S (1966) *Toward a theory of instruction*. Harvard University Press, Cambridge, Mass.

Butts, D C B and Megarry, J (1977) Teaching educational technology at a distance. In Hills, P and Gilbert, J (1977) *Aspects of Educational Technology XI*. Kogan Page, London.

Cornford, F M (1941) (trans) *The Republic of Plato*. Clarendon Press, Oxford.

Duke, R D (1971) (ed) *Proceedings National Gaming Council Tenth Annual Symposium*. University of Michigan, Ann Arbor, Michigan.

Dukes, R L and Kidder, S S (1972) Letter to the editor. *Simulation and Games*, 5, 3, 335-337.

Dukes, R L and Seidner, C (1973) Self role incongruence and role enactment in simulation games. *Simulation and Games*, 4, 2, 159-176.

Dunn, W R and Holroyd, C (1969) *Aspects of Educational Technology 2*. Methuen, London.

Dwyer, F M (1972) *A Guide for Improving Visualised Instruction*. State College, Pennsylvania.

Elder, C D (1973) Problems in the structure and use of educational simulation. *Sociology of Education*, **46**, 335-354.

Fennessey, G (1973) Simulation games and guidelines. *Simulation and Games*, **4**, 2, 205-220.

Fletcher, J L (1971a) Evaluation of learning in two social studies of simulation games. *Simulation and Games*, **2**, 3, 259-286.

Fletcher, J L (1971b) The effectiveness of simulation games as learning environments: a proposed program of research. *Simulation and Games*, **2**, 4, 473-488.

Follettie, J F (1973) Within and beyond formative and summative: an evaluation perspective for large-scale educational R & D. *Professional Paper no 23*. SW Regional Lab For Educational Research and Development, Los Alamitos, California.

Gibbs, G I and Howe, A (1974) *Academic Gaming and Simulation in Education and Training*. Kogan Page, London.

Goodman, F L (1974) An introduction to the concept of 'frame game', pp 303-307, in Belkin and Hazi (1974).

Goroff, N N (1973) Simulated incarceration experiences. *Simulation and Games*, **4**, 1, 59-70.

Greenblat, C S (1973) Teaching with simulation games. *Teaching Sociology*, **1**, 1, 62-83.

Greenblat, C S (1974) Sociological theory and the 'multiple reality' game. *Simulation and Games*, **5**, 1, 3-21.

Hemphill, J K et al (1962) *Administrative Performance and Personality*. Bureau of Publications, Columbia University, New York.

House, P (1973) Gaming at equilibrium — some observations. *Simulation and Games*, **4**, 4, 454-458.

Hubbard, G (1972) Posing the problems, pp 223-226, in Austwick and Harris (1972).

Inbar, M (1968) Individual and group effects on enjoyment and learning in a game simulating a community disaster, pp 169-190, in Boocock and Schild (1968).

Jowett, B (1953) (trans) *Dialogues of Plato* (4th revised edition), vol 1. Oxford University Press, London.

Kennedy, M I (1973) Theoretical framework for the use of urban simulation games in education and urban planning. *Simulation and Games*, **4**, 3, 331-339.

Keys, B (1974) *A rationale for the evaluation of learning in simulation and games: Piaget or Skinner*. Paper presented to NGC Meeting in Pittsburgh, October 1974.

Kolb, D et al (1974) *An experiential approach*. Prentice-Hall, Englewood Cliffs, New Jersey.

Kraft, R *et al* (1974) *Four evaluation examples: anthropological, economic, narrative and portrayal,* AERA Monograph series on Curriculum Evaluation No 7. Rand McNally, Chicago.

McAleese, R (1977) Editorial. *Programmed Learning & Educational Technology,* 14, 2, 197.

Macdonald-Ross, M (1972) Behavioural objectives and the structure of knowledge, pp 38-47, in Austwick and Harris (1972).

Macdonald-Ross, M (1973) Behavioural objectives: a critical review. *Instructional Science,* 2, 1-52.

McKenney, J L (1967) *Simulation gaming for management development.* Harvard University, Boston.

Mayo, E (1949) *The social problems of an industrial civilisation.* Routledge Kegan Paul, London.

Megarry, J (1975) A review of science games: variations on a theme of rummy. *Simulation and Games,* 6, 4, 423-437.

Megarry, J (ed) (1977) *Aspects of Simulation and Gaming.* Kogan Page, London.

Mitchell, P D (1972) The sacramental nature of behavioural objectives, pp 48-55, in Austwick and Harris (1972).

Mitchell, V F *et al* (1973) *Proceedings of the 32nd Annual Meeting of the Academy of Management.* Minneapolis, Minnesota, August 1972.

Parsons, C (1976) The new evaluation: a cautionary note. *Journal of Curriculum Studies,* 8, 2, 125-138.

Pierfy, D A (1977) Comparative simulation game research. *Simulation and Games,* 8, 2, 255-268.

Popham, W J (1975) *Educational Evaluation.* Prentice-Hall, Englewood Cliffs, New Jersey.

Ricciardi, F M *et al* (1957) *Top Management Decision Simulation: the AMA Approach.* American Management Association, New York.

Roebuck, M (1970) Factors influencing the success of programmed materials in under-equipped classrooms and inadequately staffed schools, pp 97-111, in Bajpai and Leedham (1970).

Rosenfeld, F H (1974) The educational effectiveness of simulation games: a synthesis of recent findings. Douglas College, Rutgers University, New Jersey (mimeo).

Rowntree, D (1975) Two styles of communication and their implications for learning, pp 281-293, in Baggaley *et al* (1975).

Shirts, R G (1970) Games students play. *Saturday Review,* 53, 16 May, 81-82.

Shirts, R G (1971) Review of 'Games for Growth' by A K Gordon. *Simulation and Games,* 2, 3, 377-379.

Shirts, R G (1976) Simulation games: an analysis of the last decade. *Programmed Learning & Educational Technology*, 13, 3, 37-41.

Stadsklev, R (1974) *Handbook of Simulation Gaming in Social Education Part 1: Textbook*. IHERS, Alabama.

Stanley, J C (1971) Letter to the editor. *Simulation and Games*, 2, 1, 119-122.

Steffens, H (1977) An economic planning game for the secondary school, pp 33-44, in Megarry (1977).

Stenhouse, L (1975) *Introduction to Curriculum Research and Development*. Heinemann, London.

Tansey, P J (1970) Simulation techniques in training teachers. *Simulation and Games*, 1, 3, 281-303.

Tansey, P J (ed) (1971) *Educational Aspects of Simulation*. McGraw-Hill, London.

Tansey, P J (1973) Evaluation, statistics both slammed. *Simulation/Gaming/News*, 1, 5, 4.

Tansey, P J and Unwin, D (1969a) Simulation and academic gaming: highly motivational teaching techniques, pp 171-178, in Dunn and Holroyd (1969).

Tansey, P J and Unwin, D (1969b) *Simulation and Gaming in Education*. Methuen, London.

Taylor, J L (1971) *Instructional Planning Systems: A Gaming-Simulation Approach to Urban Problems*. Cambridge University Press, Cambridge.

Taylor, J L (1976) Learning to learn: an anthropological approach to simulation evaluation. *Proceedings of 6th Annual ISAGA Conference*. Polytechnic University FAST, Milan.

Teather, D C B and Whittle, S J (1971) Classroom-based research for teachers in training. *Education for Teaching*, 86, 24-31.

Thiagarajan, S and Stolovitch, H D (1976) *Games with the Pocket Calculator*. Dymax, Menlo Park, California.

Tyler, R et al (1967) *Perspectives of Curriculum Evaluation*. AERA Monograph series on Curriculum Evaluation No 1. Rand McNally, Chicago.

Whitehead, A N (1962) *The Aims of Education and Other Essays*. Ernest Benn, London.

Whitlock, G H (1973) Management development: measuring the stimulus side of the equation, pp 268-270, in Mitchell et al (1973).

Zelmer, A E (1974) Letter to the editor. *Simulation and Games*, 5, 1, 122-125.

Index